OPC

RAIL ATLAS
Great Britain & Ireland

S. K. Baker

11th Edition

OPC

An imprint of
Ian Allan Publishing

Glossary of Abbreviations

ABP	Associated British Ports	GBRf	GB Railfreight
ARC	Amey Roadstone Co	H.L.	High Level
BnM	Bord na Móna (Peat Board)	IE	Iarnród Éireann (Irish Rail)
BSL	Bord Soláthair an Leictreachais	Junc. or Jn.	Junction
	(ESB — Irish Electricity Board)	L.L.	Low Level
BP	British Petroleum	LUL	London Underground Ltd
BPC	Bristol Port Company	MDHC	Mersey Docks & Harbour Co
C. & W.	Carriage & Wagon	MoD	Ministry of Defence
Cal-Mac	Caledonian MacBrayne	MSC	Manchester Ship Canal
C.C.	County Council	NR	Network Rail
CE	Civil Engineer	OLE	Overhead Line Equipment
C.S.	Carriage Sidings	P.S.	Power Station
D.C.	District Council	PTE	Passenger Transport Executive
DMU	Diesel Multiple Unit	P.W.	Permanent Way
Dist.	Distribution	RPS	Railway Preservation Society
D.P.	Disposal Point (Opencast Coal)	RPSI	Railway Preservation Society of Ireland
EMU	Electric Multiple Unit	S. & T.	Signal & Telegraph
EWS	English, Welsh & Scottish Railway	T. or Term.	Terminal
FLT	Freightliner Terminal	Tun.	Tunnel

Publisher's Note

Although situations are constantly changing on the railways of Britain, every effort has been made by the author to ensure complete accuracy of the maps in the book at the time of going to press.

First published 1977
2nd Edition 1978
3rd Edition 1980
4th Edition 1984, Reprinted 1985
5th Edition 1988, Reprinted 1988 and 1989
6th Edition 1990
7th Edition 1992, Reprinted 1995
8th Edition 1996, Reprinted 1998
9th Edition 2001, Reprinted 2001
10th Edition 2004, Reprinted 2005
11th Edition 2007

ISBN (10) 0 86093 602 3
ISBN (13) 978 0 86093 602 2

Published by Oxford Publishing Co

an imprint of Ian Allan Publishing Ltd, Hersham, Surrey KT12 4RG.
Printed by Ian Allan Printing Ltd, Hersham, Surrey KT12 4RG.

Code: 0704/K

Cartography by Maidenhead Cartographics, Berks

Visit the Ian Allan Publishing website at:
www.ianallanpublishing.com

Front: Freightliner Class 66 No 66566 leads a northbound empty coal train through Dent station.

Back, top: Ireland has recently seen a sharp decline in freight traffic. On 11 December 2004 an empty sugar beet train headed by diesels 169 and 124 pauses at Waterford en route to Wellington Bridge while a loaded train passes in the opposite direction.

Back, bottom: On 2 August 2006 a rake of 'Southern' Class 377 electric multiple-units heads south between Windmill Bridge Junction and East Croydon, headed by set No 377162. *All photographs S. K. Baker*

Contents

Preface to First Edition

The inspiration for this atlas was two-fold; firstly a feeling of total bewilderment by 'Llans' and 'Abers' on first visiting South Wales four years ago, and secondly a wall railway map drawn by a friend, Martin Bairstow. Since then, at university, there has been steady progress in drawing the rail network throughout Great Britain. The author feels sure that this atlas as it has finally evolved will be useful to all with an interest in railways, whether professional or enthusiast. The emphasis is on the current network since it is felt that this information is not published elsewhere.

Throughout, the main aim has been to show clearly, using expanded sheets as necessary, the railways of this country, including the whole of London Transport and the light railways. Passenger lines are distinguished by colour according to the operating company and all freight-only lines are depicted in red. The criterion for a British Rail passenger line has been takes as at least one advertised train per day in each direction. On passenger routes, to assist the traveller, single and multiple track sections with crossing loops on single lines have been shown. Symbols are used to identify both major centres of rail freight, such as collieries and power stations and railway installations such as locomotive depots and works. Secondary information, for example junction names and tunnels over 100 yards long, with lengths if over one mile has been shown

The author would like to express his thanks to members of the Oxford University Railway Society and to Nigel Bird, Chris Hammond and Richard Warson in particular for help in compiling and correcting the maps. His cousin, Dr Tony McCann deserves special thanks for removing much of the tedium by computer sorting the index, as do Oxford City Libraries for providing excellent reference facilities.

June 1977

Preface to Eleventh Edition

As I sit in the waiting room at Finse station in central Norway, at 1,222m above sea level, with snow higher than the overhead line masts and punctual trains, I am reflecting on the contrasts in the railway environment. The British and Irish networks are very varied: from the urban London tube lines or the DART to the outposts of Northern Scotland or County Mayo. Indeed, the 30 years since the first publication of this Atlas has also brought many contrasts: much has changed since the first edition. The railway of the 1970s still ran loose coupled mineral trains and passenger trains still had locomotives!

How many more editions and years of this Atlas there will be to come remains to be seen (optimistically another 30 years since I was still a teenager when the first map was produced!) What changes will occur over the next 30 years in terms of the railway network?

Many external contributions have been received and the author would like to thank everyone who has helped with information for the maps. Further information and comments are always welcome. Please contact me through the publisher: Ian Allan Publishing Ltd, Riverdene Business Park, Molesey Road, Hersham, Surrey KT12 4RG or by e-mail direct to me on stuartbaker1@hotmail.com.

Stuart Baker
York
April 2007

KEY TO ATLAS

		Surface	Tunnel	Tube
Passenger Rail Network *(With gauge where other than standard gauge: i.e. 4' 8½" Britain/5' 3" Ireland)*	Multiple Track			
	Single Track			
Municipal/Urban Railways or Irish Peat Railways *(London Underground Ltd lines indicated by code, Irish Peat lines are 3' gauge unless shown)*	Multiple Track	C	C	C
	Single Track	C	C	C
Preserved & Minor Passenger Railways *(With name, and gauge where other than standard gauge)*	Multiple Track			
	Single Track			
Freight only lines	No Single/ Multiple Distinction			

Advertised Passenger Station: Saltburn

Crossing Loop at Passenger Station: Newtown

Crossing Loop on Single Line: *Kincraig*

Unadvertised/Excursion Station: Dunleer*

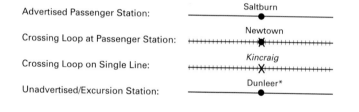

Major Power Signal Boxes	PRESTON	Line Ownership Boundaries	NR │ LUL
Carriage Sidings	⊣ C.S.	Power Station	△
Freight Marshalling Yard		Oil Refinery	●
Freightliner Terminal	⊣ FLT	Oil Terminal	○
Locomotive Depot/Stabling Point	■ BS	Cement Works or Terminal	■
Railway Works	▨	Quarry	▫
Junction Names	*Haughley Junc.*	Other Freight Terminal	⊣
Country Border		Proposed Railway	==========
County Boundary *(PTE Areas, London & Ireland only)*		Colliery (incl. Washery & Opencast site)- UK Coal unless otherwise specified	▲
Shipping Service		Freight line used for passenger diversions and with regular timetabled services.	†

DIAGRAM OF MAPS

INSETS
MAIN SHEETS
OVERLAP

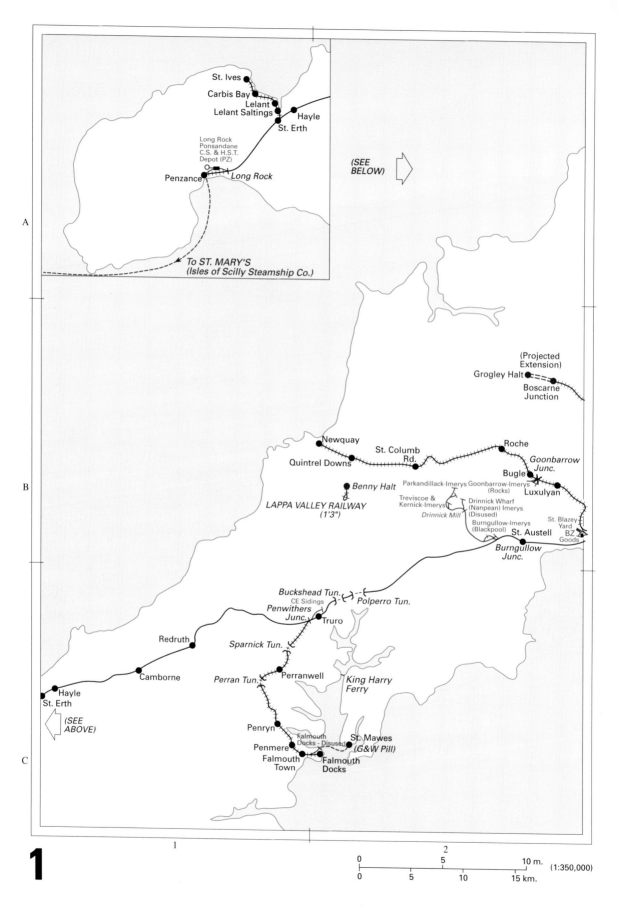

1

St. Ives
Carbis Bay
Lelant
Lelant Saltings
Hayle
St. Erth

Long Rock
Ponsandane
C.S. & H.S.T.
Depot (PZ)
Penzance — *Long Rock*

(SEE BELOW)

*To ST. MARY'S
(Isles of Scilly Steamship Co.)*

A

*(Projected
Extension)*
Grogley Halt
Boscarne
Junction

Newquay
Quintrel Downs
St. Columb
Rd.
Roche
*Goonbarrow
Junc.*
Bugle
Luxulyan

Benny Halt
*LAPPA VALLEY RAILWAY
(1'3")*

Parkandillack-Imerys Goonbarrow-Imerys
(Rocks)
Treviscoe &
Kernick-Imerys
Drinnick Mill
Drinnick Wharf
(Nanpean) Imerys
(Disused)
Burngullow-Imerys
(Blackpool)
St. Austell
St. Blazey
Yard
BZ
Goods

B

*Burngullow
Junc.*

Buckshead Tun.
CE Sidings
*Penwithers
Junc.*
Polperro Tun.

Redruth

Sparnick Tun.
Truro

Camborne

Perran Tun.
Perranwell

*King Harry
Ferry*

Hayle
St. Erth

*(SEE
ABOVE)*

Penryn

Falmouth
Docks - Disused
St. Mawes
(G&W Pill)
Penmere

C

Falmouth
Town
Falmouth
Docks

0   2   10 m.
5
0   5   10   15 km.   (1:350,000)

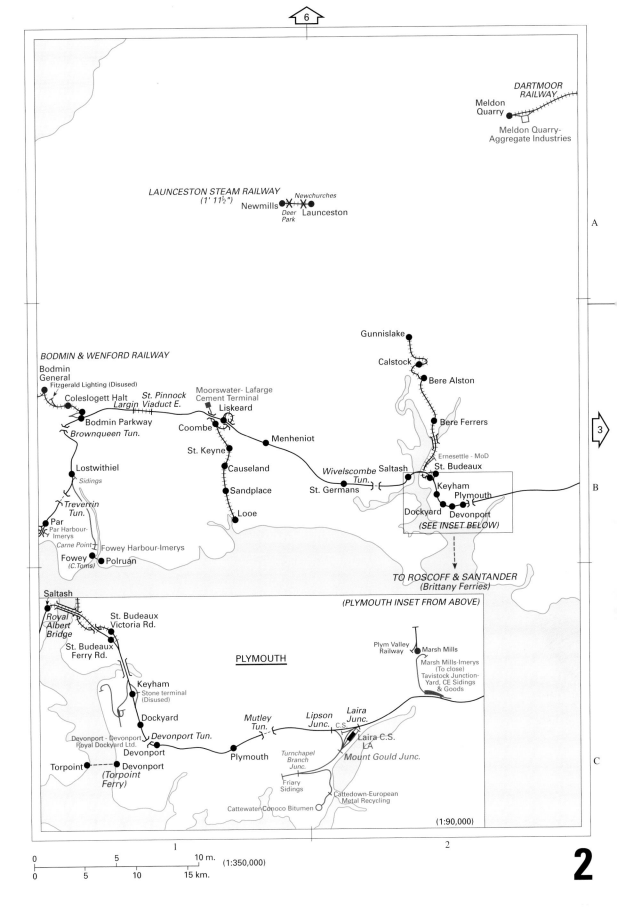

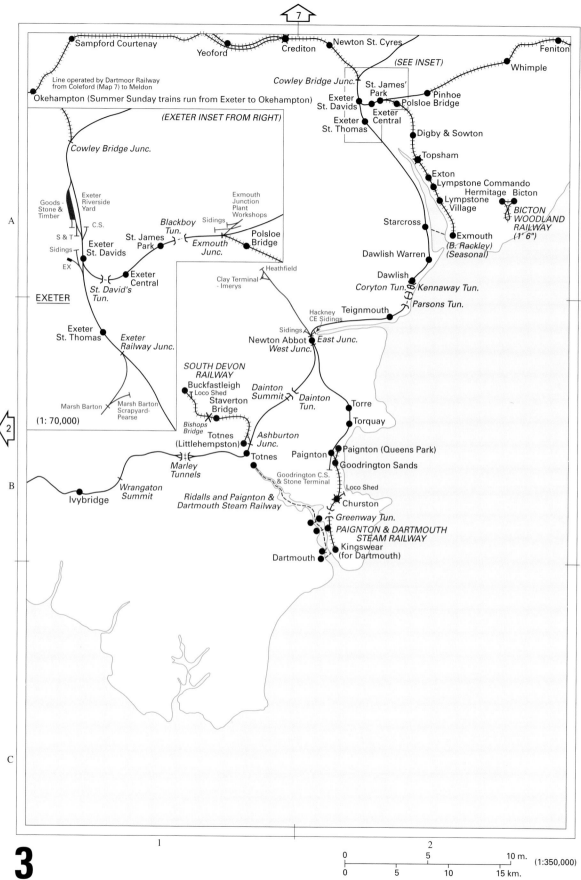

Sampford Courtenay

Yeoford

Crediton

Newton St. Cyres

(SEE INSET)

Feniton

Whimple

Line operated by Dartmoor Railway
from Coleford (Map 7) to Meldon

Cowley Bridge Junc.

St. James'
Park

Pinhoe

Okehampton (Summer Sunday trains run from Exeter to Okehampton)

Exeter
St. Davids

Polsloe Bridge

Exeter
Central

(EXETER INSET FROM RIGHT)

Exeter
St. Thomas

Digby & Sowton

Cowley Bridge Junc.

Topsham

Exmouth
Junction
Plant
Workshops

Exton
Lympstone Commando
Hermitage   Bicton

Exeter
Riverside
Yard

Sidings

Lympstone
Village

Goods -
Stone &
Timber

C.S.

Blackboy
Tun.

Polsloe
Bridge

BICTON
WOODLAND
RAILWAY
(1' 6")

S & T

Starcross

Sidings

Exeter
St. Davids

St. James
Park

Exmouth
Junc.

Exmouth
(B. Rackley)
(Seasonal)

EX

Dawlish Warren

Heathfield

Exeter
Central

Dawlish

Clay Terminal
- Imerys

Coryton Tun.   Kennaway Tun.

EXETER

St. David's
Tun.

Parsons Tun.

Hackney
CE Sidings

Teignmouth

Exeter
St. Thomas

Exeter
Railway Junc.

Sidings

Newton Abbot   East Junc.
West Junc.

Marsh Barton

Marsh Barton
Scrapyard-
Pearse

SOUTH DEVON
RAILWAY

(1: 70,000)

Buckfastleigh   Loco Shed
Staverton
Bridge

Dainton
Summit

Dainton
Tun.

Torre

Torquay

Bishops
Bridge

Totnes
(Littlehempston)

Ashburton
Junc.

Paignton   Paignton (Queens Park)

Goodrington Sands

Totnes

Marley
Tunnels

Goodrington C.S.
& Stone Terminal

Loco Shed

Ivybridge

Wrangaton
Summit

Ridalls and Paignton &
Dartmouth Steam Railway

Churston

Greenway Tun.

PAIGNTON & DARTMOUTH
STEAM RAILWAY

Kingswear
(for Dartmouth)

Dartmouth

2

3

1

2
5
10 m.

0
5
10
15 km.

(1:350,000)

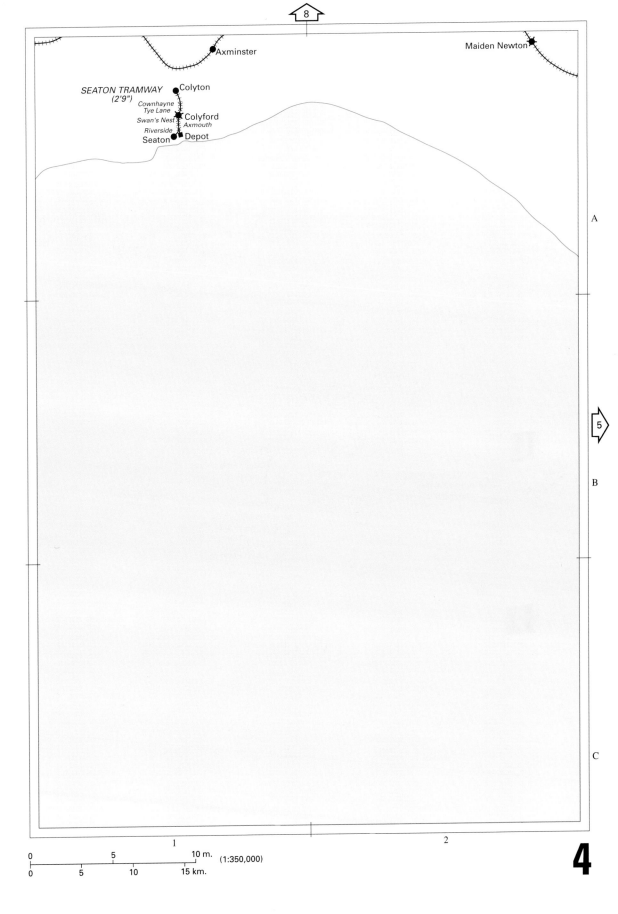

Axminster

Maiden Newton

SEATON TRAMWAY
(2'9")

Colyton

Cownhayne
Tye Lane
Swan's Nest
Riverside
Seaton

Colyford
Axmouth
Depot

8

5

A

B

C

1

2

0   5   10 m.   (1:350,000)

0   5   10   15 km.

4

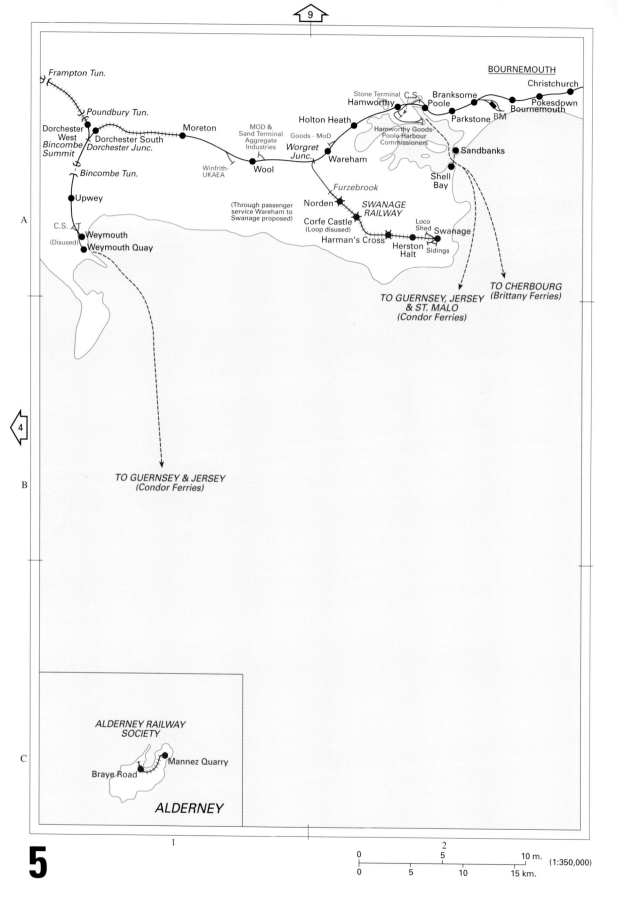

BOURNEMOUTH

Christchurch

Frampton Tun.

Poundbury Tun.

Stone Terminal C.S.
Hamworthy Poole
Branksome
Pokesdown
Bournemouth
Holton Heath
Parkstone
BM

Dorchester
West Moreton
Dorchester South
Dorchester Junc.
Bincombe
Summit

MOD &
Sand Terminal
Aggregate
Industries

Goods - MoD

Worgret
Junc.

Hamworthy Goods
Poole Harbour
Commissioners

Sandbanks

Bincombe Tun.

Winfrith-
UKAEA

Wool

Wareham

Shell
Bay

Upwey

Furzebrook

SWANAGE
RAILWAY

A

C.S.

Weymouth
Weymouth Quay

(Disused)

(Through passenger
service Wareham to
Swanage proposed)

Norden

Corfe Castle
(Loop disused)

Harman's Cross

Loco
Shed

Herston
Halt

Swanage

Sidings

TO CHERBOURG
(Brittany Ferries)

TO GUERNSEY, JERSEY
& ST. MALO
(Condor Ferries)

4

B

TO GUERNSEY & JERSEY
(Condor Ferries)

C

ALDERNEY RAILWAY
SOCIETY

Mannez Quarry

Braye Road

ALDERNEY

5

1

2
5

10 m. (1:350,000)

0
0

5

5
10

10

15 km.

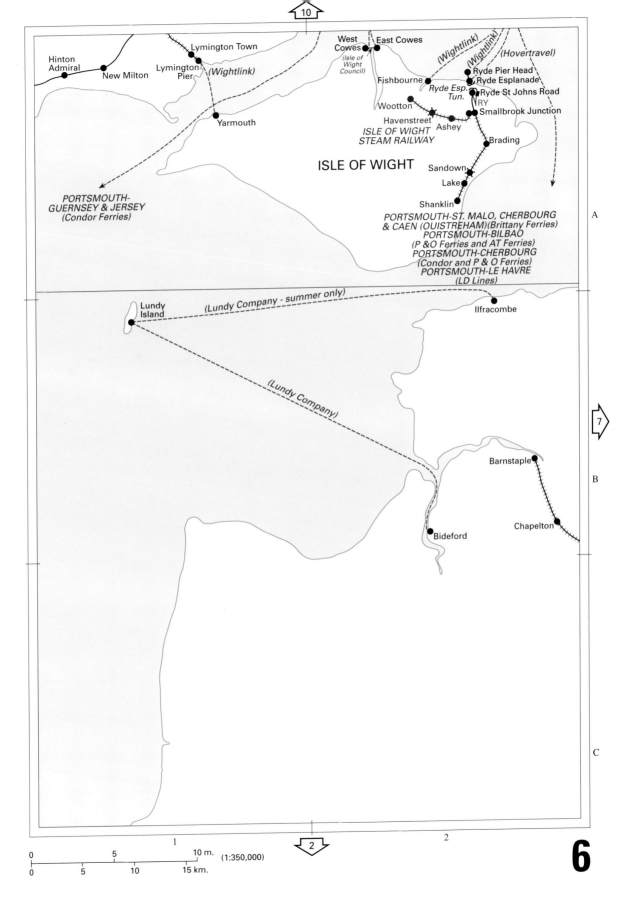

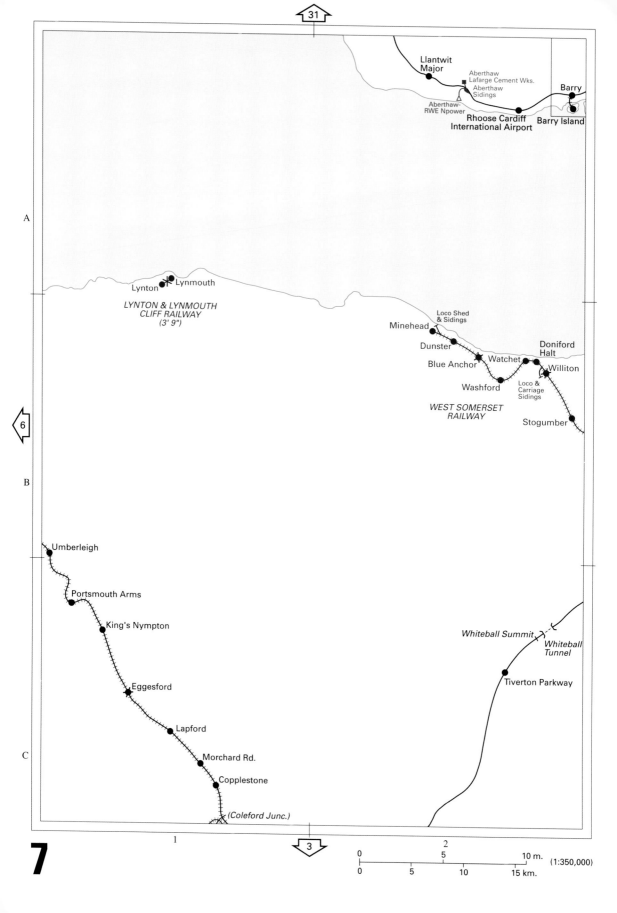

Llantwit
Major

Aberthaw
Lafarge Cement Wks.
Aberthaw
Sidings

Barry

Aberthaw-
RWE Npower

Rhoose Cardiff
International Airport

Barry Island

A

Lynmouth

Lynton

LYNTON & LYNMOUTH
CLIFF RAILWAY
(3' 9")

Loco Shed
& Sidings

Minehead

Dunster

Doniford
Halt

Blue Anchor

Watchet

Williton

Washford

Loco &
Carriage
Sidings

6

WEST SOMERSET
RAILWAY

Stogumber

B

Umberleigh

Portsmouth Arms

King's Nympton

Whiteball Summit

Whiteball
Tunnel

Eggesford

Tiverton Parkway

Lapford

Morchard Rd.

C

Copplestone

(Coleford Junc.)

7

2

0   5   10 m.   (1:350,000)

0   5   10   15 km.

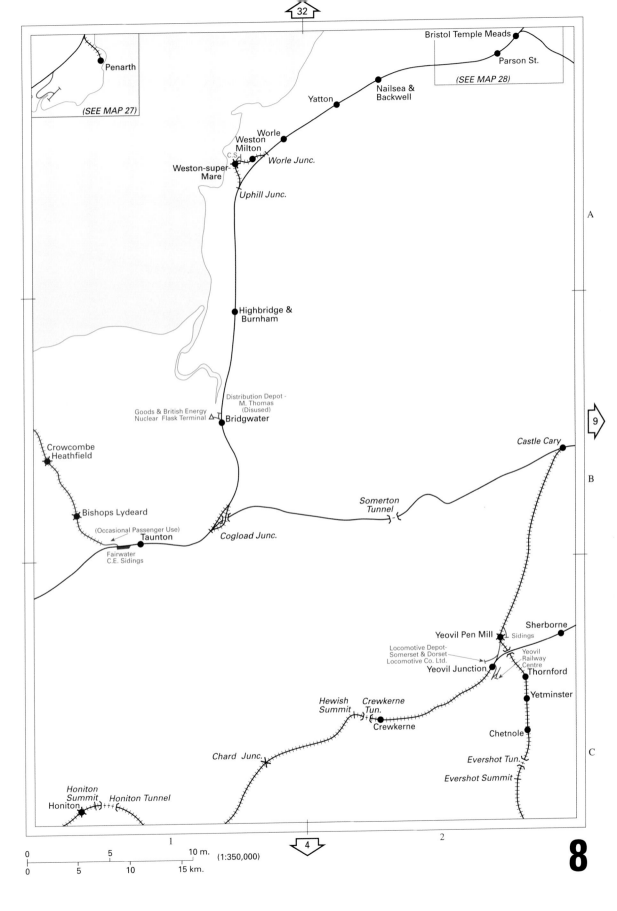

Penarth

(SEE MAP 27)

Bristol Temple Meads

Parson St.

(SEE MAP 28)

Nailsea & Backwell

Yatton

Worle

Weston Milton

C.S.

Worle Junc.

Weston-super-Mare

Uphill Junc.

A

Highbridge & Burnham

Distribution Depot - M. Thomas (Disused)

Goods & British Energy Nuclear Flask Terminal

Bridgwater

9

Castle Cary

Crowcombe Heathfield

B

Somerton Tunnel

Bishops Lydeard

(Occasional Passenger Use)

Taunton

Cogload Junc.

Fairwater C.E. Sidings

Sherborne

Yeovil Pen Mill

Sidings

Locomotive Depot - Somerset & Dorset Locomotive Co. Ltd.

Yeovil Railway Centre

Yeovil Junction

Thornford

Yetminster

Hewish Summit

Crewkerne Tun.

Crewkerne

Chetnole

Chard Junc.

Evershot Tun.

C

Evershot Summit

Honiton Summit

Honiton Tunnel

Honiton

1

2

0   5   10 m.   (1:350,000)

0   5   10   15 km.

8

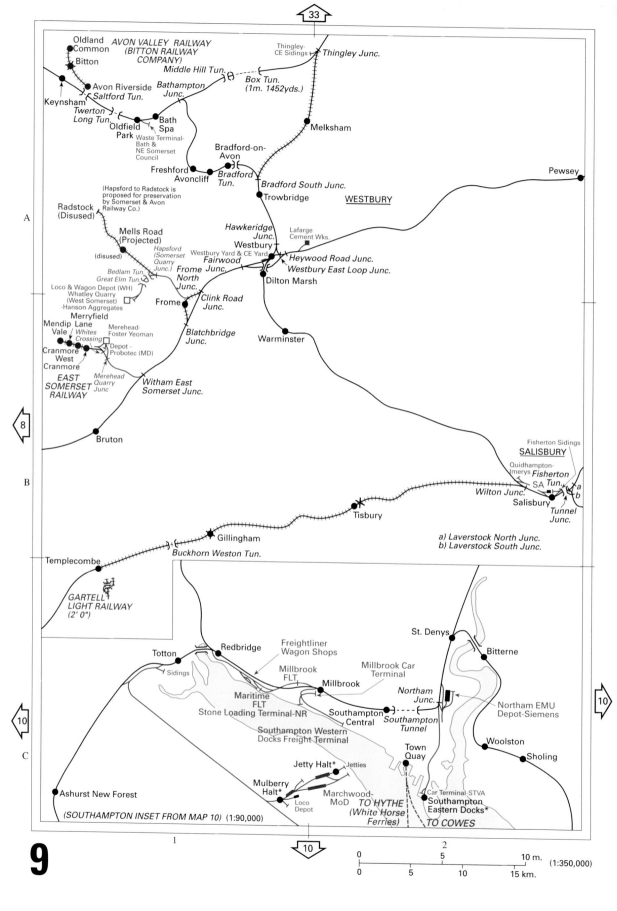

Oldland Common

AVON VALLEY RAILWAY
(BITTON RAILWAY
COMPANY)

Bitton

Thingley-
CE Sidings
Thingley Junc.

Middle Hill Tun.

Avon Riverside
Saltford Tun.
Bathampton Junc.

Box Tun.
(1m. 1452yds.)

Keynsham
Twerton Long Tun.
Oldfield Park
Bath Spa

Melksham

Waste Terminal-
Bath &
NE Somerset
Council

Bradford-on-Avon

Freshford
Avoncliff
Bradford Tun.

Bradford South Junc.

Pewsey

Trowbridge

WESTBURY

A

(Hapsford to Radstock is
proposed for preservation
by Somerset & Avon
Railway Co.)

Radstock
(Disused)

Mells Road
(Projected)

Hawkeridge Junc.
Westbury
Lafarge Cement Wks.

Heywood Road Junc.
Westbury East Loop Junc.

(disused)

Hapsford (Somerset Quarry Junc.)
Fairwood Junc.
Frome North Junc.

Westbury Yard & CE Yard

Bedlam Tun.
Great Elm Tun.
Loco & Wagon Depot (WH)
Whatley Quarry
(West Somerset)
-Hanson Aggregates

Dilton Marsh

Frome
Clink Road Junc.

Merryfield
Lane
Mendip Vale
Whites Crossing
Merehead-
Foster Yeoman

Blatchbridge Junc.

Warminster

Cranmore
West Cranmore
Depot -
Probotec (MD)

EAST
SOMERSET
RAILWAY

Merehead Quarry Junc.
Witham East Somerset Junc.

Fisherton Sidings

SALISBURY

Bruton

B

Quidhampton-Imerys
Fisherton Tun.
SA

Wilton Junc.
Salisbury
a
b

Tunnel Junc.

Tisbury

a) Laverstock North Junc.
b) Laverstock South Junc.

Gillingham
Buckhorn Weston Tun.

Templecombe

GARTELL
LIGHT RAILWAY
(2' 0")

St. Denys

Bitterne

Totton
Redbridge

Freightliner
Wagon Shops

Millbrook Car
Terminal

Sidings

Millbrook
FLT
Millbrook

Northam Junc.

Northam EMU
Depot-Siemens

Maritime
FLT
Stone Loading Terminal-NR

Southampton
Central
Southampton Tunnel

Woolston

C

Southampton Western
Docks Freight Terminal

Sholing

Town
Quay

Jetty Halt*
Jetties

Car Terminal-STVA

Ashurst New Forest

Mulberry
Halt*

Marchwood-
MoD

Southampton
Eastern Docks*

Loco
Depot

TO HYTHE
(White Horse
Ferries)

TO COWES

(SOUTHAMPTON INSET FROM MAP 10) (1:90,000)

1

9

2

0   5   10 m.
0   5   10   15 km.

(1:350,000)

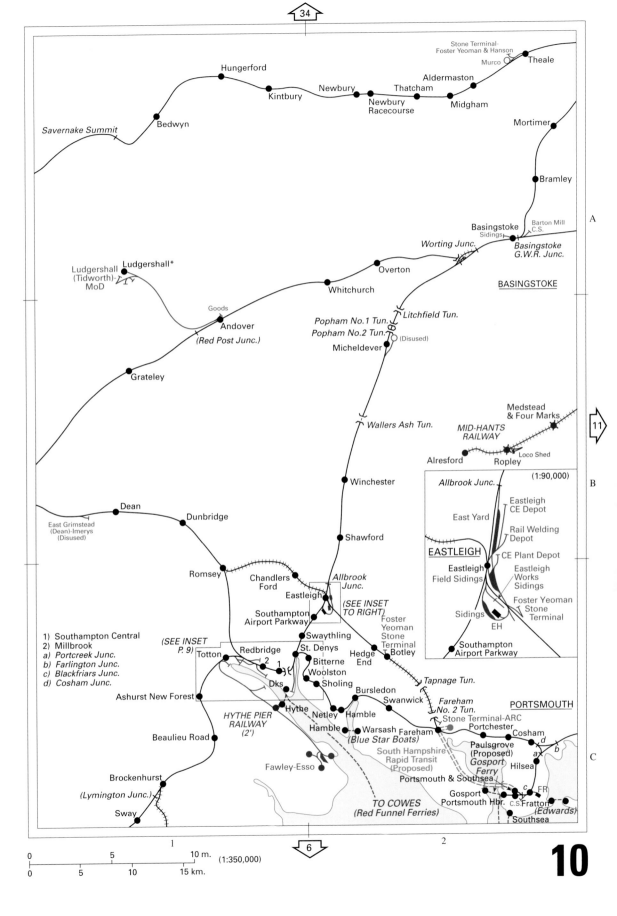

Stone Terminal-
Foster Yeoman & Hanson
Murco
Theale

Hungerford

Newbury
Kintbury
Newbury
Racecourse
Thatcham
Aldermaston
Midgham

Mortimer

Savernake Summit
Bedwyn

Bramley

Barton Mill
C.S.
Basingstoke
Sidings
Basingstoke
G.W.R. Junc.

A

Worting Junc.

BASINGSTOKE

Ludgershall*
Ludgershall
(Tidworth)-
MoD

Overton

Whitchurch

Goods

Andover
(Red Post Junc.)

Popham No.1 Tun.
Popham No.2 Tun.
Litchfield Tun.
(Disused)
Micheldever

Grateley

Medstead
& Four Marks

11

Wallers Ash Tun.

MID-HANTS
RAILWAY

Loco Shed
Alresford
Ropley

Winchester

Allbrook Junc.
(1:90,000)
B

Dean

Dunbridge

Eastleigh
CE Depot

East Yard

Rail Welding
Depot

Shawford

East Grimstead
(Dean)-Imerys
(Disused)

EASTLEIGH

CE Plant Depot

Romsey
Chandlers
Ford
Allbrook
Junc.
Eastleigh
(SEE INSET
TO RIGHT)
Eastleigh
Field Sidings
Eastleigh
Works
Sidings

Southampton
Airport Parkway
Foster
Yeoman
Stone
Terminal
Sidings
Foster Yeoman
Stone
Terminal
EH

1) Southampton Central
2) Millbrook
a) Portcreek Junc.
b) Farlington Junc.
c) Blackfriars Junc.
d) Cosham Junc.

Swaythling
St. Denys
Hedge
End
Botley
Southampton
Airport Parkway

(SEE INSET
P. 9)
Totton
Redbridge
2 1
Dks
Bitterne
Woolston
Sholing
Bursledon
Swanwick
Tapnage Tun.
Fareham
No. 2 Tun.
PORTSMOUTH

Ashurst New Forest

HYTHE PIER
RAILWAY
(2')
Hythe
Netley
Hamble
Stone Terminal-ARC
Portchester
Cosham
d
b

Hamble
Warsash
Fareham
(Blue Star Boats)
Paulsgrove
(Proposed)
Gosport
Ferry
Hilsea
a
c
C

Beaulieu Road
South Hampshire
Rapid Transit
(Proposed)
Portsmouth & Southsea

Fawley-Esso

Brockenhurst
(Lymington Junc.)
Sway
TO COWES
(Red Funnel Ferries)
Gosport
Portsmouth Hbr.
C.S
Gosport
c
FR
Fratton
(Edwards)
Southsea

0   5   10 m.   (1:350,000)
0   5   10   15 km.

10

1

2

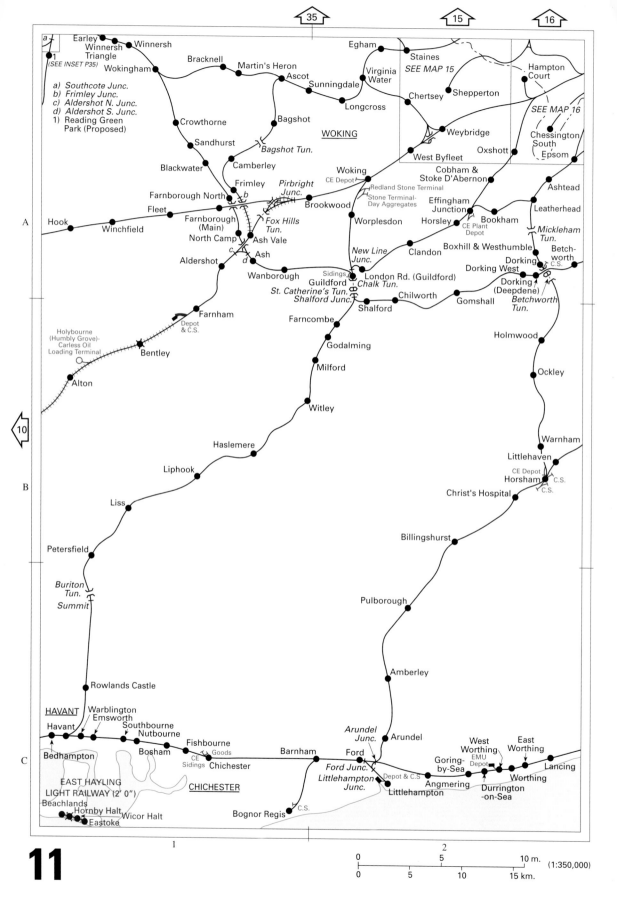

Earley
Winnersh
Winnersh Triangle
(SEE INSET P35)
1

a) Southcote Junc.
b) Frimley Junc.
c) Aldershot N. Junc.
d) Aldershot S. Junc.
1) Reading Green Park (Proposed)

Wokingham
Bracknell
Martin's Heron
Ascot
Sunningdale
Longcross
Egham
Staines
SEE MAP 15
Virginia Water
Chertsey
Shepperton
Hampton Court
SEE MAP 16
Weybridge
Oxshott
Chessington South
Epsom
West Byfleet

Crowthorne
Bagshot
Sandhurst
Bagshot Tun.
WOKING

Blackwater
Camberley
Woking
CE Depot
Cobham & Stoke D'Abernon
Ashtead

Frimley
Pirbright Junc.
Redland Stone Terminal
Stone Terminal- Day Aggregates
Effingham Junction
Leatherhead

Farnborough North
b
Brookwood
Horsley
Bookham
CE Plant Depot
Mickleham Tun.

Fleet
Worplesdon
Boxhill & Westhumble
Betchworth

A
Hook
Winchfield
Farnborough (Main)
Fox Hills Tun.
North Camp
Ash Vale
c
Ash
d
New Line Junc.
Clandon
Dorking
Dorking West
Betchworth C.S.

Aldershot
Wanborough
Guildford
Sidings
London Rd. (Guildford)
Chalk Tun.
Dorking (Deepdene)

St. Catherine's Tun.
Shalford Junc.
Chilworth
Gomshall
Betchworth Tun.

Farnham
Depot & C.S.
Farncombe
Shalford

Holybourne (Humbly Grove)-Carless Oil Loading Terminal
Bentley
Godalming
Holmwood

Milford
Ockley

Alton
Witley
Warnham

10
Haslemere
Littlehaven

B
Liphook
Horsham
CE Depot C.S.
C.S.

Liss
Christ's Hospital

Petersfield
Billingshurst

Buriton Tun.
Summit
Pulborough

Amberley

Rowlands Castle

HAVANT
Warblington
Emsworth
West Worthing
East Worthing

Havant
Southbourne
Nutbourne
Fishbourne
Arundel Junc.
Arundel
EMU Depot

Bedhampton
Bosham
Goods
Barnham
Ford
Goring-by-Sea
Lancing

C
CE Sidings
Chichester
Ford Junc.
Littlehampton Junc.
Depot & C.S.
Angmering
Worthing
Durrington-on-Sea

EAST HAYLING LIGHT RAILWAY (2' 0")
CHICHESTER
Littlehampton

Beachlands
Hornby Halt
Wicor Halt
Bognor Regis
C.S.

Eastoke

11

1   2
0   5   10 m.
0   5   10   15 km.   (1:350,000)

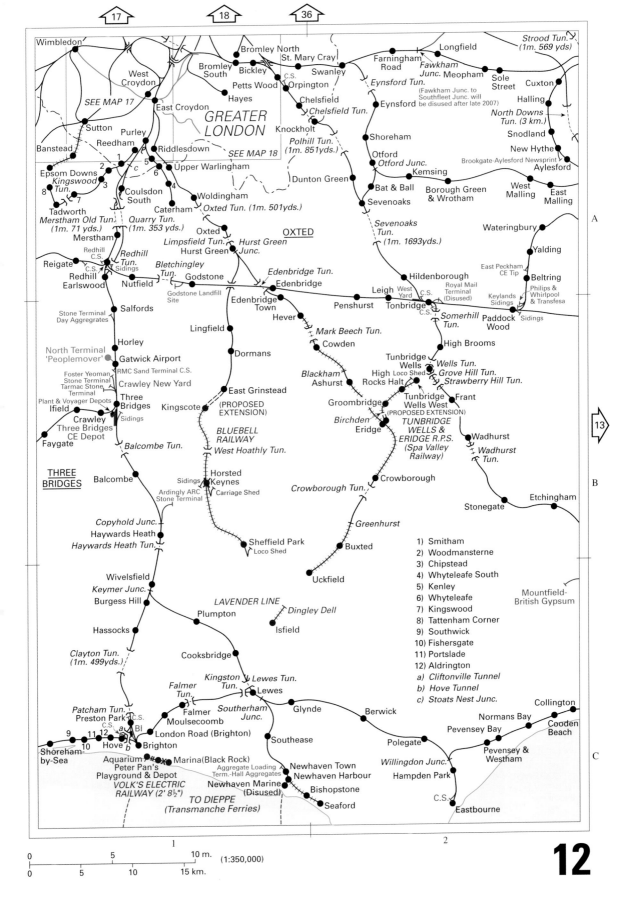

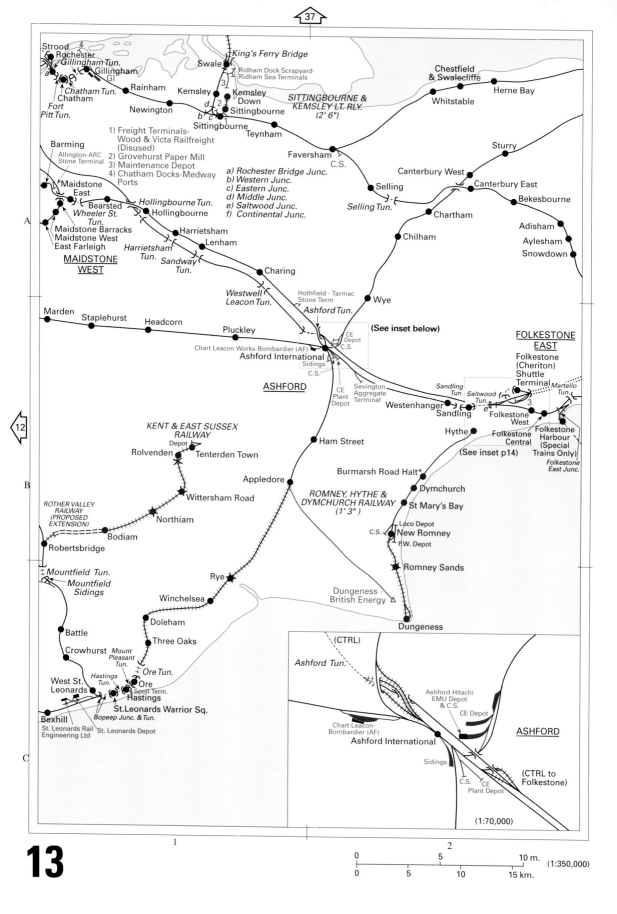

Strood
Rochester
Gillingham Tun.
Gillingham
Gl
Chatham Tun.
Chatham
Fort
Pitt Tun.
Barming
Allington-ARC
Stone Terminal
Maidstone
East
Bearsted
Wheeler St.
Tun.
Hollingbourne Tun.
Maidstone Barracks
Maidstone West
East Farleigh
MAIDSTONE
WEST
Hollingbourne
Harrietsham
Harrietsham Tun.
Lenham
Sandway Tun.
Charing
Westwell
Leacon Tun.
Ashford Tun.

Rainham
Newington
Kemsley
Kemsley
Down
Sittingbourne
Teynham
Swale
King's Ferry Bridge
Ridham Dock Scrapyard-
Ridham Sea Terminals
SITTINGBOURNE &
KEMSLEY LT. RLY.
(2' 6")

Faversham
C.S.
Selling
Selling Tun.
Chilham
Wye
Hothfield - Tarmac
Stone Term

Chestfield
& Swalecliffe
Whitstable
Herne Bay
Sturry
Canterbury West
Canterbury East
Bekesbourne
Chartham
Adisham
Aylesham
Snowdown

1) Freight Terminals-
Wood & Victa Railfreight
(Disused)
2) Grovehurst Paper Mill
3) Maintenance Depot
4) Chatham Docks-Medway
Ports

a) Rochester Bridge Junc.
b) Western Junc.
c) Eastern Junc.
d) Middle Junc.
e) Saltwood Junc.
f) Continental Junc.

Marden
Staplehurst
Headcorn
Pluckley
Chart Leacon Works-Bombardier (AF)
Ashford International
Sidings
C.S.
ASHFORD
CE
Depot
C.S.
(See inset below)
CE
Plant Depot
Sevington
Aggregate Terminal
Westenhanger
Sandling

FOLKESTONE
EAST
Folkestone
(Cheriton)
Shuttle
Terminal
Sandling Tun.
Saltwood Tun.
f
e
3
Martello
Tun.
Folkestone
West

KENT & EAST SUSSEX
RAILWAY
Depot
Rolvenden
Tenterden Town

ROTHER VALLEY
RAILWAY
(PROPOSED
EXTENSION)
Robertsbridge
Bodiam
Wittersham Road
Northiam

Appledore
Ham Street
Burmarsh Road Halt*
ROMNEY, HYTHE &
DYMCHURCH RAILWAY
(1' 3")
Dymchurch
St Mary's Bay
C.S.
New Romney
Loco Depot
P.W. Depot
Romney Sands

Hythe
Folkestone
Central
(See inset p14)
Folkestone
Harbour
(Special
Trains Only)
Folkestone
East Junc.

Mountfield Tun.
Mountfield
Sidings
Rye
Winchelsea
Doleham
Three Oaks
Battle
Crowhurst
Mount
Pleasant
Tun.
Ore Tun.
West St.
Leonards
Hastings Tun.
Ore
Spoil Term.
Hastings
St.Leonards Warrior Sq.
Bexhill
St. Leonards Rail
Engineering Ltd
Bopeep Junc. & Tun.
St. Leonards Depot

Dungeness -
British Energy
Dungeness

(CTRL)
Ashford Tun.
Chart Leacon-
Bombardier (AF)
Ashford International
Sidings
C.S.
CE
Plant Depot
Ashford-Hitachi
EMU Depot
& C.S.
CE Depot
ASHFORD
(CTRL to
Folkestone)
(1:70,000)

A
12
B
C

1
2
0   5   10 m.
0   5   10   15 km.
(1:350,000)

13

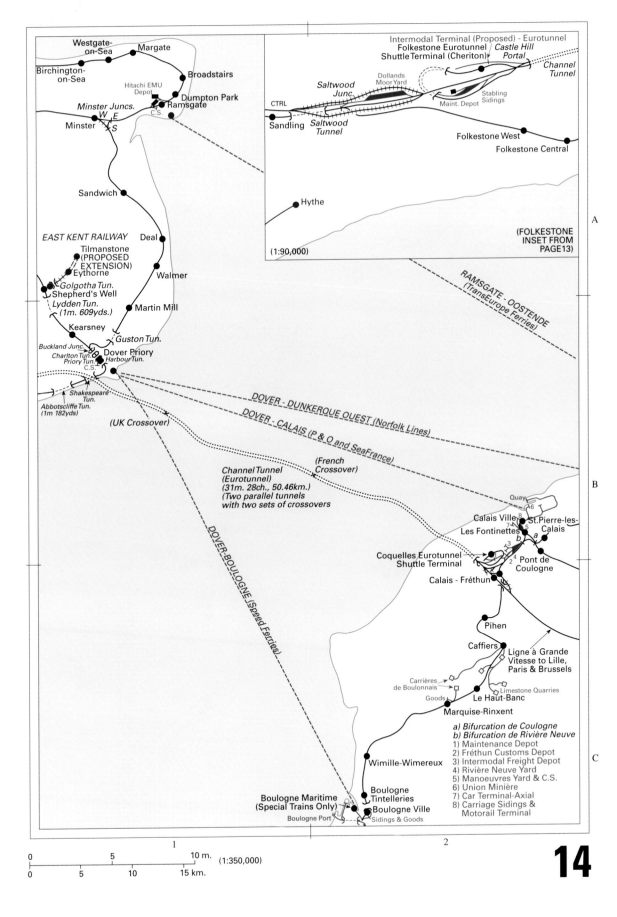

Westgate-on-Sea
Margate
Birchington-on-Sea
Broadstairs
Hitachi EMU Depot
Dumpton Park
Minster Juncs.
Ramsgate
W E
C.S.
Minster
S

Sandwich

EAST KENT RAILWAY
Deal
Tilmanstone
(PROPOSED EXTENSION)
Eythorne
Walmer
Golgotha Tun.
Shepherd's Well
Lydden Tun.
Martin Mill
(1m. 609yds.)
Kearsney
Guston Tun.
Buckland Junc.
Dover Priory
Charlton Tun.
Priory Tun.
Harbour Tun.
C.S.
Shakespeare Tun.
Abbotscliffe
Tun.
(1m 182yds)

(UK Crossover)

DOVER - DUNKERQUE OUEST (Norfolk Lines)
DOVER - CALAIS (P & O and SeaFrance)

(French Crossover)
Channel Tunnel
(Eurotunnel)
(31m. 28ch., 50.46km.)
(Two parallel tunnels
with two sets of crossovers

DOVER - BOULOGNE (Speed Ferries)

RAMSGATE - OOSTENDE
(TransEurope Ferries)

(FOLKESTONE INSET FROM PAGE 13)

Intermodal Terminal (Proposed) - Eurotunnel
Folkestone Eurotunnel *Castle Hill*
Shuttle Terminal (Cheriton) *Portal*
Dollands *Channel*
Moor Yard *Tunnel*
Saltwood
Junc.
Stabling
Sidings
CTRL Maint. Depot
Sandling *Saltwood*
Tunnel
Folkestone West
Folkestone Central

Hythe

A

(1:90,000)

B

Quay
6
Calais Ville 8 St. Pierre-les-
7 Calais
Les Fontinettes 5
b *a*
3
Coquelles Eurotunnel 2 4 Pont de
Shuttle Terminal Coulogne
Calais - Fréthun

Pihen

Caffiers
Ligne à Grande
Vitesse to Lille,
Paris & Brussels
Carrières
de Boulonnais Limestone Quarries
Goods Le Haut-Banc
Marquise-Rinxent

C

a) Bifurcation de Coulogne
b) Bifurcation de Rivière Neuve
1) Maintenance Depot
2) Fréthun Customs Depot
3) Intermodal Freight Depot
4) Rivière Neuve Yard
5) Manoeuvres Yard & C.S.
6) Union Minière
7) Car Terminal-Axial
8) Carriage Sidings &
   Motorail Terminal

Wimille-Wimereux

Boulogne
Tintelleries
Boulogne Maritime
(Special Trains Only) Boulogne Ville
Boulogne Port Sidings & Goods

---

0   5   10 m.   (1:350,000)
0   5   10   15 km.

1   2

14

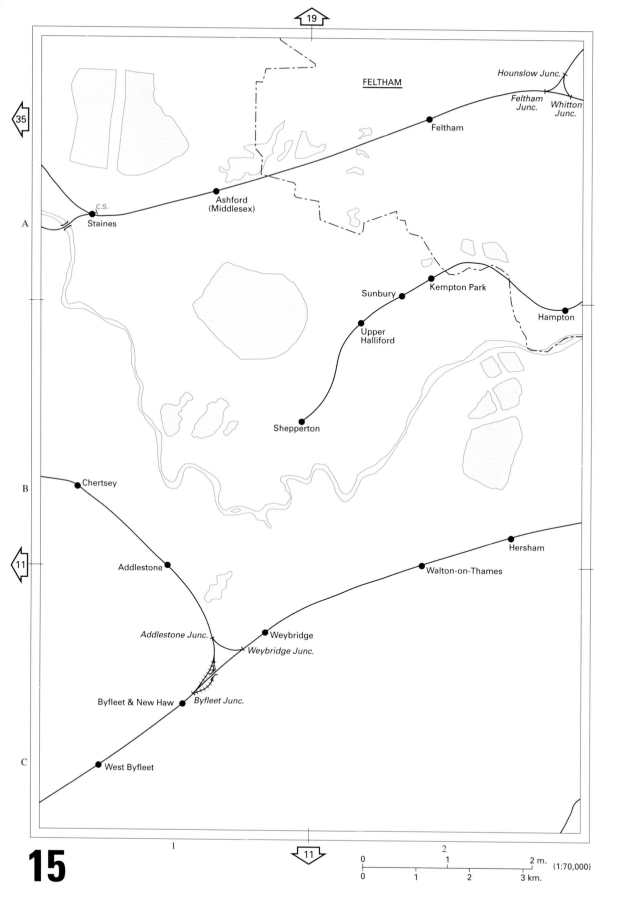

35

FELTHAM

Hounslow Junc.

Feltham Junc.

Whitton Junc.

Feltham

A

C.S.

Staines

Ashford
(Middlesex)

Sunbury

Kempton Park

Hampton

Upper
Halliford

Shepperton

B

Chertsey

Hersham

Addlestone

Walton-on-Thames

11

Addlestone Junc.

Weybridge

Weybridge Junc.

Byfleet & New Haw

Byfleet Junc.

C

West Byfleet

15

0   1   2 m.

0   1   2   3 km.

(1:70,000)

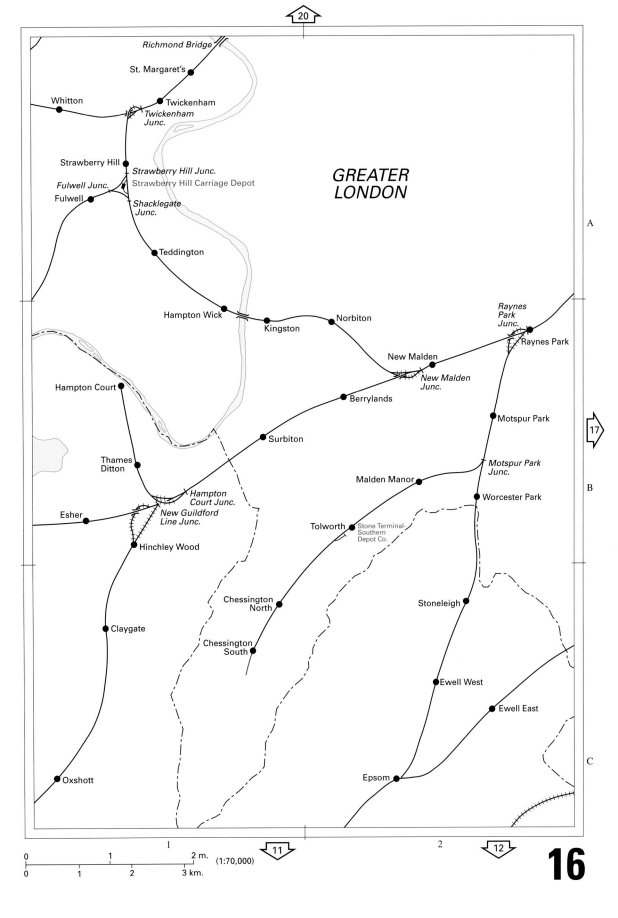

Richmond Bridge

St. Margaret's

Whitton

Twickenham

Twickenham Junc.

Strawberry Hill

Strawberry Hill Junc.

Strawberry Hill Carriage Depot

Fulwell Junc.

Fulwell

Shacklegate Junc.

GREATER LONDON

A

Teddington

Hampton Wick

Kingston

Norbiton

Raynes Park Junc.

Raynes Park

New Malden

New Malden Junc.

Hampton Court

Berrylands

Motspur Park

17

Surbiton

Thames Ditton

Motspur Park Junc.

Malden Manor

B

Esher

Hampton Court Junc.

New Guildford Line Junc.

Worcester Park

Tolworth

Stone Terminal-Southern Depot Co.

Hinchley Wood

Claygate

Chessington North

Stoneleigh

Chessington South

Ewell West

Ewell East

C

Oxshott

Epsom

0   1   2 m.   (1:70,000)

0   1   2   3 km.

16

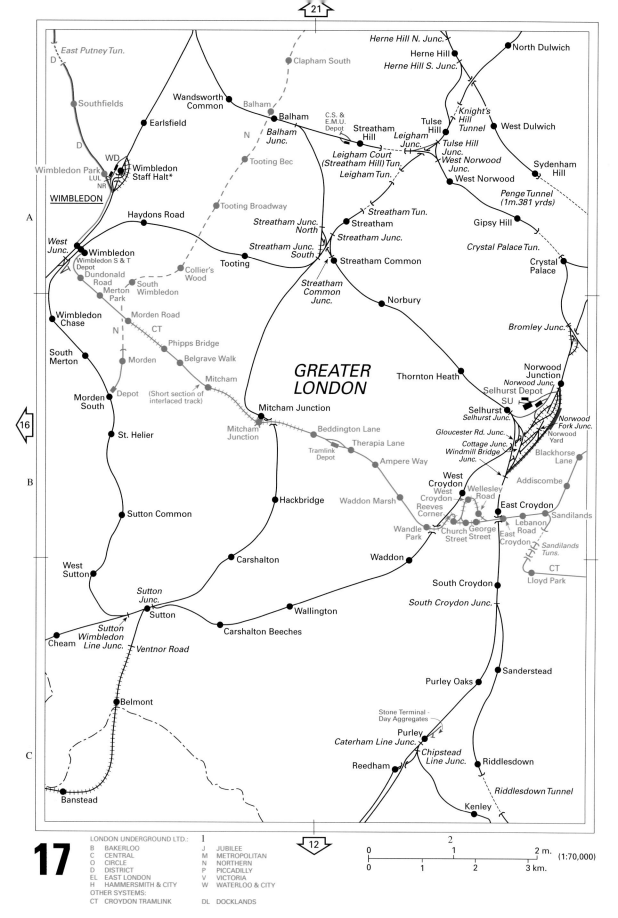

Crofton Park

Honor Oak Park

Hither Green

Lee Junc.

Lee

HG

CE & CE Plant Depot

Lee Spur. Junc.

Catford

Catford Bridge

Grove Park Down Freight Yard

Grove Park Up C.S. (St Mildreds)

Mottingham

New Eltham

Grove Park Down C.S. (Bramdean)

Forest Hill

E.M.U. Depot

Bellingham c.s.

Grove Park

Grove Park Junc.

Sydenham

Chislehurst Tunnels

A

Sydenham Junc.

Lower Sydenham

Beckenham Hill

Elmstead Woods

Penge East

New Beckenham

Sundridge Park

Ravensbourne

New Beckenham Junc.

C.S.

Beckenham Junction

Penge West

Bromley North

Anerley

Kent House

Beckenham Road

Beckenham Junction

Shortlands Junc.

Chislehurst

Avenue Road

Clock House

Shortlands

Bickley Junc.

Chislehurst Junc.

Birkbeck

St.Mary Cray Junc.

Birkbeck

Bromley South

Bickley

Harrington Road

Elmers End

Hawkwood Junc.

CT

Petts Wood Junc.

Arena

Eden Park

Petts Wood

Woodside

GREATER LONDON

12

B

West Wickham

Hayes

Coombe Lane

CT

Addington Village

Fieldway

Gravel Hill

King Henry's Drive

New Addington

C

0   1   2 m.   (1:70,000)

0   1   2   3 km.

1

LONDON UNDERGROUND LTD.: 2
B   BAKERLOO   J   JUBILEE
C   CENTRAL   M   METROPOLITAN
O   CIRCLE   N   NORTHERN
D   DISTRICT   P   PICCADILLY
EL   EAST LONDON   V   VICTORIA
H   HAMMERSMITH & CITY   W   WATERLOO & CITY
OTHER SYSTEMS:
CT   CROYDON TRAMLINK   DL   DOCKLANDS

18

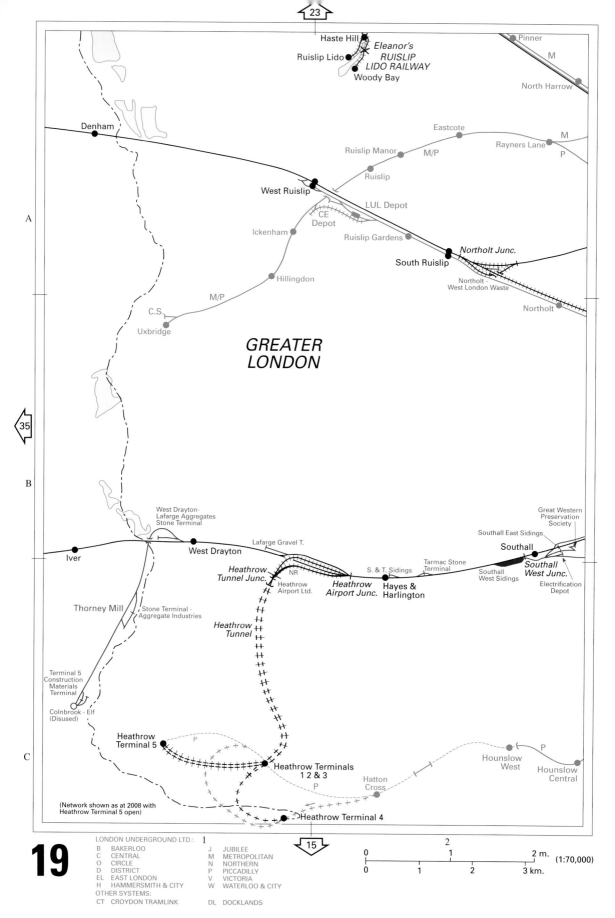

Haste Hill
Ruislip Lido
Eleanor's
RUISLIP
LIDO RAILWAY
Woody Bay

Pinner
M
North Harrow

Denham

Eastcote
M
Ruislip Manor
M/P
Rayners Lane
M
P

Ruislip

West Ruislip

LUL Depot

CE
Depot

Northolt Junc.

A

Ickenham

Ruislip Gardens

South Ruislip

Hillingdon

Northolt -
West London Waste

Northolt

M/P

C.S.

Uxbridge

**GREATER
LONDON**

B

West Drayton-
Lafarge Aggregates
Stone Terminal

Great Western
Preservation
Society

Southall East Sidings

Southall

Iver

West Drayton

Lafarge Gravel T.

NR

*Heathrow
Tunnel Junc.*

Heathrow
Airport Ltd.

*Heathrow
Airport Junc.*

Hayes &
Harlington

S. & T. Sidings

Tarmac Stone
Terminal

Southall
West Sidings

*Southall
West Junc.*

Electrification
Depot

Thorney Mill

Stone Terminal -
Aggregate Industries

*Heathrow
Tunnel*

Terminal 5
Construction
Materials
Terminal

Colnbrook - Elf
(Disused)

Heathrow
Terminal 5

P

C

Heathrow Terminals
1 2 & 3

Hatton
Cross

P

Hounslow
West

P

Hounslow
Central

(Network shown as at 2008 with
Heathrow Terminal 5 open)

Heathrow Terminal 4

19

1

2

0   1   2 m.
0   1   2   3 km.

(1:70,000)

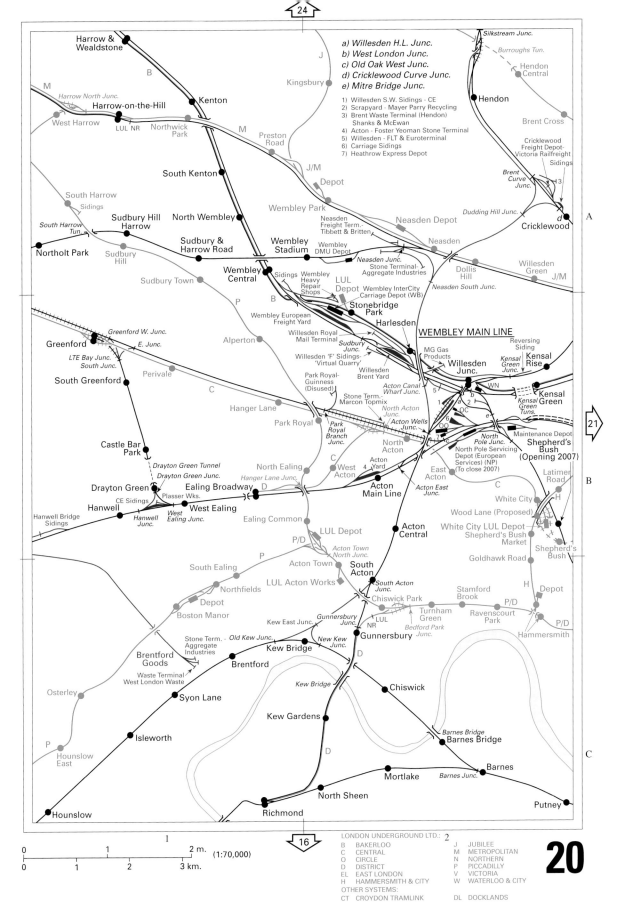

a) Willesden H.L. Junc.
b) West London Junc.
c) Old Oak West Junc.
d) Cricklewood Curve Junc.
e) Mitre Bridge Junc.

1) Willesden S.W. Sidings - CE
2) Scrapyard - Mayer Parry Recycling
3) Brent Waste Terminal (Hendon)
   Shanks & McEwan
4) Acton - Foster Yeoman Stone Terminal
5) Willesden - FLT & Euroterminal
6) Carriage Sidings
7) Heathrow Express Depot

Harrow & Wealdstone

Silkstream Junc.

Burroughs Tun.

J

Kingsbury

Hendon Central

M

Hendon

Harrow North Junc.

Kenton

West Harrow

LUL NR

Northwick Park

M

Preston Road

Brent Cross

Cricklewood Freight Depot-Victoria Railfreight Sidings

Harrow-on-the-Hill

South Kenton

Wembley Park

J/M

Depot

Brent Curve Junc.

H3

Sudbury Hill Harrow

North Wembley

Dudding Hill Junc.

Cricklewood

A

South Harrow Tun.

Sudbury & Harrow Road

Wembley Park

Neasden Freight Term.- Tibbett & Britten

Neasden Depot

Northolt Park

South Harrow Sidings

Wembley Stadium

Neasden

Willesden Green

J/M

Sudbury Hill

Wembley DMU Depot

Neasden Junc.
Stone Terminal- Aggregate Industries

Dollis Hill

Wembley Central

P

Sidings

Wembley Heavy Repair Shops

LUL Depot

Neasden South Junc.

Sudbury Town

B

Wembley European Freight Yard

Wembley InterCity Carriage Depot (WB)

Stonebridge Park

Harlesden

WEMBLEY MAIN LINE

Reversing Siding

Willesden Royal Mail Terminal

Sudbury Junc.

MG Gas Products

Kensal Green Junc.

Kensal Rise

Greenford

Greenford W. Junc.

E. Junc.

Willesden 'F' Sidings- 'Virtual Quarry'

Willesden Junc.

WN

Kensal Rise

LTE Bay Junc.
South Junc.

Perivale

C

Park Royal- Guinness (Disused)

Willesden Brent Yard

Acton Canal Wharf Junc.

5

Kensal Green Tuns.

Kensal Green

South Greenford

Stone Term.- Marcon Topmix

North Acton Junc.

1 a b 2

OC

21

Hanger Lane

Park Royal

Acton Wells Junc.

North Pole Junc.

Maintenance Depot

Castle Bar Park

Park Royal Branch Junc.

North Acton

6

OO

e

Shepherd's Bush (Opening 2007)

Drayton Green Tunnel
Drayton Green Junc.

North Acton Servicing Depot (European Services) (NP) (To close 2007)

Latimer Road

B

Drayton Green

North Ealing

C

West Acton

4

Acton Yard

East Acton

White City

Wood Lane (Proposed)

H

Hanwell

CE Sidings

Plasser Wks.

Ealing Broadway

D

Hanger Lane Junc.

Acton East Junc.

Acton Main Line

White City LUL Depot

Shepherd's Bush Market

Hanwell Bridge Sidings

Hanwell Junc.

West Ealing Junc.

West Ealing

South Acton

Acton Central

Goldhawk Road

H

Shepherd's Bush

Depot

Ealing Common

LUL Depot

P/D

Acton Town North Junc.

South Ealing

P

South Acton

South Acton Junc.

Stamford Brook

Ravenscourt Park

P/D

Northfields

Acton Town

Chiswick Park

Turnham Green

G

Depot

LUL Acton Works

LUL NR

P/D

Boston Manor

Kew East Junc.

Gunnersbury Junc.

Bedford Park Junc.

Hammersmith

Stone Term. Aggregate Industries

Old Kew Junc.

New Kew Junc.

Gunnersbury

Brentford Goods

Kew Bridge

D

Osterley

Waste Terminal West London Waste

Brentford

Kew Bridge

Chiswick

Syon Lane

Kew Gardens

Barnes Bridge

P

Isleworth

Barnes Bridge

Hounslow East

D

Barnes

C

Mortlake

Barnes Junc.

North Sheen

Putney

Hounslow

Richmond

1

0   1   2 m.   (1:70,000)

0   1   2   3 km.

LONDON UNDERGROUND LTD.: 2

B   BAKERLOO
C   CENTRAL
O   CIRCLE
D   DISTRICT
EL   EAST LONDON
H   HAMMERSMITH & CITY
OTHER SYSTEMS:
CT   CROYDON TRAMLINK

J   JUBILEE
M   METROPOLITAN
N   NORTHERN
P   PICCADILLY
V   VICTORIA
W   WATERLOO & CITY

DL   DOCKLANDS

20

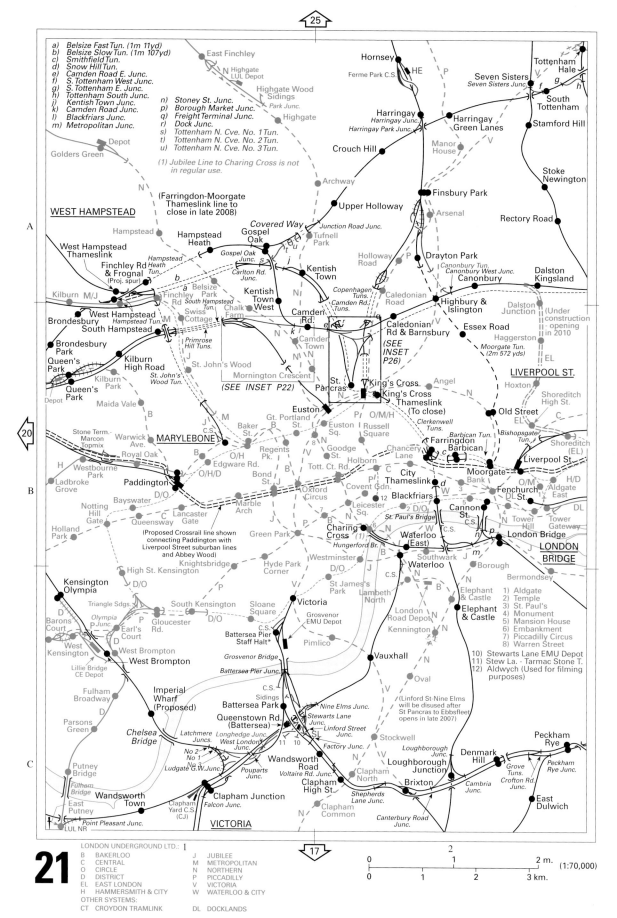

a) Belsize Fast Tun. (1m 11yd)
b) Belsize Slow Tun. (1m 107yd)
c) Smithfield Tun.
d) Snow Hill Tun.
e) Camden Road E. Junc.
f) S. Tottenham West Junc.
g) S. Tottenham E. Junc.
h) Tottenham South Junc.
j) Kentish Town Junc.
k) Camden Road Junc.
l) Blackfriars Junc.
m) Metropolitan Junc.

n) Stoney St. Junc.
p) Borough Market Junc.
q) Freight Terminal Junc.
r) Dock Junc.
s) Tottenham N. Cve. No. 1 Tun.
t) Tottenham N. Cve. No. 2 Tun.
u) Tottenham N. Cve. No. 3 Tun.

(1) Jubilee Line to Charing Cross is not in regular use.

(Farringdon-Moorgate Thameslink line to close in late 2008)

WEST HAMPSTEAD

1) Aldgate
2) Temple
3) St. Paul's
4) Monument
5) Mansion House
6) Embankment
7) Piccadilly Circus
8) Warren Street
10) Stewarts Lane EMU Depot
11) Stew La. - Tarmac Stone T.
12) Aldwych (Used for filming purposes)

(Linford St-Nine Elms will be disused after St Pancras to Ebbsfleet opens in late 2007)

(Proposed Crossrail line shown connecting Paddington with Liverpool Street suburban lines and Abbey Wood)

(Under construction - opening in 2010)

LIVERPOOL ST.

LONDON BRIDGE

VICTORIA

21

LONDON UNDERGROUND LTD.:

B   BAKERLOO
C   CENTRAL
O   CIRCLE
D   DISTRICT
EL EAST LONDON
H   HAMMERSMITH & CITY

J   JUBILEE
M   METROPOLITAN
N   NORTHERN
P   PICCADILLY
V   VICTORIA
W   WATERLOO & CITY

OTHER SYSTEMS:
CT CROYDON TRAMLINK   DL DOCKLANDS

0   1   2 m.
0   1   2   3 km.

(1:70,000)

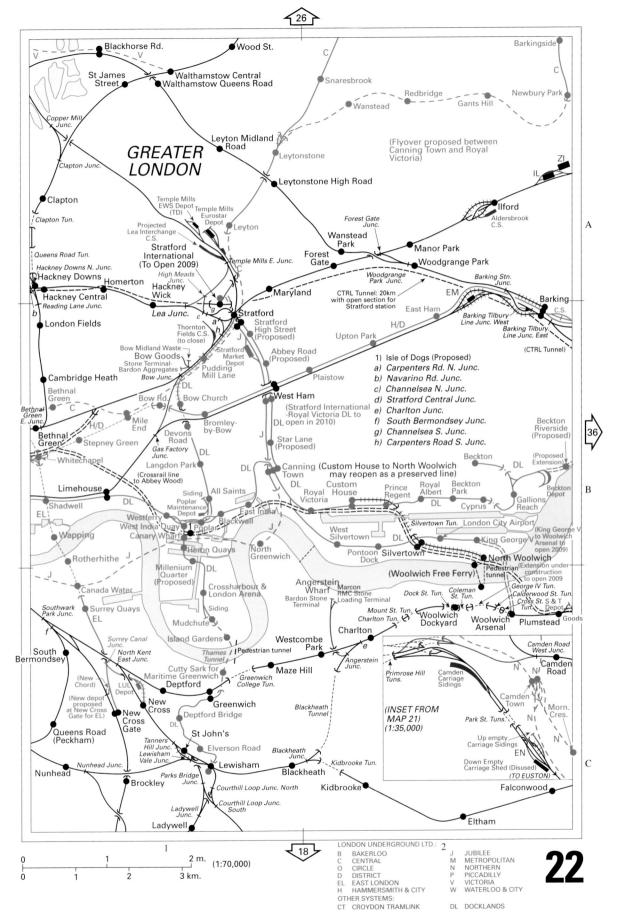

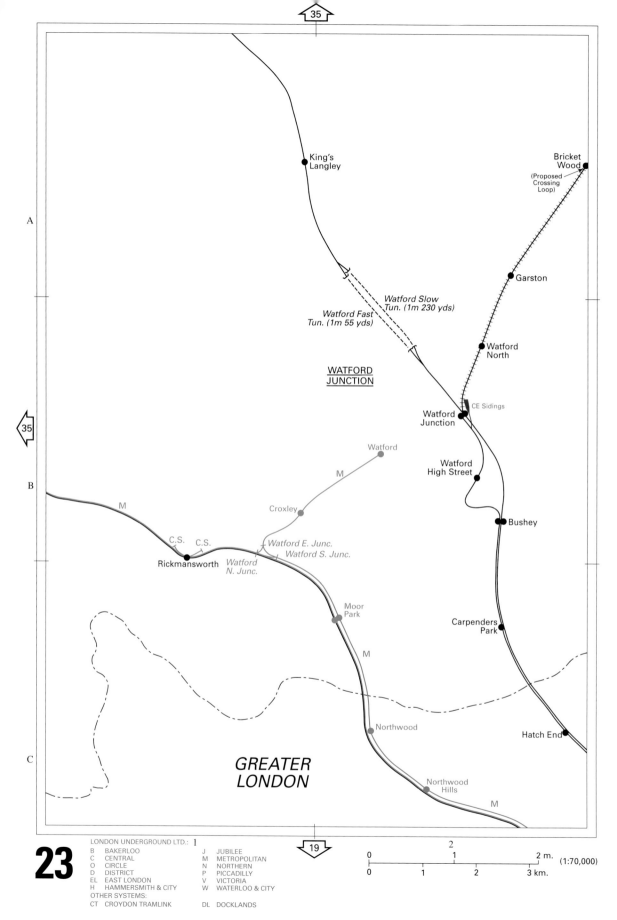

King's
Langley

Bricket
Wood

(Proposed
Crossing
Loop)

A

Garston

*Watford Slow
Tun. (1m 230 yds)*

*Watford Fast
Tun. (1m 55 yds)*

Watford
North

WATFORD
JUNCTION

CE Sidings

Watford
Junction

Watford

M

Watford
High Street

B

Croxley

Bushey

M

C.S. C.S.

Watford E. Junc.
Watford S. Junc.

Rickmansworth

*Watford
N. Junc.*

Moor
Park

Carpenders
Park

M

Northwood

Hatch End

C

GREATER
LONDON

Northwood
Hills

M

23

LONDON UNDERGROUND LTD.: 1

B	BAKERLOO	J	JUBILEE
C	CENTRAL	M	METROPOLITAN
O	CIRCLE	N	NORTHERN
D	DISTRICT	P	PICCADILLY
EL	EAST LONDON	V	VICTORIA
H	HAMMERSMITH & CITY	W	WATERLOO & CITY

OTHER SYSTEMS:
CT CROYDON TRAMLINK   DL DOCKLANDS

2
1
2 m.

0
0   1   2   3 km.

(1:70,000)

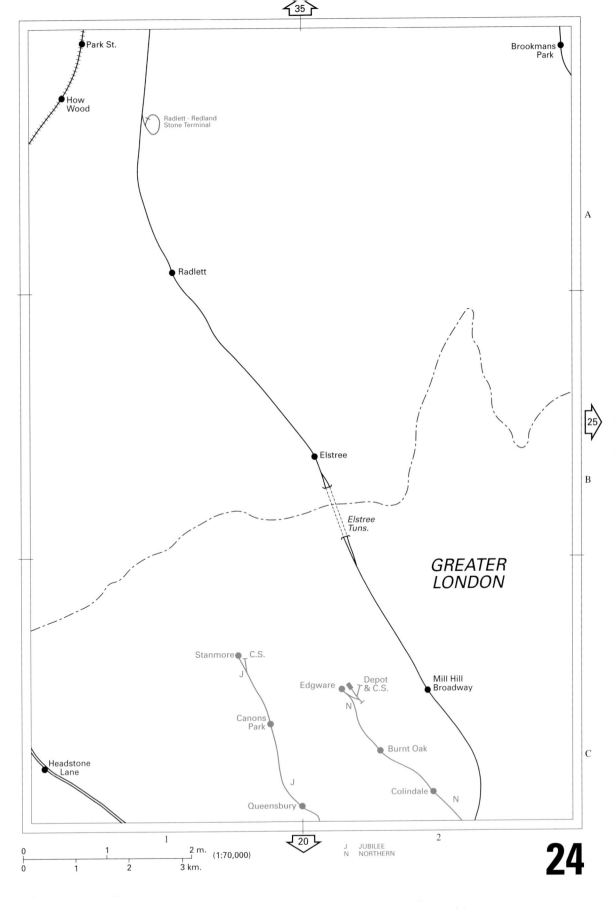

Park St.

Brookmans
Park

How
Wood

Radlett - Redland
Stone Terminal

Radlett

A

25

Elstree

B

Elstree
Tuns.

GREATER
LONDON

Stanmore C.S.

J

Depot
& C.S.

Mill Hill
Broadway

Edgware

N

Canons
Park

Burnt Oak

C

Headstone
Lane

J

Colindale

N

Queensbury

1

2 m. (1:70,000)

2

0   1   2 m.

0   1   2   3 km.

J   JUBILEE
N   NORTHERN

24

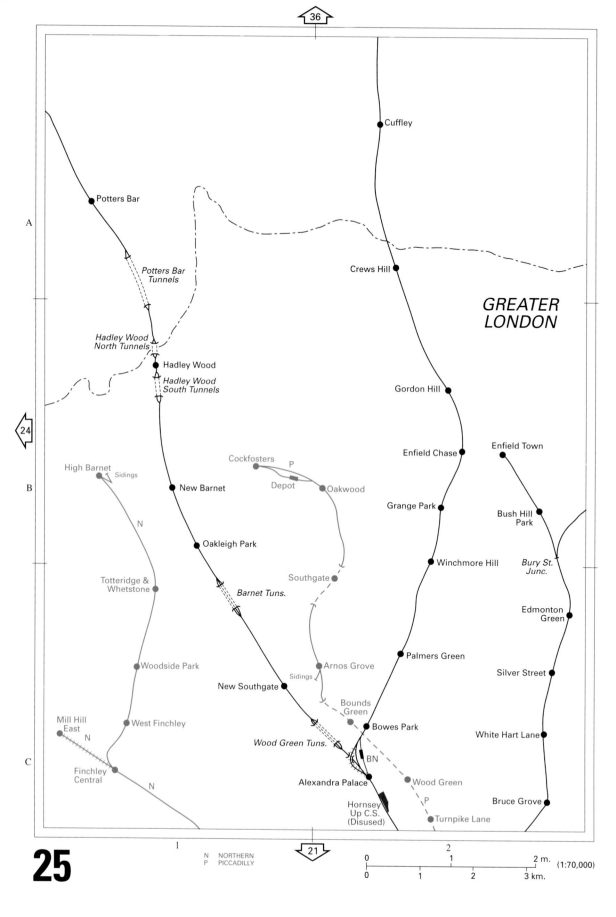

Cuffley

Potters Bar

A

Crews Hill

*GREATER
LONDON*

*Potters Bar
Tunnels*

*Hadley Wood
North Tunnels*

Hadley Wood

*Hadley Wood
South Tunnels*

Gordon Hill

Enfield Chase

Enfield Town

High Barnet
Sidings

B

Cockfosters

P

Depot

Oakwood

New Barnet

Grange Park

Bush Hill
Park

N

Oakleigh Park

Winchmore Hill

*Bury St.
Junc.*

Totteridge &
Whetstone

Barnet Tuns.

Southgate

Edmonton
Green

Woodside Park

Arnos Grove

Palmers Green

Silver Street

Sidings

New Southgate

Bounds
Green

Mill Hill
East

N

West Finchley

Bowes Park

White Hart Lane

C

Wood Green Tuns.

BN

Finchley
Central

N

Wood Green

Bruce Grove

Alexandra Palace

Hornsey
Up C.S.
(Disused)

P

Turnpike Lane

25

1

2

N   NORTHERN
P   PICCADILLY

0   1   2 m.

0   1   2   3 km.

(1:70,000)

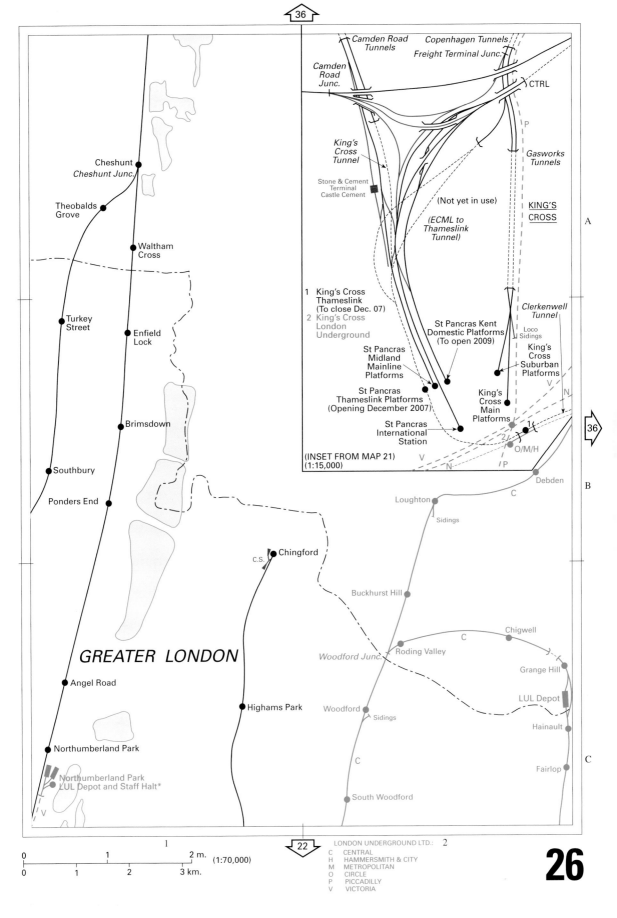

Camden Road
Tunnels
Copenhagen Tunnels
Freight Terminal Junc.

Camden
Road
Junc.

CTRL

P

King's
Cross
Tunnel

Gasworks
Tunnels

Stone & Cement
Terminal
Castle Cement

(Not yet in use)

KING'S
CROSS

A

(ECML to
Thameslink
Tunnel)

Clerkenwell
Tunnel

1 King's Cross
   Thameslink
   (To close Dec. 07)
2 King's Cross
   London
   Underground

St Pancras Kent
Domestic Platforms
(To open 2009)

Loco
Sidings

King's
Cross
Suburban
Platforms

St Pancras
Midland
Mainline
Platforms

King's
Cross
Main
Platforms

V

N

St Pancras
Thameslink Platforms
(Opening December 2007)

St Pancras
International
Station

36

1

2

O/M/H

(INSET FROM MAP 21)
(1:15,000)

V

N

P

B

Cheshunt
Cheshunt Junc.

Theobalds
Grove

Waltham
Cross

Debden

C

Loughton

Sidings

Turkey
Street

Enfield
Lock

Buckhurst Hill

Chigwell

Brimsdown

C

Woodford Junc.

Roding Valley

Grange Hill

Southbury

LUL Depot

Ponders End

GREATER LONDON

C.S.

Chingford

Woodford

Sidings

Hainault

Angel Road

Highams Park

C

Fairlop

Northumberland Park

Northumberland Park
LUL Depot and Staff Halt*

South Woodford

C

V

LONDON UNDERGROUND LTD.:   2
C   CENTRAL
H   HAMMERSMITH & CITY
M   METROPOLITAN
O   CIRCLE
P   PICCADILLY
V   VICTORIA

0   1   2 m.   (1:70,000)
0   1   2   3 km.

26

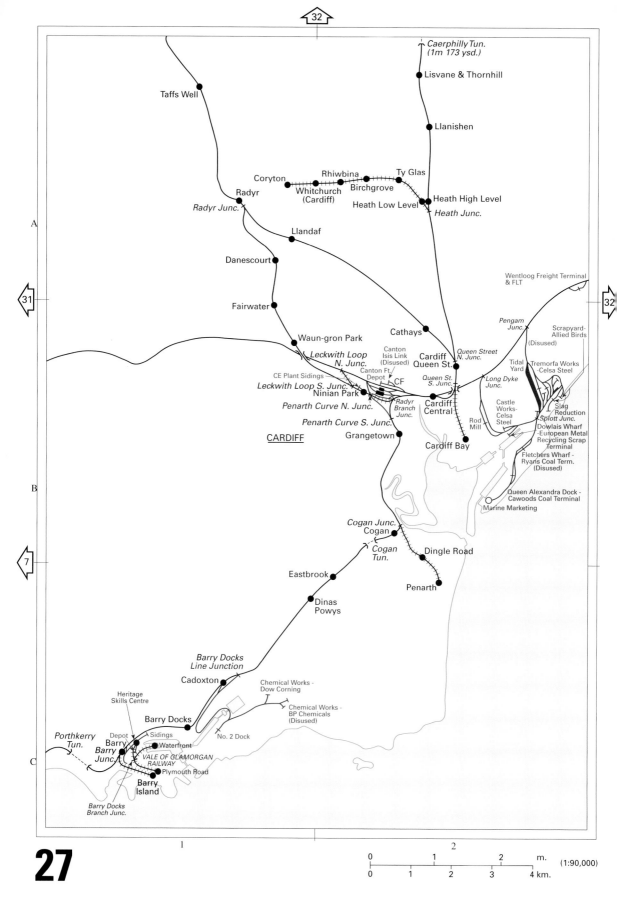

Caerphilly Tun.
(1m 173 ysd.)

Lisvane & Thornhill

Taffs Well

Llanishen

Coryton
Rhiwbina
Ty Glas
Whitchurch
(Cardiff)
Birchgrove
Radyr
Heath High Level
Heath Low Level
Radyr Junc.
Heath Junc.

Llandaf

Danescourt

Wentloog Freight Terminal
& FLT

Fairwater

Cathays

*Pengam
Junc.*

Scrapyard-
Allied Birds
(Disused)

Waun-gron Park

*Leckwith Loop
N. Junc.*
Canton
Isis Link
(Disused)
Cardiff
Queen St.
*Queen Street
N. Junc.*

Tidal
Yard

Tremorfa Works
-Celsa Steel

CE Plant Sidings
Canton Ft.
Depot
CF

Long Dyke
Junc.

Leckwith Loop S. Junc.
Ninian Park
*Queen St.
S. Junc.*

Castle
Works-
Celsa
Steel

Slag
Reduction

Penarth Curve N. Junc.
*Radyr
Branch
Junc.*
Cardiff
Central
Splott Junc.

Penarth Curve S. Junc.
Rod
Mill
Dowlais Wharf
-European Metal
Recycling Scrap
Terminal

CARDIFF
Grangetown
Cardiff Bay

Fletchers Wharf -
Ryans Coal Term.
(Disused)

Queen Alexandra Dock -
Cawoods Coal Terminal
Marine Marketing

Cogan Junc.
Cogan

Dingle Road

*Cogan
Tun.*

Eastbrook

Penarth

Dinas
Powys

*Barry Docks
Line Junction*
Cadoxton

Chemical Works -
Dow Corning

Chemical Works -
BP Chemicals
(Disused)

Heritage
Skills Centre

Barry Docks

No. 2 Dock

*Porthkerry
Tun.*
Depot
Sidings

Barry
Barry
Junc.
Waterfront

*VALE OF GLAMORGAN
RAILWAY*
Plymouth Road

Barry
Island

*Barry Docks
Branch Junc.*

27

0   1   2   m.
0   1   2   3   4 km.

(1:90,000)

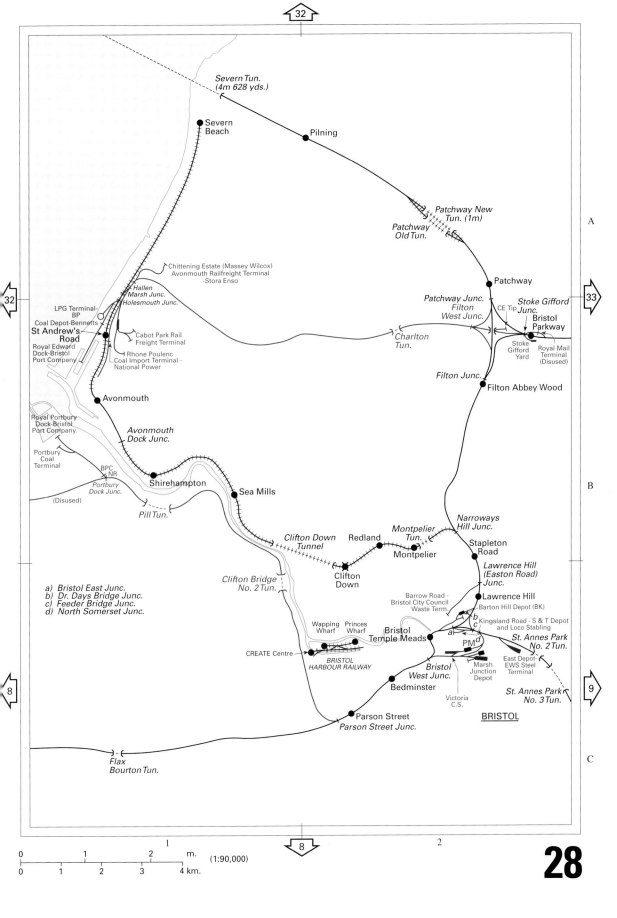

Severn Tun.
(4m 628 yds.)

● Severn
  Beach

● Pilning

A

Patchway New
Tun. (1m)

Patchway
Old Tun.

└ Chittening Estate (Massey Wilcox)
  Avonmouth Railfreight Terminal
  -Stora Enso

Hallen
Marsh Junc.
Holesmouth Junc.

● Patchway

Patchway Junc.
Filton
West Junc.

CE Tip

Stoke Gifford
Junc.

Bristol
Parkway

LPG Terminal-
BP
Coal Depot-Bennetts
St Andrew's
Road

Royal Edward
Dock-Bristol
Port Company

┌ Cabot Park Rail
  Freight Terminal

└ Rhone Poulenc
  Coal Import Terminal -
  National Power

Charlton
Tun.

Stoke
Gifford
Yard

Royal Mail
Terminal
(Disused)

Filton Junc.

● Filton Abbey Wood

● Avonmouth

Royal Portbury
Dock-Bristol
Port Company

Avonmouth
Dock Junc.

Portbury
Coal
Terminal

BPC
NR

Portbury
Dock Junc.

(Disused)

● Shirehampton

Pill Tun.

● Sea Mills

B

Clifton Down
Tunnel

● Redland

Montpelier
Tun.

Narroways
Hill Junc.

● Stapleton
  Road

● Montpelier

Clifton Bridge
No. 2 Tun.

✦ Clifton
  Down

Lawrence Hill
(Easton Road)
Junc.

Barrow Road -
Bristol City Council
Waste Term.

● Lawrence Hill

Barton Hill Depot (BK)

a) Bristol East Junc.
b) Dr. Days Bridge Junc.
c) Feeder Bridge Junc.
d) North Somerset Junc.

Kingsland Road - S & T Depot
and Loco Stabling

b
a *c*
d

St. Annes Park
No. 2 Tun.

Wapping
Wharf

Princes
Wharf

Bristol
Temple Meads

PM

East Depot-
EWS Steel
Terminal

CREATE Centre

BRISTOL
HARBOUR RAILWAY

Bristol
West Junc.

Marsh
Junction
Depot

St. Annes Park
No. 3 Tun.

● Bedminster

Victoria
C.S.

BRISTOL

● Parson Street
Parson Street Junc.

C

Flax
Bourton Tun.

0   1   2   m.   (1:90,000)
0 1 2 3 4 km.

1

2

28

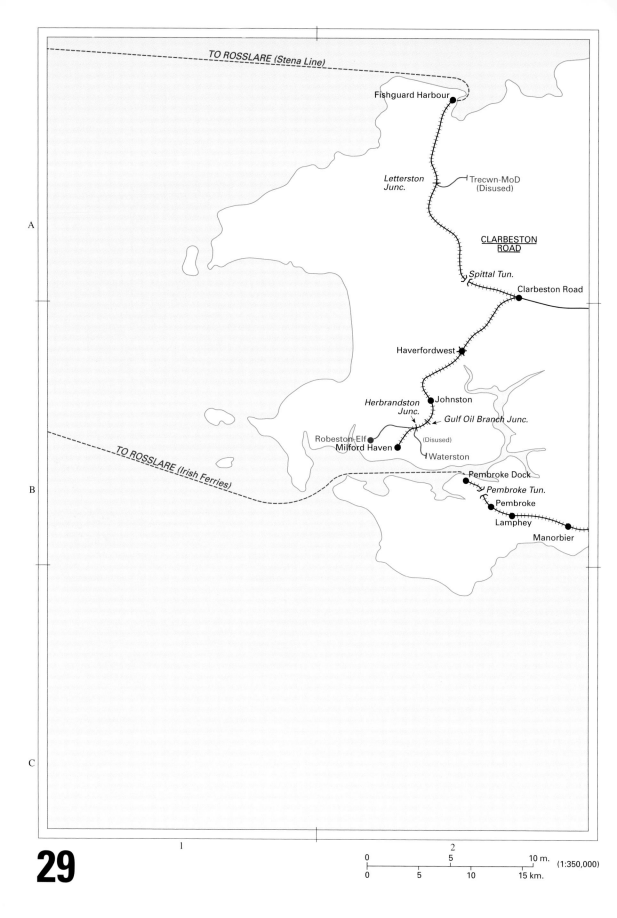

TO ROSSLARE (Stena Line)

Fishguard Harbour

Letterston Junc.

Trecwn-MoD (Disused)

CLARBESTON ROAD

Spittal Tun.

Clarbeston Road

Haverfordwest

Johnston

Herbrandston Junc.

Gulf Oil Branch Junc.

Robeston-Elf

Milford Haven

(Disused)

Waterston

TO ROSSLARE (Irish Ferries)

Pembroke Dock

Pembroke Tun.

Pembroke

Lamphey

Manorbier

A

B

C

1

2

29

0   5   10 m.
0   5   10   15 km.

(1:350,000)

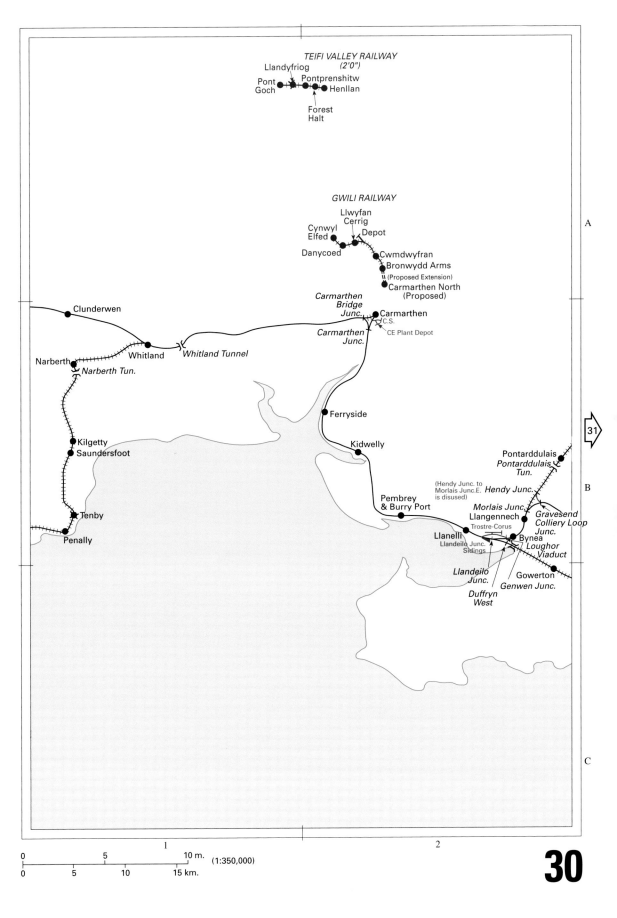

TEIFI VALLEY RAILWAY
(2'0")

Llandyfriog
Pont Goch   Pontprenshitw
           Henllan
Forest Halt

GWILI RAILWAY

Llwyfan Cerrig
Cynwyl Elfed   Depot
Danycoed
Cwmdwyfran
Bronwydd Arms
(Proposed Extension)
Carmarthen North (Proposed)

Clunderwen

Carmarthen Bridge Junc.
Carmarthen
C.S.
CE Plant Depot

Carmarthen Junc.

Narberth
Whitland   *Whitland Tunnel*
Narberth Tun.

Ferryside

Kidwelly

Kilgetty
Saundersfoot

Pontarddulais
Pontarddulais Tun.

Pembrey & Burry Port

(Hendy Junc. to Morlais Junc.E. is disused)   *Hendy Junc.*

Morlais Junc.
Llangennech
Trostre-Corus   *Gravesend Colliery Loop Junc.*

Tenby
Penally

Llanelli
Llandeilo Junc. Sidings
Llandeilo Junc.
Duffryn West
Bynea   *Loughor Viaduct*
Gowerton
Genwen Junc.

A

31

B

C

1   2

0   5   10 m.   (1:350,000)
0   5   10   15 km.

30

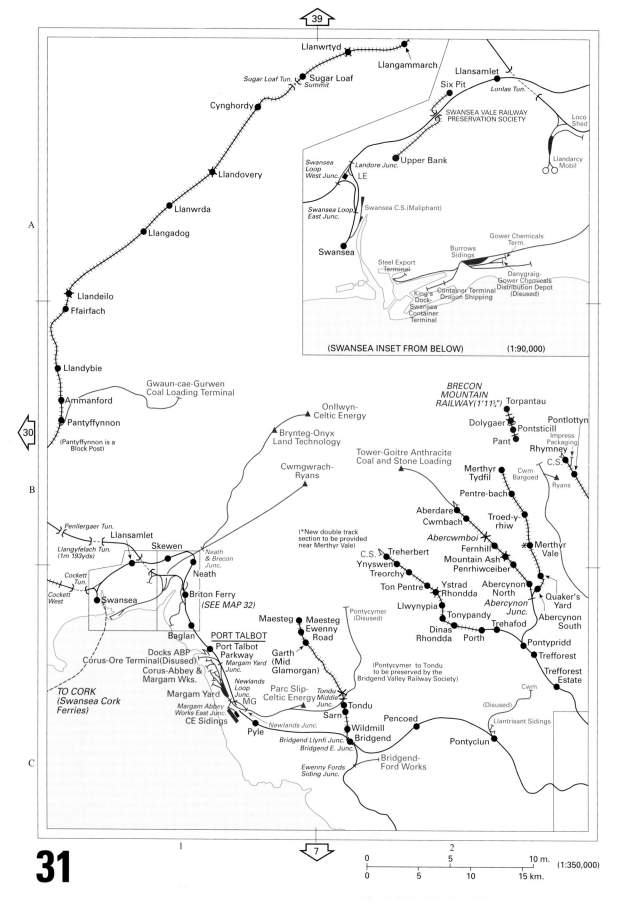

(SWANSEA INSET FROM BELOW) **(1:90,000)**

Llanwrtyd
Llangammarch
Sugar Loaf Tun.
Summit
Sugar Loaf
Swansea Loaf Tun.
Cynghordy
Llandovery
Llanwrda
Llangadog

A

Llandeilo
Ffairfach

Llandybie
Ammanford
Pantyffynnon
(Pantyffynnon is a
Block Post)

Six Pit
Llansamlet
Lonlas Tun.
SWANSEA VALE RAILWAY
PRESERVATION SOCIETY
Loco
Shed
Upper Bank
Llandarcy
Mobil
*Swansea Loop
West Junc.*
Landore Junc.
LE
*Swansea Loop
East Junc.*
Swansea C.S.(Maliphant)
Swansea
Steel Export
Terminal
Burrows
Sidings
Gower Chemicals
Term.
King's
Dock-
Swansea
Container
Terminal
Container Terminal
Dragon Shipping
Danygraig-
Gower Chemicals
Distribution Depot
(Disused)

Gwaun-cae-Gurwen
Coal Loading Terminal

30

Onllwyn-
Celtic Energy
Brynteg-Onyx
Land Technology
Cwmgwrach-
Ryans

Tower-Goitre Anthracite
Coal and Stone Loading

*BRECON
MOUNTAIN
RAILWAY(1'11¾")*
Torpantau
Dolygaer
Pontlottyn
Pontsticill
Pant
Rhymney
Impress
Packaging
C.S.

B

Merthyr
Tydfil
*Cwm
Bargoed*
Ryans
Pentre-bach

(*New double track
section to be provided
near Merthyr Vale)

Aberdare
Cwmbach
Troed-y-
rhiw
Abercwmboi
Merthyr
Vale
Penllergaer Tun.
Llangyfelach Tun.
(1m 193yds)
Llansamlet
Skewen
*Neath &
Brecon
Junc,*
Neath
Cockett
Tun.
Cockett
West
Swansea
Briton Ferry
(SEE MAP 32)

C.S.
Treherbert
Ynyswen
Treorchy
Ton Pentre
Llwynypia
Fernhill
Mountain Ash
Penrhiwceiber
Ystrad
Rhondda
Abercynon
North
*Abercynon
Junc.*
Quaker's
Yard
Abercynon
South

Maesteg
Maesteg
Ewenny
Road
Garth
(Mid
Glamorgan)
Parc Slip-
Celtic Energy

Baglan
PORT TALBOT
Port Talbot
Parkway
*Margam Yard
Junc.*
Docks ABP
Corus-Ore Terminal(Disused)
Corus-Abbey &
Margam Wks.
*Newlands
Loop Junc.*
Margam Yard
MG
*Margam Abbey
Works East Junc.*
CE Sidings
Pyle
Newlands Junc.

*TO CORK
(Swansea Cork
Ferries)*

C

Pontycymer
(Disused)
Tonypandy
Dinas
Rhondda
Porth
Trehafod
Pontypridd
Trefforest
Trefforest
Estate
Cwm
(Disused)

(Pontycymer to Tondu
to be preserved by the
Bridgend Valley Railway
Society)

*Tondu
Middle
Junc.*
Tondu
Sarn
Wildmill
Bridgend
Bridgend Llynfi Junc.
Bridgend E. Junc.
*Ewenny Fords
Siding Junc.*
Pencoed
Bridgend-
Ford Works
Llantrisant Sidings
Pontyclun

31

1

2

0   5   10 m.
0   5   10   15 km.
(1:350,000)

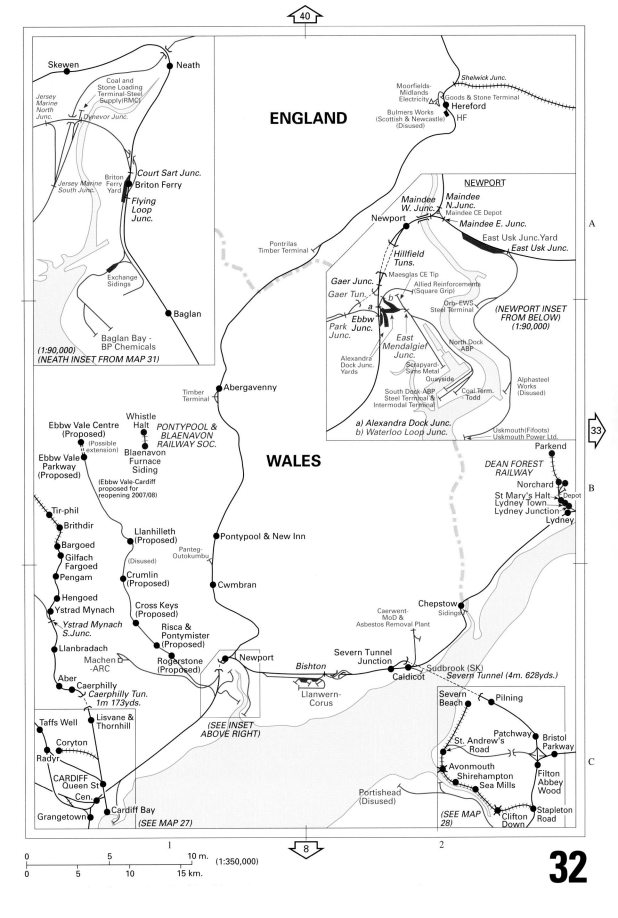

ENGLAND

Skewen · Neath

Coal and Stone Loading Terminal-Steel Supply (RMC)

Jersey Marine North Junc.

Dynevor Junc.

Court Sart Junc.
Briton Ferry Yard
Briton Ferry

Flying Loop Junc.

Jersey Marine South Junc.

Exchange Sidings

Baglan

Baglan Bay - BP Chemicals

(1:90,000)
(NEATH INSET FROM MAP 31)

Moorfields-Midlands Electricity

Shelwick Junc.

Goods & Stone Terminal
Hereford
HF

Bulmers Works (Scottish & Newcastle) (Disused)

NEWPORT

Maindee W.Junc.
Maindee N.Junc.
Maindee CE Depot
Newport
Maindee E. Junc.

East Usk Junc.Yard
East Usk Junc.

Hillfield Tuns.

Pontrilas Timber Terminal

Maesglas CE Tip

Gaer Junc.
Gaer Tun.
Allied Reinforcements (Square Grip)
a *b*
Orb- EWS Steel Terminal

Park Junc.
Ebbw Junc.
East Mendalgief Junc.

(NEWPORT INSET FROM BELOW)
(1:90,000)

North Dock-ABP

Alexandra Dock Junc. Yards
Scrapyard-Sims Metal Quayside

South Dock-ABP Steel Terminal & Intermodal Terminal
Coal Term.- Todd
Alphasteel Works (Disused)

a) Alexandra Dock Junc.
b) Waterloo Loop Junc.

Uskmouth(Fifoots)
Uskmouth Power Ltd.

A

33

Timber Terminal
Abergavenny

Whistle Halt
Ebbw Vale Centre (Proposed)
(Possible extension)
Ebbw Vale Parkway (Proposed)

PONTYPOOL & BLAENAVON RAILWAY SOC.
Blaenavon Furnace Siding

WALES

(Ebbw Vale-Cardiff proposed for reopening 2007/08)

DEAN FOREST RAILWAY

Parkend

Norchard
St Mary's Halt
Lydney Town
Lydney Junction
Depot
Lydney

B

Tir-phil
Brithdir

Llanhilleth (Proposed)
(Disused)
Panteg-Outokumbu

Pontypool & New Inn

Bargoed
Gilfach Fargoed
Pengam

Crumlin (Proposed)

Cwmbran

Chepstow
Sidings

Caerwent-MoD & Asbestos Removal Plant

Hengoed
Ystrad Mynach
Ystrad Mynach S.Junc.

Cross Keys (Proposed)

Risca & Pontymister (Proposed)

Llanbradach
Machen -ARC

Rogerstone (Proposed)

Newport

Bishton

Severn Tunnel Junction
Caldicot
Sudbrook (SK)
Severn Tunnel (4m. 628yds.)

Aber
Caerphilly
Caerphilly Tun. 1m 173yds.

Lisvane & Thornhill

Llanwern-Corus

Severn Beach
Pilning

Taffs Well
Coryton

Radyr

(SEE INSET ABOVE RIGHT)

Patchway
St. Andrew's Road
Bristol Parkway

C

CARDIFF
Queen St
Cen.

Grangetown
Cardiff Bay
(SEE MAP 27)

Portishead (Disused)

Avonmouth
Shirehampton
Sea Mills

Filton Abbey Wood

(SEE MAP 28)

Clifton Down
Stapleton Road

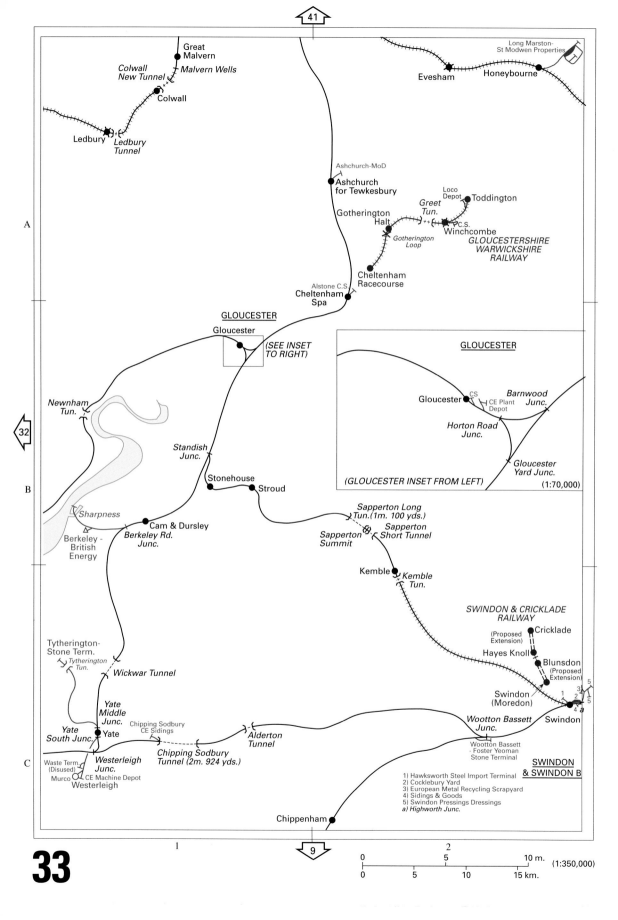

Great Malvern

Malvern Wells

*Colwall
New Tunnel*

Colwall

Long Marston-
St Modwen Properties

Evesham

Honeybourne

Ledbury

*Ledbury
Tunnel*

Ashchurch-MoD

Ashchurch
for Tewkesbury

Loco
Depot

*Greet
Tun.*

Toddington

Gotherington
Halt

C.S.

Winchcombe

*GLOUCESTERSHIRE
WARWICKSHIRE
RAILWAY*

*Gotherington
Loop*

A

Cheltenham
Racecourse

Alstone C.S.

Cheltenham
Spa

GLOUCESTER

Gloucester

*(SEE INSET
TO RIGHT)*

GLOUCESTER

Gloucester

CS

CE Plant
Depot

*Barnwood
Junc.*

*Horton Road
Junc.*

*Newnham
Tun.*

32

(GLOUCESTER INSET FROM LEFT)

*Gloucester
Yard Junc.*

(1:70,000)

*Standish
Junc.*

B

Stonehouse

Stroud

*Sapperton Long
Tun.(1m. 100 yds.)*

Sharpness

Cam & Dursley

Berkeley -
British
Energy

*Berkeley Rd.
Junc.*

*Sapperton
Summit*

*Sapperton
Short Tunnel*

Kemble

*Kemble
Tun.*

*SWINDON & CRICKLADE
RAILWAY*

Cricklade

*(Proposed
Extension)*

Hayes Knoll

Blunsdon

*(Proposed
Extension)*

*Tytherington-
Stone Term.*

*Tytherington
Tun.*

Wickwar Tunnel

Swindon
(Moredon)

*Yate
Middle
Junc.*

Chipping Sodbury
CE Sidings

3
2
4

5
1
5

1

Swindon

*Yate
South Junc.*

Yate

*Alderton
Tunnel*

*Wootton Bassett
Junc.*

C

Waste Term.
(Disused)

*Westerleigh
Junc.*

Murco

CE Machine Depot

Westerleigh

*Chipping Sodbury
Tunnel (2m. 924 yds.)*

Wootton Bassett
- Foster Yeoman
Stone Terminal

SWINDON
& SWINDON B

1) Hawksworth Steel Import Terminal
2) Cocklebury Yard
3) European Metal Recycling Scrapyard
4) Sidings & Goods
5) Swindon Pressings Dressings
a) Highworth Junc.

Chippenham

I

9

0   2
0   5   10 m.   (1:350,000)
0   5   10   15 km.

33

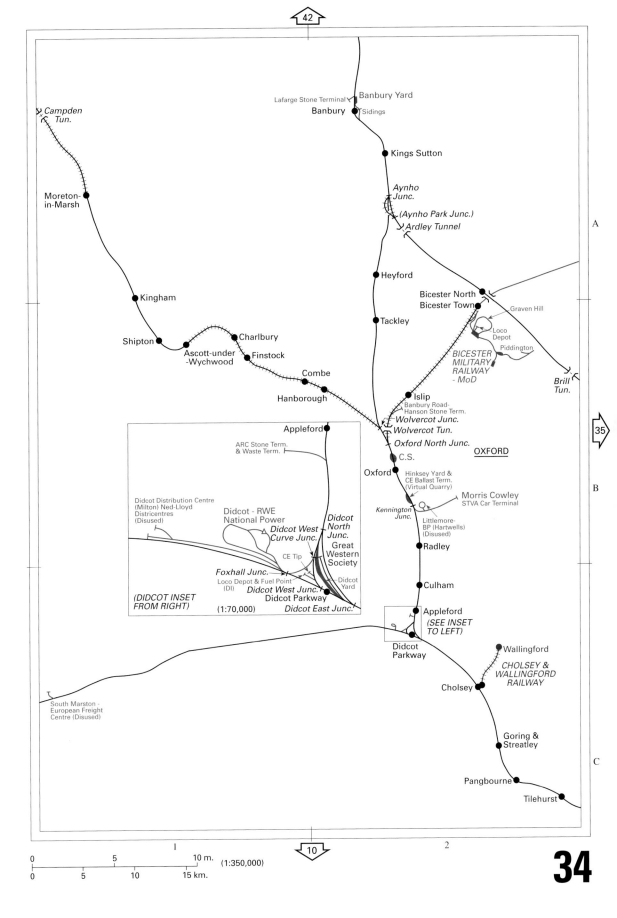

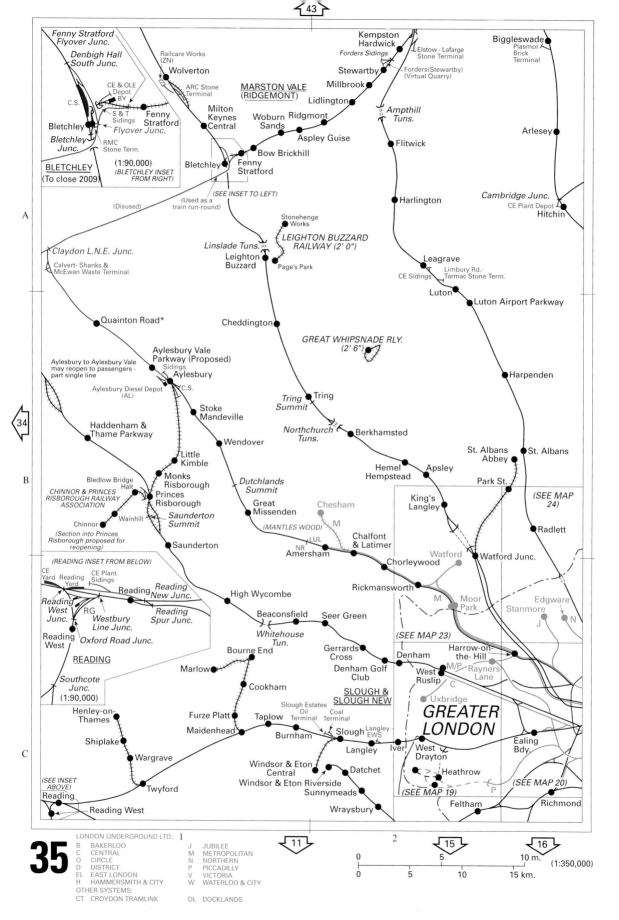

BLETCHLEY INSET:

Fenny Stratford
Flyover Junc.

Denbigh Hall
South Junc.

Railcare Works (ZN)

Wolverton

CE & OLE Depot BY

ARC Stone Terminal

C.S.

S & T Sidings

Fenny Stratford

Bletchley

Bletchley Flyover Junc.
Junc.

RMC Stone Term.

BLETCHLEY
(To close 2009)

(1:90,000)
(BLETCHLEY INSET FROM RIGHT)

MAIN MAP:

Kempston Hardwick

Elstow - Lafarge Stone Terminal

Forders Sidings

Stewartby

Forders(Stewartby) (Virtual Quarry)

Millbrook

MARSTON VALE
(RIDGEMONT)

Milton Keynes Central

Woburn Sands

Ridgmont

Lidlington

Ampthill Tuns.

Aspley Guise

Flitwick

Bow Brickhill

Bletchley

Fenny Stratford

(SEE INSET TO LEFT)

(Disused)

(Used as a train run-round)

(SEE INSET TO LEFT)

Harlington

Biggleswade

Plasmor Brick Terminal

Arlesey

Cambridge Junc.
CE Plant Depot

Hitchin

A

Claydon L.N.E. Junc.

Calvert- Shanks & McEwan Waste Terminal

Stonehenge Works

LEIGHTON BUZZARD RAILWAY (2' 0")

Linslade Tuns.

Leighton Buzzard

Page's Park

Cheddington

GREAT WHIPSNADE RLY.
(2' 6")

Leagrave

CE Sidings

Limbury Rd.- Tarmac Stone Term.

Luton

Luton Airport Parkway

Quainton Road*

Aylesbury Vale Parkway (Proposed)

Aylesbury to Aylesbury Vale may reopen to passengers - part single line

Sidings

Aylesbury

Aylesbury Diesel Depot (AL)

C.S.

Stoke Mandeville

Wendover

Tring Summit

Tring

Northchurch Tuns.

Berkhamsted

Harpenden

St. Albans Abbey

St. Albans

34

B

Haddenham & Thame Parkway

Little Kimble

Bledlow Bridge Halt

Monks Risborough

CHINNOR & PRINCES RISBOROUGH RAILWAY ASSOCIATION

Princes Risborough

Wainhill

Chinnor

(Section into Princes Risborough proposed for reopening)

Saunderton Summit

Saunderton

Dutchlands Summit

Great Missenden

(MANTLES WOOD)

Chesham

M

Chalfont & Latimer

NR

LUL

Amersham

Chorleywood

Hemel Hempstead

Apsley

King's Langley

Watford

Park St.

Watford Junc.

(SEE MAP 24)

Radlett

Rickmansworth

M

Moor Park

(SEE MAP 23)

Edgware

Stanmore

J

N

READING INSET:

CE Yard

Reading Yard

CE Plant Sidings

Reading

Reading New Junc.

Reading West Junc.

RG

Westbury Line Junc.

Reading Spur Junc.

Reading West

Oxford Road Junc.

READING

Southcote Junc.
(1:90,000)

High Wycombe

Beaconsfield

Seer Green

Whitefield Tun.

Gerrards Cross

Denham Golf Club

Denham

Harrow-on-the-Hill

West Ruslip

M/P

Rayners Lane

C

SLOUGH & SLOUGH NEW

Uxbridge

GREATER LONDON

Bourne End

Marlow

Cookham

Furze Platt

Henley-on-Thames

Shiplake

Wargrave

Twyford

(SEE INSET ABOVE)

Reading

Reading West

Maidenhead

Taplow

Slough Estates Oil Terminal

Coal Terminal

Slough

Langley EWS

Burnham

Langley

Iver

West Drayton

Ealing Bdy.

Windsor & Eton Central

Windsor & Eton Riverside

Datchet

Heathrow

Sunnymeads

Wraysbury

(SEE MAP 19)

P

(SEE MAP 20)

Feltham

Richmond

C

35

LONDON UNDERGROUND LTD.:
B BAKERLOO
C CENTRAL
O CIRCLE
D DISTRICT
EL EAST LONDON
H HAMMERSMITH & CITY
OTHER SYSTEMS:
CT CROYDON TRAMLINK

J JUBILEE
M METROPOLITAN
N NORTHERN
P PICCADILLY
V VICTORIA
W WATERLOO & CITY

DL DOCKLANDS

0 5 10 m.
0 5 10 15 km.

(1:350,000)

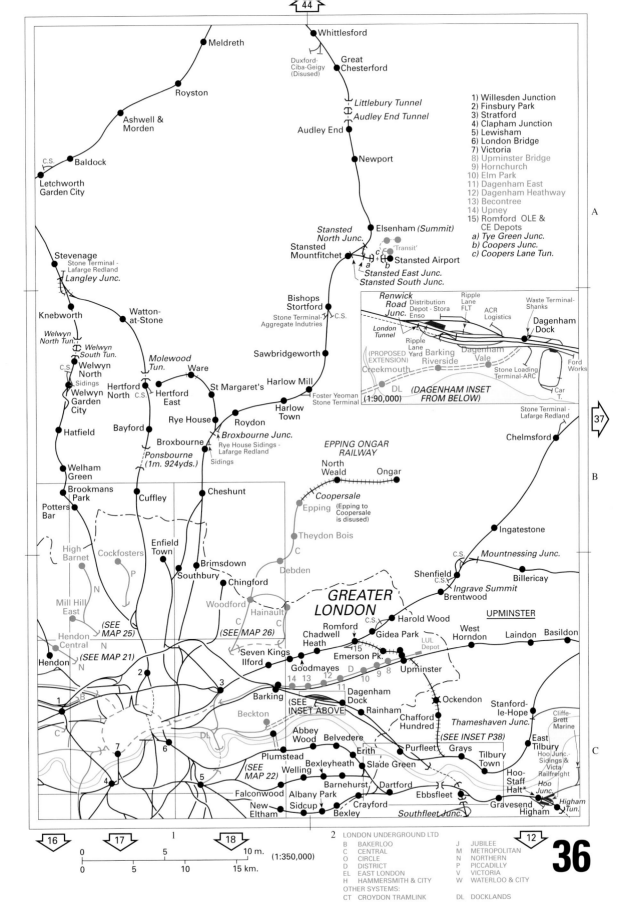

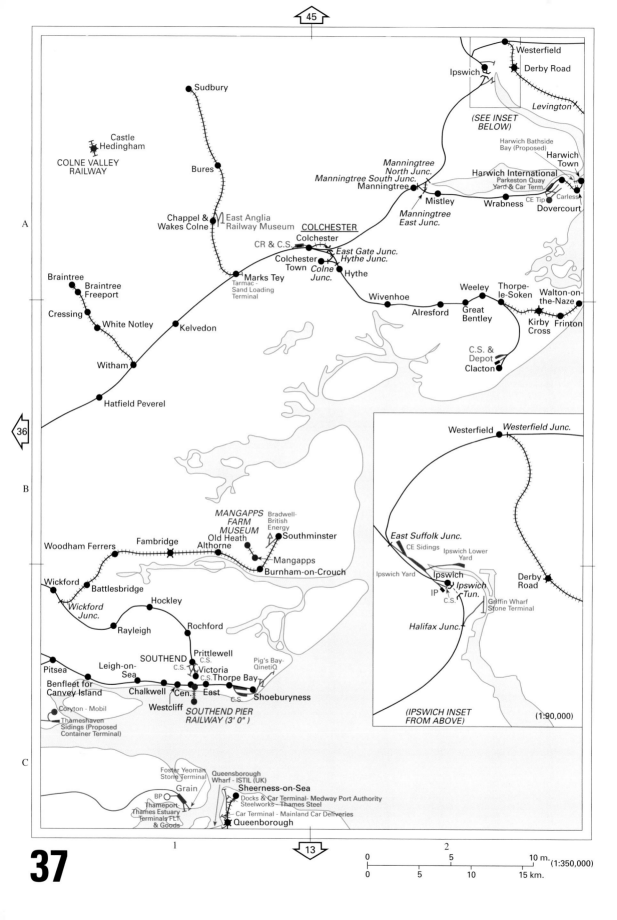

Sudbury

Castle Hedingham
COLNE VALLEY RAILWAY

Bures

Ipswich
Westerfield
Derby Road

(SEE INSET BELOW)

Levington

Chappel & Wakes Colne
East Anglia Railway Museum

Manningtree North Junc.
Manningtree South Junc.
Manningtree

Harwich Bathside Bay (Proposed)
Harwich Town
Harwich International
Parkeston Quay Yard & Car Term.
Carless
Dovercourt
CE Tip

COLCHESTER

A

CR & C.S.
Colchester
East Gate Junc.
Hythe Junc.
Colchester Town
Colne Junc.
Hythe

Manningtree East Junc.
Mistley
Wrabness

Marks Tey
Tarmac - Sand Loading Terminal

Weeley
Thorpe-le-Soken
Walton-on-the-Naze

Braintree
Braintree Freeport

Wivenhoe
Alresford
Great Bentley
Kirby Cross
Frinton

Cressing
White Notley

Kelvedon

Witham

C.S. & Depot
Clacton

36

Hatfield Peverel

B

Westerfield
Westerfield Junc.

MANGAPPS FARM MUSEUM
Bradwell-British Energy

Old Heath
Althorne
Southminster
East Suffolk Junc.
CE Sidings
Ipswich Lower Yard

Woodham Ferrers
Fambridge
Ipswich Yard
Ipswich
IP
Ipswich Tun.
C.S.
Derby Road

Mangapps
Burnham-on-Crouch

Griffin Wharf Stone Terminal

Wickford
Battlesbridge
Hockley
Wickford Junc.

Halifax Junc.

Rayleigh
Rochford

Pitsea
SOUTHEND
Prittlewell
C.S.
Victoria
Pig's Bay-QinetiQ
Leigh-on-Sea
C.S.
C.S. **Thorpe Bay**
Benfleet for Canvey Island
Chalkwell
Cen.
East
C.S.
Shoeburyness
Coryton - Mobil
Westcliff
SOUTHEND PIER RAILWAY (3' 0")

(IPSWICH INSET FROM ABOVE)
(1:90,000)

Thameshaven Sidings (Proposed Container Terminal)

C

Foster Yeoman Stone Terminal
Queensborough Wharf - ISTIL (UK)
Sheerness-on-Sea
Grain
BP
Thameport Thames Estuary Terminals FLT & Goods
Docks & Car Terminal- Medway Port Authority
Steelworks - Thames Steel
Car Terminal - Mainland Car Deliveries
Queenborough

37

0   5   10 m. (1:350,000)
0   5   10   15 km.

1   2

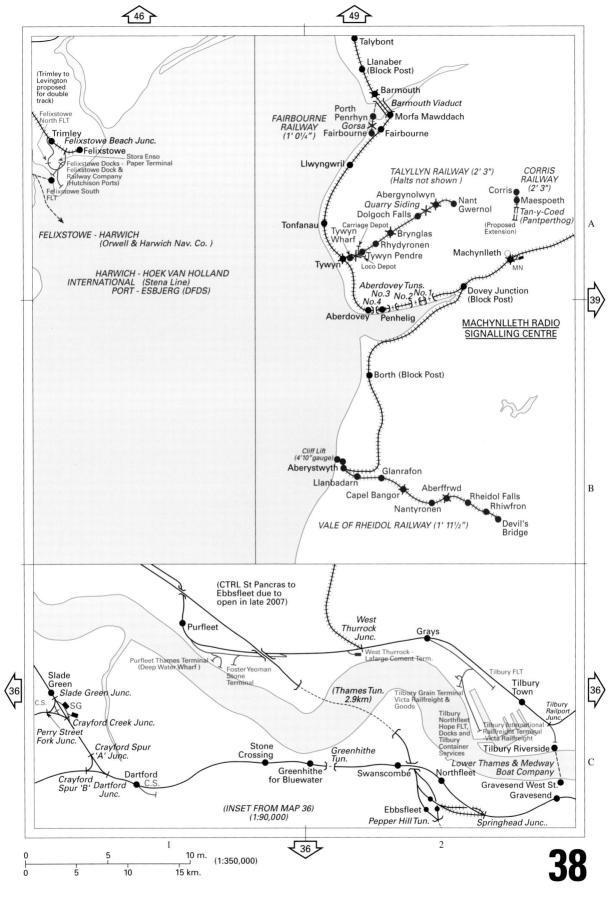

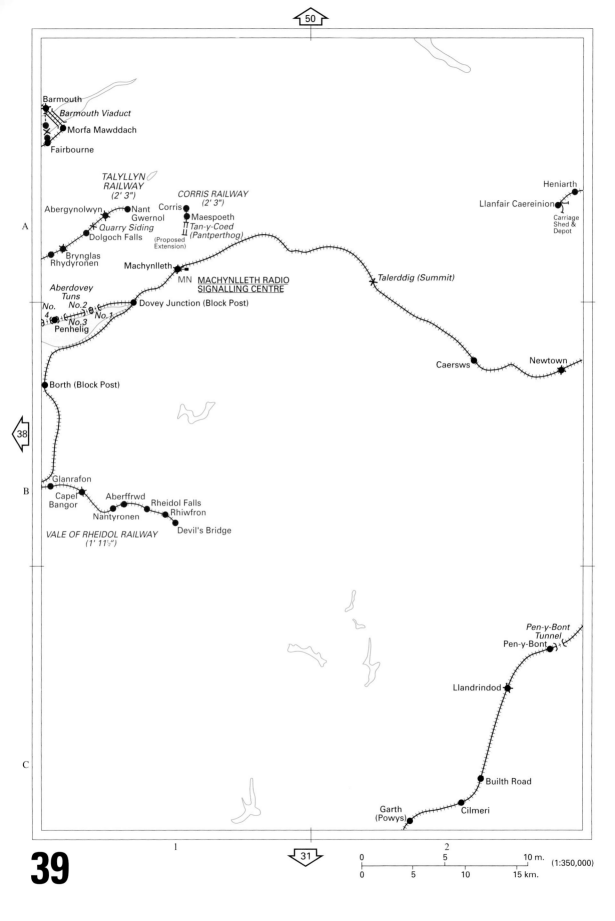

Barmouth
Barmouth Viaduct
Morfa Mawddach
Fairbourne

*TALYLLYN
RAILWAY
(2' 3")*

*CORRIS RAILWAY
(2' 3")*

Heniarth
Llanfair Caereinion

Corris
Maespoeth
Abergynolwyn
Nant
Gwernol
Quarry Siding
Dolgoch Falls
Tan-y-Coed
(Pantperthog)
(Proposed
Extension)

Carriage
Shed &
Depot

A

Brynglas
Rhydyronen
Machynlleth
MN MACHYNLLETH RADIO
SIGNALLING CENTRE

Talerddig (Summit)

*Aberdovey
Tuns*
No. No.2
No.1
4 No.3
Penhelig
Dovey Junction (Block Post)

Caersws
Newtown

Borth (Block Post)

B

Glanrafon
Capel
Bangor
Aberffrwd
Nantyronen
Rheidol Falls
Rhiwfron
Devil's Bridge

*VALE OF RHEIDOL RAILWAY
(1' 11½")*

*Pen-y-Bont
Tunnel*
Pen-y-Bont

Llandrindod

C

Builth Road

Garth
(Powys)
Cilmeri

1

0   2
5
10 m. (1:350,000)

0   5   10   15 km.

39

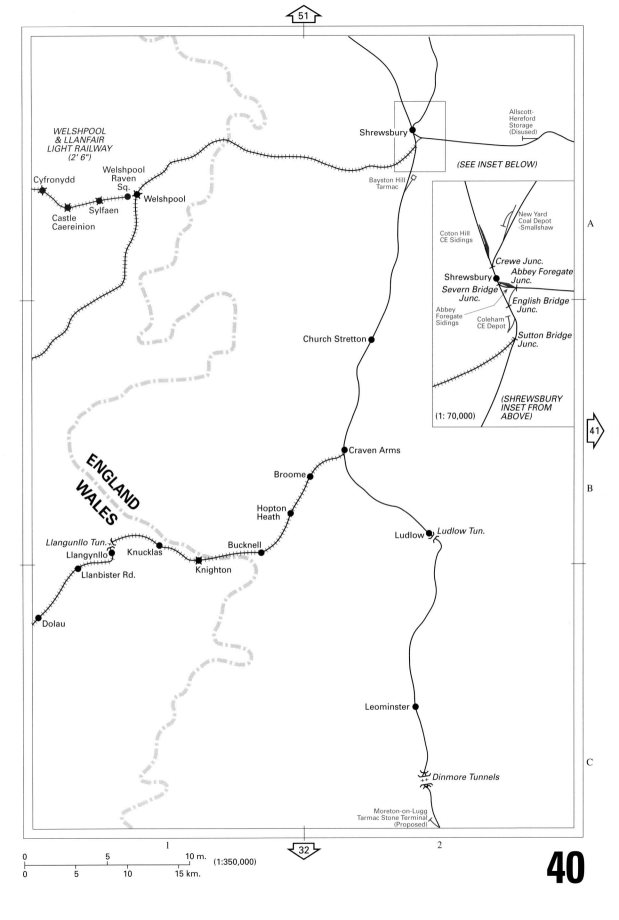

*WELSHPOOL
& LLANFAIR
LIGHT RAILWAY
(2' 6")*

Cyfronydd

Welshpool
Raven Sq.

Sylfaen

Castle
Caereinion

Welshpool

Shrewsbury

Allscott-
Hereford
Storage
(Disused)

(SEE INSET BELOW)

Bayston Hill
Tarmac

New Yard
Coal Depot
-Smallshaw

Coton Hill
CE Sidings

Crewe Junc.

*Abbey Foregate
Junc.*

Shrewsbury

*Severn Bridge
Junc.*

Abbey
Foregate
Sidings

Coleham
CE Depot

*English Bridge
Junc.*

*Sutton Bridge
Junc.*

A

Church Stretton

*(SHREWSBURY
INSET FROM
ABOVE)*

(1: 70,000)

41

Craven Arms

Broome

ENGLAND

WALES

Hopton
Heath

B

Ludlow   *Ludlow Tun.*

Llangunllo Tun.

Llangynllo

Knucklas

Bucknell

Llanbister Rd.

Knighton

Dolau

Leominster

C

Dinmore Tunnels

Moreton-on-Lugg
Tarmac Stone Terminal
(Proposed)

0   5   10 m.   (1:350,000)

0   5   10   15 km.

1

2

40

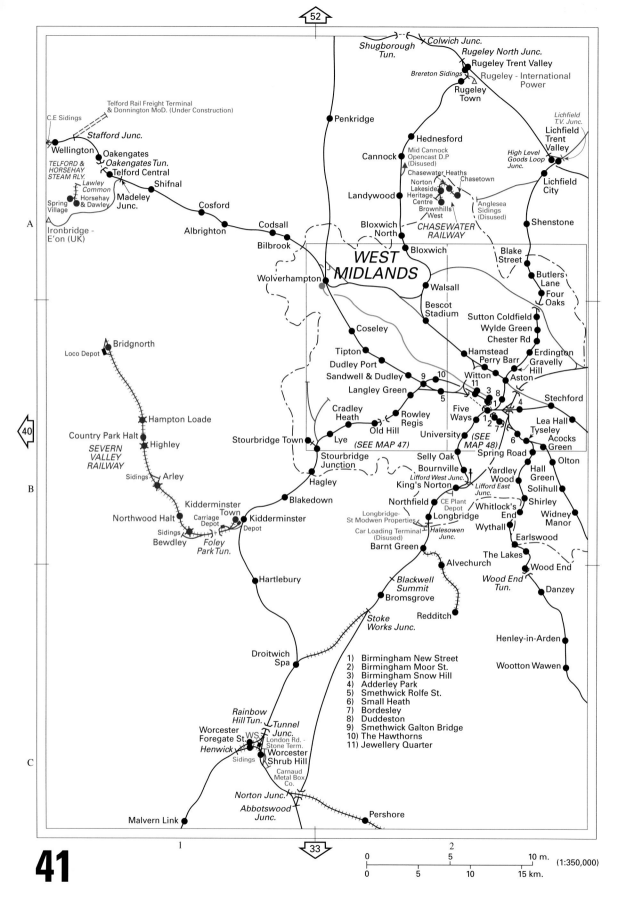

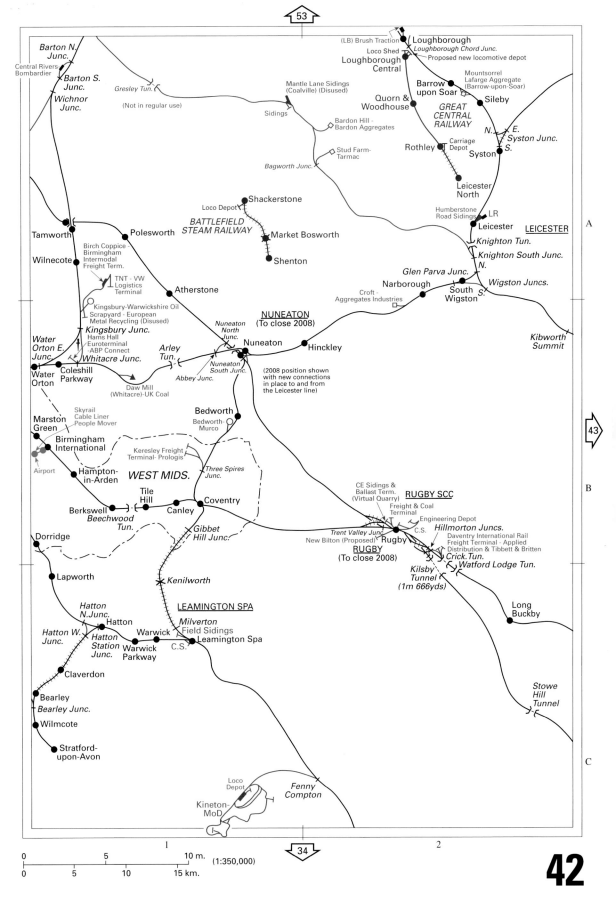

Barton N. Junc.
Central Rivers Bombardier
Barton S. Junc.
Wichnor Junc.
Gresley Tun.
(Not in regular use)

Mantle Lane Sidings (Coalville) (Disused)
Sidings
Bardon Hill - Bardon Aggregates
Stud Farm - Tarmac
Bagworth Junc.

(LB) Brush Traction — **Loughborough**
Loco Shed — *Loughborough Chord Junc.*
Loughborough Central — Proposed new locomotive depot
Barrow upon Soar — Mountsorrel Lafarge Aggregate (Barrow-upon-Soar)
Quorn & Woodhouse — **Sileby**
GREAT CENTRAL RAILWAY
N. — E.
S. Syston Junc.
Carriage Depot
Rothley — **Syston**
Leicester North

Humberstone Road Sidings
Leicester — LR
LEICESTER — A
Knighton Tun.
Knighton South Junc.
N.

Shackerstone
Loco Depot
BATTLEFIELD STEAM RAILWAY
Market Bosworth
Shenton

Tamworth — **Polesworth**
Wilnecote
Birch Coppice - Birmingham Intermodal Freight Term.
TNT - VW Logistics Terminal
Kingsbury-Warwickshire Oil
Scrapyard - European Metal Recycling (Disused)
Kingsbury Junc.
Hams Hall Euroterminal - ABP Connect
Whitacre Junc.
Coleshill Parkway
Water Orton
Water Orton E. Junc.
Daw Mill (Whitacre)-UK Coal

Atherstone

Glen Parva Junc.
Narborough
Croft - Aggregates Industries
South Wigston
Wigston Juncs.
S.
Kibworth Summit

NUNEATON (To close 2008)
Nuneaton North Junc.
Nuneaton — **Hinckley**
Arley Tun.
Nuneaton South Junc.
Abbey Junc.
(2008 position shown with new connections in place to and from the Leicester line)

Bedworth
Bedworth-Murco
Skyrail Cable Liner People Mover
Marston Green
Birmingham International
Airport
Hampton-in-Arden
Keresley Freight Terminal- Prologis
Three Spires Junc.
WEST MIDS.

CE Sidings & Ballast Term. (Virtual Quarry)
RUGBY SCC
Freight & Coal Terminal
— B
Engineering Depot
Hillmorton Juncs.

Tile Hill
Berkswell
Beechwood Tun.
Canley — **Coventry**
Dorridge
Gibbet Hill Junc.

Trent Valley Junc.
C.S.
New Bilton (Proposed)
RUGBY (To close 2008) — **Rugby**
Daventry International Rail Freight Terminal - Applied Distribution & Tibbett & Britten
Crick. Tun.
Watford Lodge Tun.
Kilsby Tunnel (1m 666yds)

Lapworth
Kenilworth
LEAMINGTON SPA
Long Buckby

Hatton N.Junc.
Hatton
Milverton
Field Sidings
Hatton W. Junc.
Hatton Station Junc.
Warwick
Warwick Parkway
C.S.
Leamington Spa

Claverdon
Stowe Hill Tunnel

Bearley
Bearley Junc.
Wilmcote
Stratford-upon-Avon
— C

Loco Depot
Fenny Compton
Kineton-MoD

0 —— 5 —— 10 m. (1:350,000)
0 —— 5 —— 10 —— 15 km.

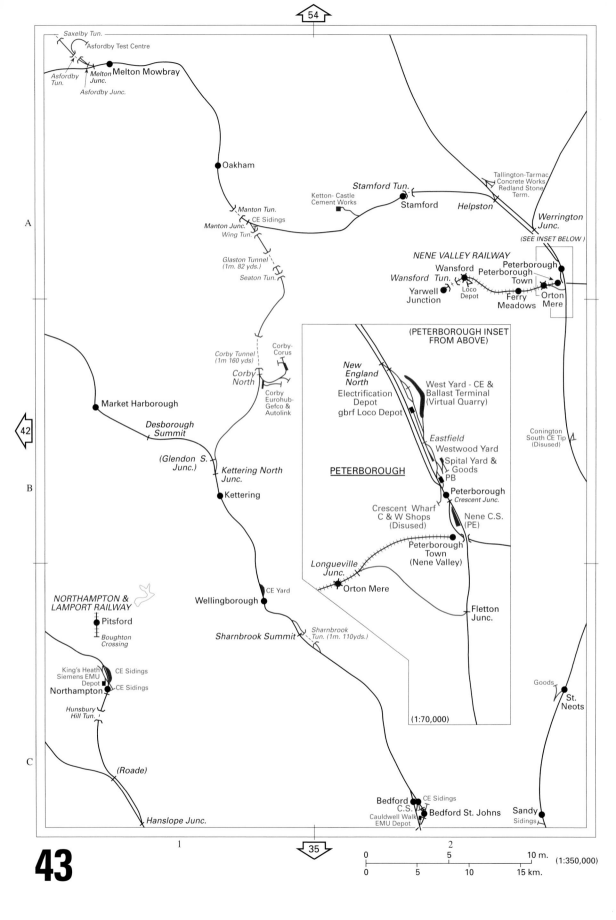

Saxelby Tun.
Asfordby Test Centre
Asfordby Tun.
Melton Junc.
Asfordby Junc.
Melton Mowbray
Oakham

Stamford Tun.
Ketton- Castle Cement Works
Stamford
Helpston

Tallington-Tarmac Concrete Works Redland Stone Term.
Werrington Junc.

Manton Tun.
CE Sidings
Manton Junc.
Wing Tun.

(SEE INSET BELOW)

A

NENE VALLEY RAILWAY

Glaston Tunnel (1m. 82 yds.)
Seaton Tun.

Wansford Tun.
Wansford
Peterborough
Peterborough Town
Yarwell Junction
Loco Depot
Ferry Meadows
Orton Mere

Corby Tunnel (1m 160 yds.)
Corby-Corus
Corby North
Corby Eurohub-Gefco & Autolink

(PETERBOROUGH INSET FROM ABOVE)

New England North
Electrification Depot
gbrf Loco Depot

West Yard - CE & Ballast Terminal (Virtual Quarry)

Market Harborough

Desborough Summit

Eastfield
Westwood Yard
Spital Yard & Goods
PB

PETERBOROUGH

Conington South CE Tip (Disused)

42

(Glendon S. Junc.)

Kettering North Junc.

Peterborough
Crescent Junc.

Crescent Wharf C & W Shops (Disused)

Nene C.S. (PE)

B

Kettering

Peterborough Town (Nene Valley)

Longueville Junc.
Orton Mere

CE Yard
Wellingborough

Fletton Junc.

NORTHAMPTON & LAMPORT RAILWAY

Pitsford
Boughton Crossing

Sharnbrook Summit
Sharnbrook Tun. (1m. 110yds.)

(1:70,000)

King's Heath Siemens EMU Depot
CE Sidings
CE Sidings
Northampton

Goods
St. Neots

Hunsbury Hill Tun.

C

(Roade)

Bedford C.S.
CE Sidings
Bedford St. Johns

Sandy
Sidings

Cauldwell Walk EMU Depot

Hanslope Junc.

1

2
5
10 m.
(1:350,000)

0   5   10   15 km.

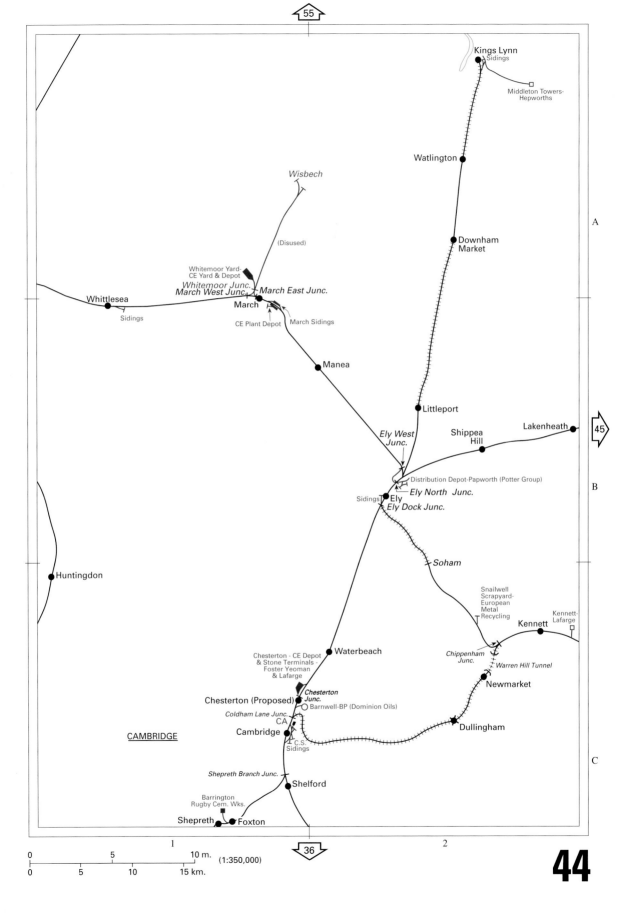

Kings Lynn
Sidings

Middleton Towers-
Hepworths

Watlington

A

Downham
Market

Wisbech

(Disused)

Whitemoor Yard-
CE Yard & Depot
Whitemoor Junc.
March West Junc. *March East Junc.*
March
CE Plant Depot
March Sidings

Whittlesea
Sidings

Manea

Littleport

Ely West Junc.

Shippea Hill

Lakenheath

45

Distribution Depot-Papworth (Potter Group)

Ely North Junc.

Sidings Ely
Ely Dock Junc.

B

Soham

Huntingdon

Snailwell
Scrapyard-
European
Metal
Recycling

Kennett-
Lafarge

Kennett

*Chippenham
Junc.*

Warren Hill Tunnel

Waterbeach

Chesterton - CE Depot
& Stone Terminals -
Foster Yeoman
& Lafarge

Newmarket

*Chesterton
Junc.*

Chesterton (Proposed)
Barnwell-BP (Dominion Oils)

Coldham Lane Junc.
CA
Cambridge

Dullingham

C.S.
Sidings

<u>CAMBRIDGE</u>

C

Shepreth Branch Junc.
Shelford

Barrington
Rugby Cem. Wks.
Shepreth Foxton

0 ___ 5 ___ 10 m.   (1:350,000)
0 _ 5 _ 10 _ 15 km.

1

2

44

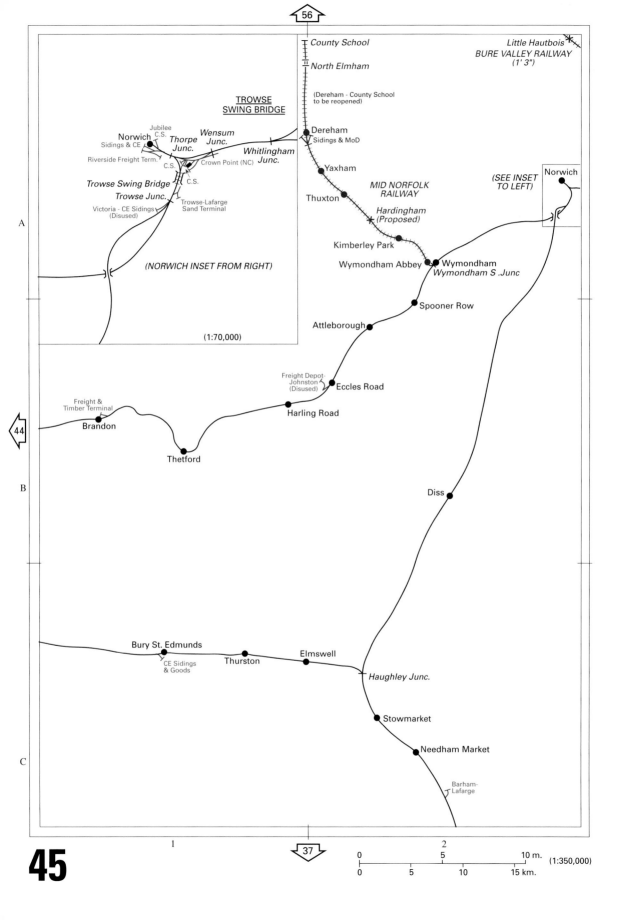

County School

North Elmham

(Dereham - County School
to be reopened)

Little Hautbois
BURE VALLEY RAILWAY
(1' 3")

TROWSE
SWING BRIDGE

Jubilee
C.S.
Norwich
Sidings & CE
Riverside Freight Term.

Thorpe
Junc.
C.S.

Wensum
Junc.

Whitlingham
Junc.

Crown Point (NC)

Trowse Swing Bridge
Trowse Junc.

Victoria - CE Sidings
(Disused)

Trowse-Lafarge
Sand Terminal

(NORWICH INSET FROM RIGHT)

(1:70,000)

Dereham
Sidings & MoD

Yaxham

Thuxton

MID NORFOLK
RAILWAY

Hardingham
(Proposed)

Kimberley Park

Wymondham Abbey

Wymondham

Wymondham S .Junc

(SEE INSET
TO LEFT)

Norwich

Spooner Row

Attleborough

Freight Depot-
Johnston
(Disused)

Eccles Road

Harling Road

Freight &
Timber Terminal
Brandon

Thetford

Diss

A

44

B

Bury St. Edmunds
CE Sidings
& Goods

Thurston

Elmswell

Haughley Junc.

Stowmarket

Needham Market

Barham-
Lafarge

C

45

1

2

5

10 m.

(1:350,000)

0   5   10   15 km.

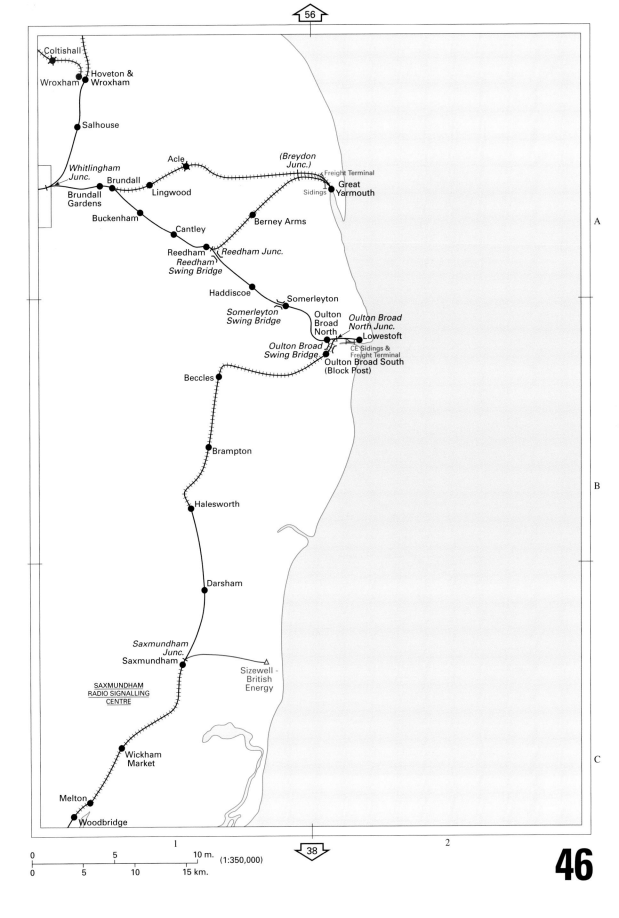

Coltishall

Hoveton &
Wroxham

Wroxham

Salhouse

*Whitlingham
Junc.*

Brundall

Acle

*(Breydon
Junc.)*

Freight Terminal

Brundall
Gardens

Lingwood

Sidings

Great
Yarmouth

Buckenham

Cantley

Berney Arms

Reedham

Reedham Junc.

*Reedham
Swing Bridge*

Haddiscoe

Somerleyton

*Somerleyton
Swing Bridge*

Oulton
Broad
North

*Oulton Broad
North Junc.*

Lowestoft

*Oulton Broad
Swing Bridge*

CE Sidings &
Freight Terminal

Oulton Broad South
(Block Post)

Beccles

Brampton

Halesworth

Darsham

*Saxmundham
Junc.*

Saxmundham

Sizewell -
British
Energy

SAXMUNDHAM
RADIO SIGNALLING
CENTRE

Wickham
Market

Melton

Woodbridge

A

B

C

1

2

0   5   10 m.
(1:350,000)

0   5   10   15 km.

46

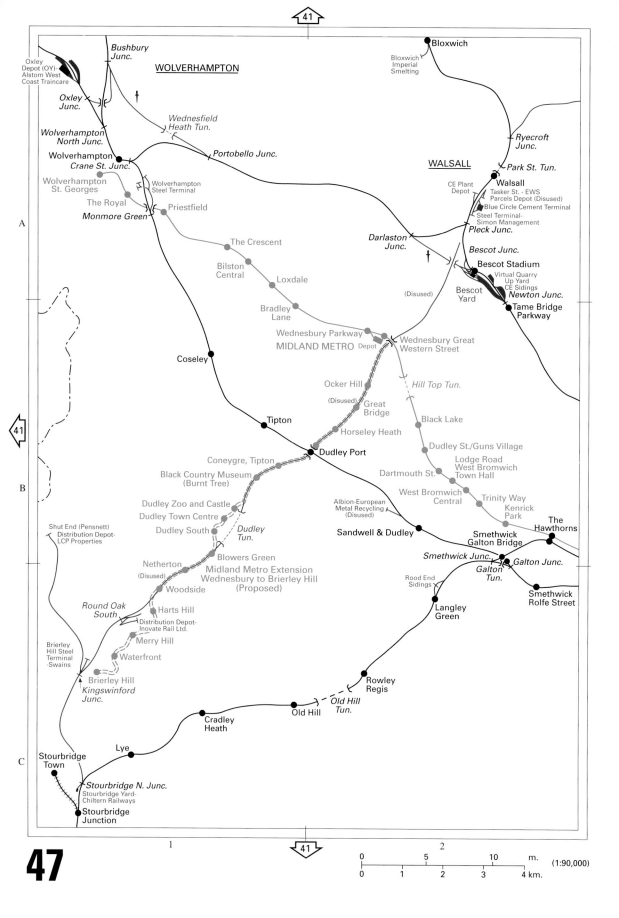

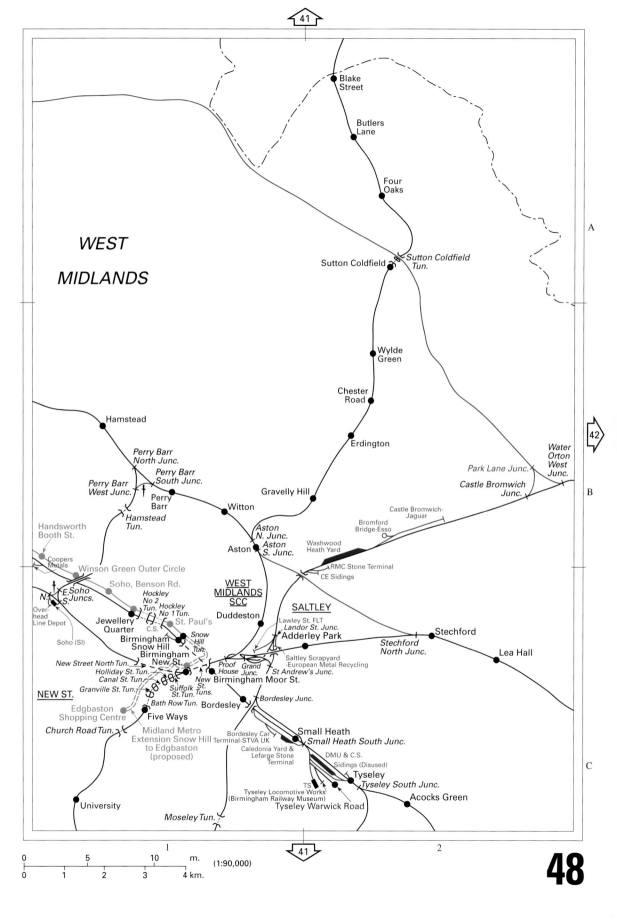

WEST

MIDLANDS

Blake
Street

Butlers
Lane

Four
Oaks

A

Sutton Coldfield
Tun.

Sutton Coldfield

Wylde
Green

Chester
Road

Hamstead

Erdington

Water
Orton
West
Junc.

Perry Barr
North Junc.

Perry Barr
South Junc.

Park Lane Junc.

Castle Bromwich
Junc.

B

Perry Barr
West Junc.

Perry
Barr

Gravelly Hill

Hamstead
Tun.

Witton

Castle Bromwich-
Jaguar

Handsworth
Booth St.

Aston
N. Junc.
Aston
S. Junc.

Bromford
Bridge-Esso

Coopers
Metals

Aston

Washwood
Heath Yard

Winson Green Outer Circle

Soho, Benson Rd.

WEST
MIDLANDS
SCC

RMC Stone Terminal

CE Sidings

N.
E. Soho
S.
Juncs.

Hockley
No 2
Tun.

Hockley
No 1 Tun.

Duddeston

SALTLEY

Stechford

Over-
head
Line Depot

Jewellery
Quarter

C.S.

St. Paul's

Lawley St. FLT

Landor St. Junc.

Stechford
North Junc.

Lea Hall

Soho (SI)

Birmingham
Snow Hill

Snow
Hill
Tun.

Adderley Park

New Street North Tun.

Birmingham
New St.

Proof
House

Grand
Junc.

Saltley Scrapyard
-European Metal Recycling

Holliday St. Tun.

New
St.
Tuns.

St Andrew's Junc.

NEW ST.

Canal St. Tun.

Granville St. Tun.

Suffolk
St. Tun.

Birmingham Moor St.

Bath Row Tun.

Bordesley

Bordesley Junc.

Edgbaston
Shopping Centre

Five Ways

Small Heath

Small Heath South Junc.

Church Road Tun.

Midland Metro
Extension Snow Hill
to Edgbaston
(proposed)

Bordesley Car
Terminal-STVA UK

Caledonia Yard &
Lefarge Stone
Terminal

DMU & C.S.

Sidings (Disused)

C

Tyseley

Tyseley South Junc.

TS

University

Tyseley Locomotive Works
(Birmingham Railway Museum)

Tyseley Warwick Road

Acocks Green

Moseley Tun.

0   5   10   m.   (1:90,000)

0   1   2   3   4 km.

1   2

48

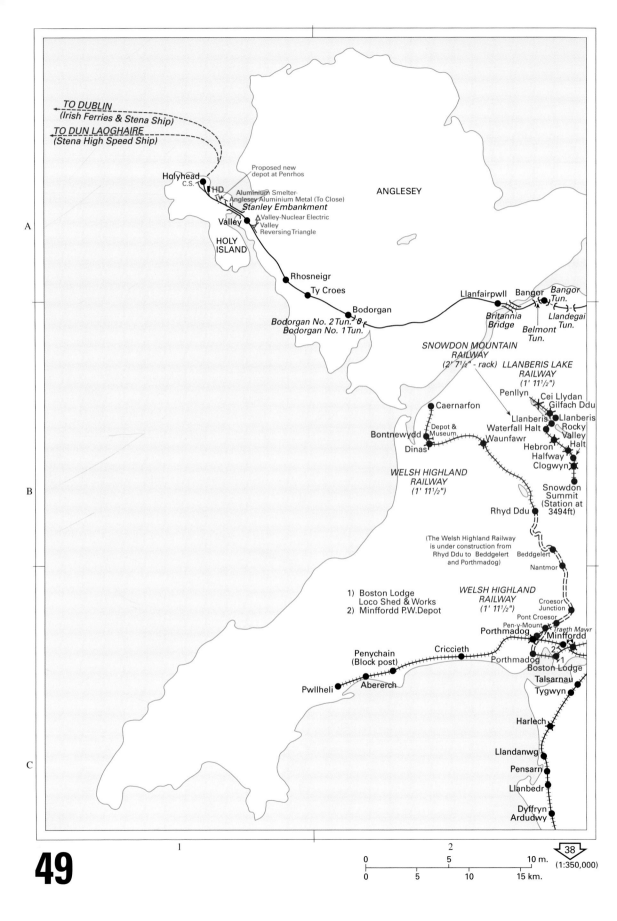

TO DUBLIN
(Irish Ferries & Stena Ship)

TO DUN LAOGHAIRE
(Stena High Speed Ship)

ANGLESEY

Proposed new
depot at Penrhos

Holyhead
C.S.
HD

Aluminium Smelter-
Anglesey Aluminium Metal (To Close)
Stanley Embankment

Valley

Valley-Nuclear Electric
Valley
Reversing Triangle

HOLY
ISLAND

A

Rhosneigr

Ty Croes

Bodorgan

Bodorgan No. 2 Tun.
Bodorgan No. 1 Tun.

Llanfairpwll

Bangor

*Bangor
Tun.*

*Britannia
Bridge*

*Belmont
Tun.*

*Llandegai
Tun.*

*SNOWDON MOUNTAIN
RAILWAY*
(2' 7¹/₂" - rack)

*LLANBERIS LAKE
RAILWAY*
(1' 11¹/₂")

Penllyn

Cei Llydan
Gilfach Ddu

Caernarfon

Llanberis

Llanberis

Depot &
Museum

Waterfall Halt

Rocky
Valley
Halt

Bontnewydd

Waunfawr

Dinas

Hebron

Halfway

Clogwyn

*WELSH HIGHLAND
RAILWAY*
(1' 11¹/₂")

Snowdon
Summit
(Station at
3494ft)

Rhyd Ddu

(The Welsh Highland Railway
is under construction from
Rhyd Ddu to Beddgelert
and Porthmadog)

Beddgelert

Nantmor

1) Boston Lodge
Loco Shed & Works
2) Minffordd P.W.Depot

*WELSH HIGHLAND
RAILWAY*
(1' 11¹/₂")

Croesor
Junction

Pont Croesor

Pen-y-Mount

Traeth Mawr

Porthmadog

Minffordd

2

Penychain
(Block post)

Criccieth

Porthmadog

1

Boston Lodge

Talsarnau

Pwllheli

Abererch

Tygwyn

Harlech

Llandanwg

Pensarn

C

Llanbedr

Dyffryn
Ardudwy

49

38
(1:350,000)

0   5   10 m.
0   5   10   15 km.

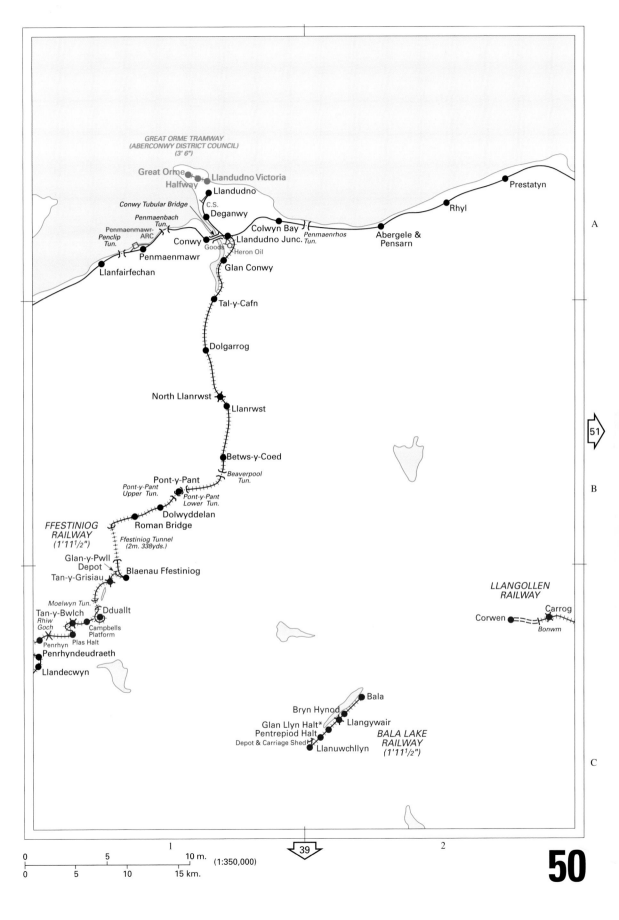

GREAT ORME TRAMWAY
(ABERCONWY DISTRICT COUNCIL)
(3' 6")

Great Orme
Halfway
Llandudno Victoria

Prestatyn

Llandudno

C.S.
Conwy Tubular Bridge
Deganwy
Rhyl

Penmaenbach
Tun.
Penmaenmawr-
Penclip
Tun.
Colwyn Bay
Penmaenrhos
Tun.
Abergele &
Pensarn

Penmaenmawr-
ARC
Conwy
Goods
Llandudno Junc.

Penmaenmawr
Heron Oil

Llanfairfechan
Glan Conwy

A

Tal-y-Cafn

Dolgarrog

North Llanrwst

Llanrwst

51

Betws-y-Coed

Pont-y-Pant
Beaverpool
Tun.

B

Pont-y-Pant
Upper Tun.
Pont-y-Pant
Lower Tun.
Dolwyddelan

FFESTINIOG
RAILWAY
(1'11½")

Roman Bridge

Ffestiniog Tunnel
(2m. 338yds.)

Glan-y-Pwll
Depot
Tan-y-Grisiau
Blaenau Ffestiniog

LLANGOLLEN
RAILWAY

Moelwyn Tun.
Tan-y-Bwlch
Dduallt
Corwen
Carrog

Rhiw
Goch
Campbells
Platform
Bonwm

Penrhyn
Plas Halt
Penrhyndeudraeth

Llandecwyn

Bala

Bryn Hynod

Glan Llyn Halt*
Llangywair
Pentrepiod Halt
Depot & Carriage Shed
Llanuwchllyn
BALA LAKE
RAILWAY
(1'11½")

C

1
10 m.
(1:350,000)

2

0   5   10 m.
0   5   10   15 km.

39

50

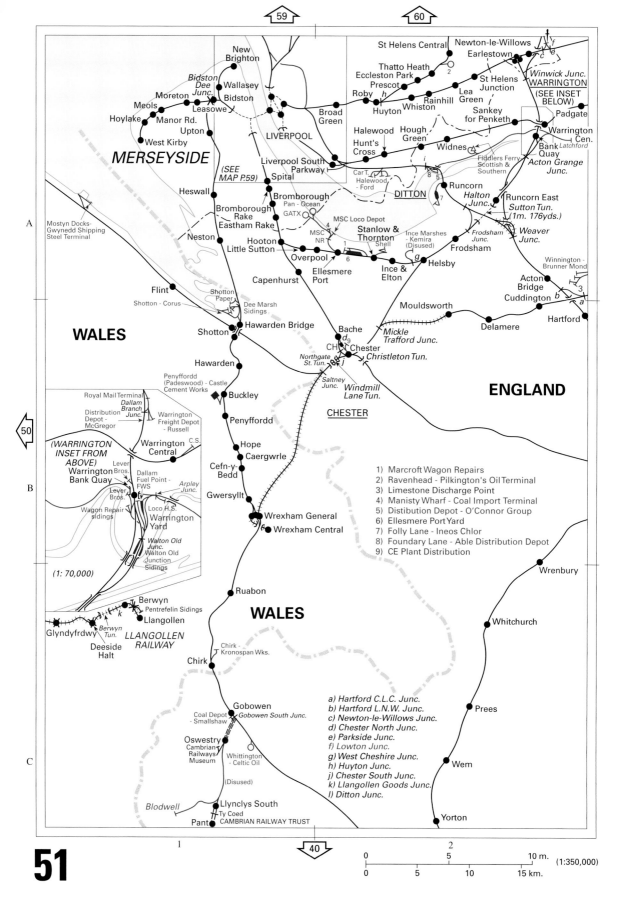

New Brighton
Wallasey
Bidston *Dee Junc.*
Moreton
Bidston
Meols
Leasowe
Hoylake
Manor Rd.
Upton
West Kirby
Broad Green

MERSEYSIDE

St Helens Central
Newton-le-Willows
Earlestown
Thatto Heath
Eccleston Park
Prescot
St Helens Junction
Roby *h*
Rainhill
Lea Green
Whiston
Sankey for Penketh
WARRINGTON (SEE INSET BELOW)
Padgate
Winwick Junc.
Warrington Cen.
Huyton
Halewood
Hough Green
Widnes
Bank Quay *Latchford*
Acton Grange Junc.
Fiddlers Ferry Scottish & Southern

(SEE MAP P.59)

Heswall
Spital
LIVERPOOL
Liverpool South Parkway
Hunt's Cross
Car T.
Halewood - Ford
DITTON

Mostyn Docks-Gwynedd Shipping Steel Terminal

A

Bromborough
Pan - Ocean
GATX
Bromborough Rake
Eastham Rake
Hooton
Little Sutton
Overpool
Ellesmere Port
Ince & Elton
MSC NR
MSC Loco Depot
Stanlow & Thornton
Shell
Ince Marshes - Kemira (Disused)
Frodsham
Frodsham Junc.
Helsby *g*
Runcorn
Halton Junc.
Runcorn East
Sutton Tun. (1m. 176yds.)
Weaver Junc.
Neston
Capenhurst

Winnington - Brunner Mond
Acton Bridge
Cuddington *b*
Hartford *a*

Flint
Shotton Paper
Shotton - Corus
Dee Marsh Sidings
Mouldsworth
Delamere

WALES

Shotton
Hawarden Bridge
Bache *d*
CH. Chester
Mickle Trafford Junc.
Christleton Tun.
Northgate St. Tun.
Hawarden

ENGLAND

Penyffordd (Padeswood) - Castle Cement Works
Buckley
Saltney Junc.
Windmill Lane Tun.
Penyffordd
CHESTER

50

Royal Mail Terminal
Dallam Branch Junc.
Distribution Depot - McGregor
Warrington Freight Depot - Russell
Hope
Caergwrle
Warrington Central
C.S.
(WARRINGTON INSET FROM ABOVE)
Warrington Bank Quay
Lever Bros.
Dallam Fuel Point - FWS
Lever Bros.
Arpley Junc.
Cefn-y-Bedd
Gwersyllt

B

Wagon Repair sidings
Loco H.S.
Warrington Yard
Wrexham General
Wrexham Central

1) Marcroft Wagon Repairs
2) Ravenhead - Pilkington's Oil Terminal
3) Limestone Discharge Point
4) Manisty Wharf - Coal Import Terminal
5) Distibution Depot - O'Connor Group
6) Ellesmere Port Yard
7) Folly Lane - Ineos Chlor
8) Foundary Lane - Able Distribution Depot
9) CE Plant Distribution

Walton Old Junc.
Walton Old Junction Sidings

(1: 70,000)

Wrenbury

Berwyn
Pentrefelin Sidings
Llangollen
Berwyn Tun.
Glyndyfrdwy
Deeside Halt
LLANGOLLEN RAILWAY

Ruabon
WALES

Whitchurch

Chirk - Kronospan Wks.
Chirk

a) Hartford C.L.C. Junc.
b) Hartford L.N.W. Junc.
c) Newton-le-Willows Junc.
d) Chester North Junc.
e) Parkside Junc.
f) Lowton Junc.
g) West Cheshire Junc.
h) Huyton Junc.
j) Chester South Junc.
k) Llangollen Goods Junc.
l) Ditton Junc.

C

Coal Depot - Smallshaw
Gobowen
Gobowen South Junc.
Oswestry
Cambrian Railways Museum
Whittington - Celtic Oil
(Disused)
Prees

Wem

Blodwell
Llynclys South
Ty Coed
CAMBRIAN RAILWAY TRUST
Pant

Yorton

1
40
2
5
10 m.
0
5
10
15 km.
(1:350,000)

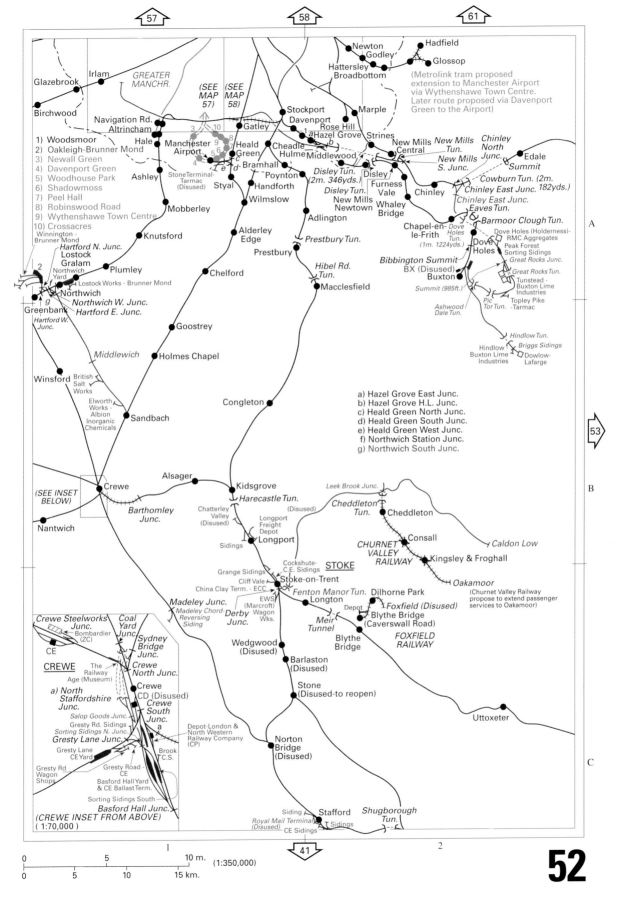

Glazebrook
Irlam
Birchwood
GREATER MANCHR.

(SEE MAP 57)
(SEE MAP 58)

Navigation Rd.
Altrincham
Hale
Manchester Airport
Heald Green
Ashley
Bramhall
Styal
Poynton
Handforth
Mobberley
Wilmslow
Knutsford
Adlington
Alderley Edge
Prestbury
Prestbury Tun.
Chelford
Hibel Rd. Tun.
Goostrey
Macclesfield

Newton
Godley
Hadfield
Glossop
Hattersley
Broadbottom
Marple

(Metrolink tram proposed extension to Manchester Airport via Wythenshawe Town Centre. Later route proposed via Davenport Green to the Airport)

Stockport
Davenport
Rose Hill
Gatley
Hazel Grove
Strines
Cheadle
Hulme
Middlewood
Disley Tun. (2m. 346yds.)
Disley Tun.
Furness Vale
New Mills Newtown
Whaley Bridge

New Mills Central
New Mills S. Junc.
New Mills Tun.
Disley
Chinley North Junc.
Edale
Summit
Cowburn Tun. (2m. 182yds.)
Chinley East Junc.
Eaves Tun.
Chapel-en-le-Frith
Dove Holes Tun. (1m. 1224yds.)
Barmoor Clough Tun.
Dove Holes (Holderness) - RMC Aggregates
Peak Forest Sorting Sidings
Great Rocks Junc.
Dove Holes
Bibbington Summit
BX (Disused)
Buxton
Summit (985ft.)
Ashwood Dale Tun.
Pic Tor Tun.
Great Rocks Tun.
Tunstead - Buxton Lime Industries
Topley Pike -Tarmac

Hindlow Tun.
Hindlow
Buxton Lime Industries
Briggs Sidings
Dowlow- Lafarge

1) Woodsmoor
2) Oakleigh-Brunner Mond
3) Newall Green
4) Davenport Green
5) Woodhouse Park
6) Shadowmoss
7) Peel Hall
8) Robinswood Road
9) Wythenshawe Town Centre
10) Crossacres

Winnington - Brunner Mond
Hartford N. Junc.
Lostock Gralam
Northwich Yard
Plumley
Lostock Works - Brunner Mond
Northwich
Northwich W. Junc.
Hartford E. Junc.
Greenbank
Hartford W. Junc.

Winsford
British Salt Works
Elworth Works - Albion Inorganic Chemicals
Middlewich
Holmes Chapel
Sandbach
Congleton

a) Hazel Grove East Junc.
b) Hazel Grove H.L. Junc.
c) Heald Green North Junc.
d) Heald Green South Junc.
e) Heald Green West Junc.
f) Northwich Station Junc.
g) Northwich South Junc.

Alsager
Crewe
(SEE INSET BELOW)
Barthomley Junc.
Nantwich

Kidsgrove
Harecastle Tun.
Chatterley Valley (Disused)
(Disused)
Longport Freight Depot
Sidings
Longport
Leek Brook Junc.
Cheddleton Tun.
Cheddleton
Consall
CHURNET VALLEY RAILWAY
Kingsley & Froghall
Caldon Low
Oakamoor
(Churnet Valley Railway propose to extend passenger services to Oakamoor)

Cockshute C.E. Sidings
STOKE
Grange Sidings
Cliff Vale
China Clay Term. - ECC
Stoke-on-Trent
Fenton Manor Tun.
Longton
Dilhorne Park
Foxfield (Disused)
Blythe Bridge (Caverswall Road)
EWS (Marcroft) Wagon Wks.
Madeley Junc.
Madeley Chord- Reversing Siding
Derby Junc.
Meir Tunnel
Blythe Bridge
FOXFIELD RAILWAY
Wedgwood (Disused)
Barlaston (Disused)
Stone (Disused-to reopen)
Uttoxeter

Norton Bridge (Disused)
Shugborough Tun.
Stafford
Siding
Royal Mail Terminal (Disused)
CE Sidings
Sidings

CREWE INSET

Crewe Steelworks Junc.
Bombardier (ZC)
CE
CREWE
The Railway Age (Museum)
a) North Staffordshire Junc.
Salop Goods Junc.
Gresty Rd. Sidings
Sorting Sidings N. Junc.
Gresty Lane Junc.
Gresty Lane CE Yard
Gresty Rd Wagon Shops
Gresty Road - CE
Basford Hall Yard & CE Ballast Term.
Sorting Sidings South
Basford Hall Junc.
Coal Yard Junc.
Sydney Bridge Junc.
Crewe North Junc.
Crewe CD (Disused)
Crewe South Junc.
a
Depot-London & North Western Railway Company (CP)
Brook T.C.S.
(CREWE INSET FROM ABOVE)
(1:70,000)

A

B

53

C

0   5   10 m.
0   5   10   15 km.
(1:350,000)

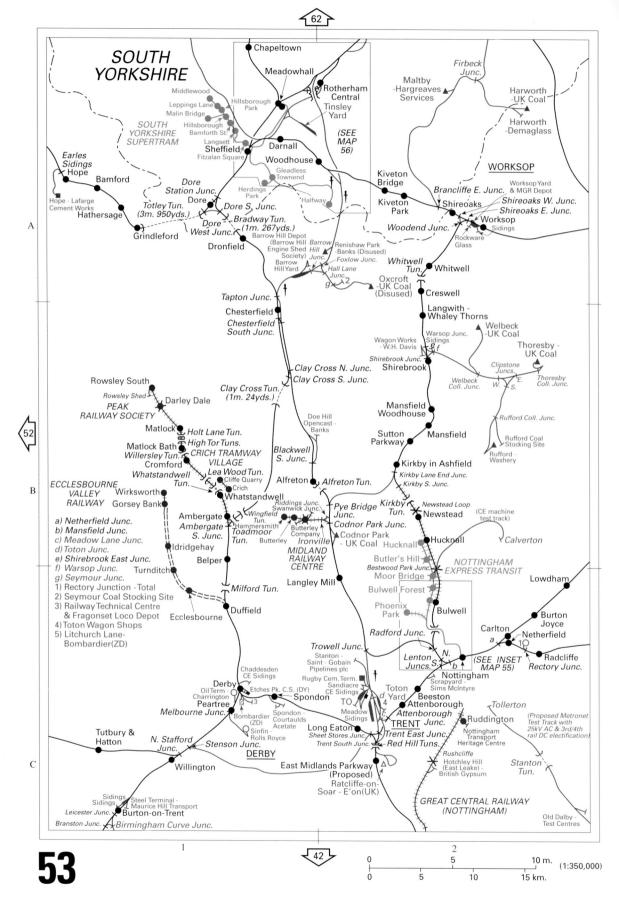

SOUTH YORKSHIRE

Chapeltown

Meadowhall

Middlewood
Leppings Lane
Malin Bridge
Hillsborough Park
Rotherham Central
Tinsley Yard

Maltby -Hargreaves Services
Firbeck Junc.
Harworth -UK Coal
Harworth -Demaglass

SOUTH YORKSHIRE SUPERTRAM
Hillsborough Bamforth St.
Langsett
Sheffield
Fitzalan Square
Darnall
Woodhouse
(SEE MAP 56)

WORKSOP

Earles Sidings Hope
Bamford

Dore Station Junc.
Dore
Gleadless Townend
Herdings Park
Halfway
Kiveton Bridge
Brancliffe E. Junc.
Shireoaks
Worksop Yard & MGR Depot
Shireoaks W. Junc.
Shireoaks E. Junc.
Worksop

Hope - Lafarge Cement Works
Hathersage
Totley Tun. (3m. 950yds.)
Dore S. Junc.
Dore West Junc.
Bradway Tun. (1m. 267yds.)
Kiveton Park
Woodend Junc.
Sidings
Rockware Glass

Grindleford
Dronfield
Barrow Hill Depot (Barrow Hill Engine Shed Society)
Barrow Hill Junc.
Barrow Hill Yard
Renishaw Park -Banks (Disused)
Foxlow Junc.
Hall Lane Junc.
Oxcroft -UK Coal (Disused)
Whitwell Tun.
Whitwell
Creswell
Langwith -Whaley Thorns
Welbeck -UK Coal
Thoresby - UK Coal

Tapton Junc.
Chesterfield
Chesterfield South Junc.
Warsop Junc. Sidings
Wagon Works - W.H. Davis
Welbeck Coll. Junc.
Clipstone Juncs.
Thoresby Coll. Junc.

Rowsley South
Rowsley Shed
PEAK RAILWAY SOCIETY
Darley Dale
Clay Cross N. Junc.
Clay Cross S. Junc.
Clay Cross Tun. (1m. 24yds.)
Shirebrook Junc.
Shirebrook
Mansfield Woodhouse
Rufford Coll. Junc.
Rufford Coal Stocking Site
Rufford Washery

Matlock
Holt Lane Tun.
High Tor Tuns.
Doe Hill Opencast - Banks
Matlock Bath
Willersley Tun.
CRICH TRAMWAY VILLAGE
Cromford
Whatstandwell Tun.
Lea Wood Tun.
Cliffe Quarry
Crich
Blackwell S. Junc.
Mansfield
Sutton Parkway

ECCLESBOURNE VALLEY RAILWAY
Wirksworth
Gorsey Bank
Whatstandwell
Alfreton
Alfreton Tun.
Kirkby in Ashfield
Kirkby Lane End Junc.
Kirkby S. Junc.

a) Netherfield Junc.
b) Mansfield Junc.
c) Meadow Lane Junc.
d) Toton Junc.
e) Shirebrook East Junc.
f) Warsop Junc.
g) Seymour Junc.
1) Rectory Junction - Total
2) Seymour Coal Stocking Site
3) Railway Technical Centre & Fragonset Loco Depot
4) Toton Wagon Shops
5) Litchurch Lane- Bombardier(ZD)

Ambergate
Ambergate S. Junc.
Wingfield Tun.
Hammersmith
Toadmoor Tun.
Butterley
Butterley Company
Ironville
MIDLAND RAILWAY CENTRE
Riddings Junc.
Swanwick Junc.
Pye Bridge Junc.
Codnor Park Junc.
Codnor Park - UK Coal
Kirkby Tun.
Newstead Loop
Newstead
(CE machine test track)
Calverton

Idridgehay
Belper
Langley Mill
Hucknall
Butler's Hill
Bestwood Park Junc.
Moor Bridge
NOTTINGHAM EXPRESS TRANSIT
Lowdham

Turnditch
Milford Tun.
Bulwell Forest
Phoenix Park
Bulwell
Burton Joyce
Carlton
Netherfield

Ecclesbourne
Duffield
Radford Junc.
Radcliffe
Rectory Junc.

Trowell Junc.
Stanton - Saint - Gobain Pipelines plc
Rugby Cem. Term.
Sandiacre CE Sidings
Lenton Juncs. N. S.
(SEE INSET MAP 55)

Chaddesden CE Sidings
Derby
Oil Term
Charrington
Peartree
Etches Pk. C.S. (DY)
Spondon
Scrapyard - Sims McIntyre
Nottingham
Toton Yard
Beeston
Tollerton

Melbourne Junc.
Bombardier (ZD)
Spondon - Courtaulds Acetate
Sinfin - Rolls Royce
Meadow Sidings
Attenborough
Attenborough Junc.
Ruddington
Nottingham Transport Heritage Centre
(Proposed Metronet Test Track with 25kV AC & 3rd/4th rail DC electrification)

Tutbury & Hatton
N. Stafford Junc.
Stenson Junc.
DERBY
Long Eaton
Sheet Stores Junc.
TRENT
Trent East Junc.
Red Hill Tuns.
Trent South Junc.
Rushcliffe
Hotchley Hill (East Leake) - British Gypsum
Stanton Tun.

Willington
East Midlands Parkway (Proposed)
Ratcliffe-on-Soar - E'on(UK)

Sidings
Steel Terminal - Maurice Hill Transport
Leicester Junc.
Burton-on-Trent
Branston Junc.
Birmingham Curve Junc.
GREAT CENTRAL RAILWAY (NOTTINGHAM)
Old Dalby - Test Centres

53

1
2
0   5   10 m.
0   5   10   15 km.
(1:350,000)

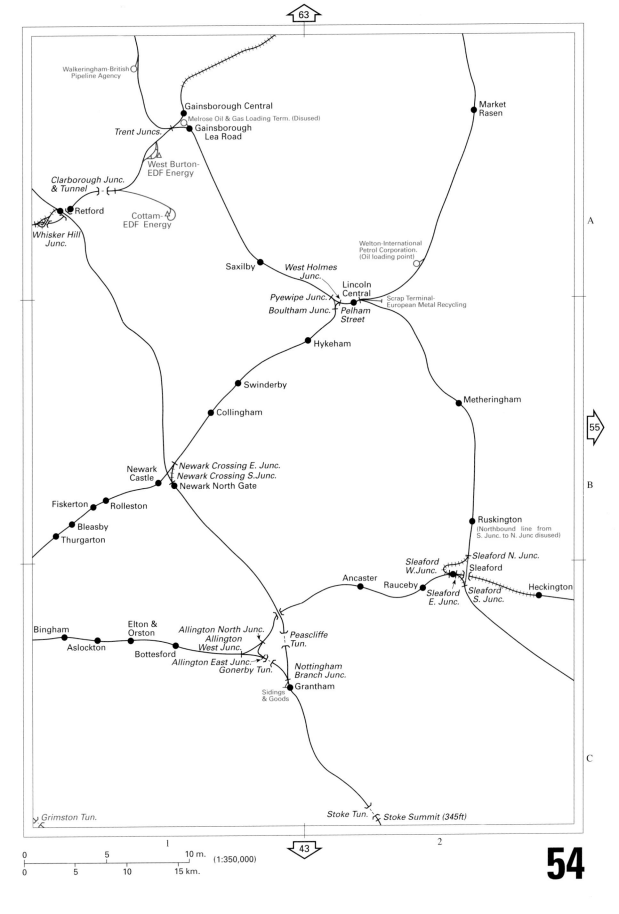

Walkeringham-British
Pipeline Agency

Gainsborough Central

Market
Rasen

Melrose Oil & Gas Loading Term. (Disused)

Trent Juncs.

Gainsborough
Lea Road

West Burton-
EDF Energy

*Clarborough Junc.
& Tunnel*

Retford

Cottam-
EDF Energy

A

*Whisker Hill
Junc.*

Welton-International
Petrol Corporation.
(Oil loading point)

Saxilby

*West Holmes
Junc.*

Lincoln
Central

Pyewipe Junc.

Scrap Terminal-
European Metal Recycling

Boultham Junc.

Pelham
Street

Hykeham

Swinderby

Metheringham

Collingham

55

Newark
Castle

Newark Crossing E. Junc.
Newark Crossing S.Junc.

Newark North Gate

B

Fiskerton

Rolleston

Ruskington

Bleasby

(Northbound line from
S. Junc. to N. Junc disused)

Thurgarton

Sleaford N. Junc.

Ancaster

*Sleaford
W.Junc.*

Sleaford

Rauceby

Heckington

Bingham

Elton &
Orston

Allington North Junc.
*Allington
West Junc.*

*Sleaford
E. Junc.*

*Sleaford
S. Junc.*

Aslockton

*Peascliffe
Tun.*

Bottesford

Allington East Junc.
Gonerby Tun.

*Nottingham
Branch Junc.*

Grantham

Sidings
& Goods

C

Grimston Tun.

Stoke Tun.   *Stoke Summit (345ft)*

0   5   10 m.   (1:350,000)

0   5   10   15 km.

54

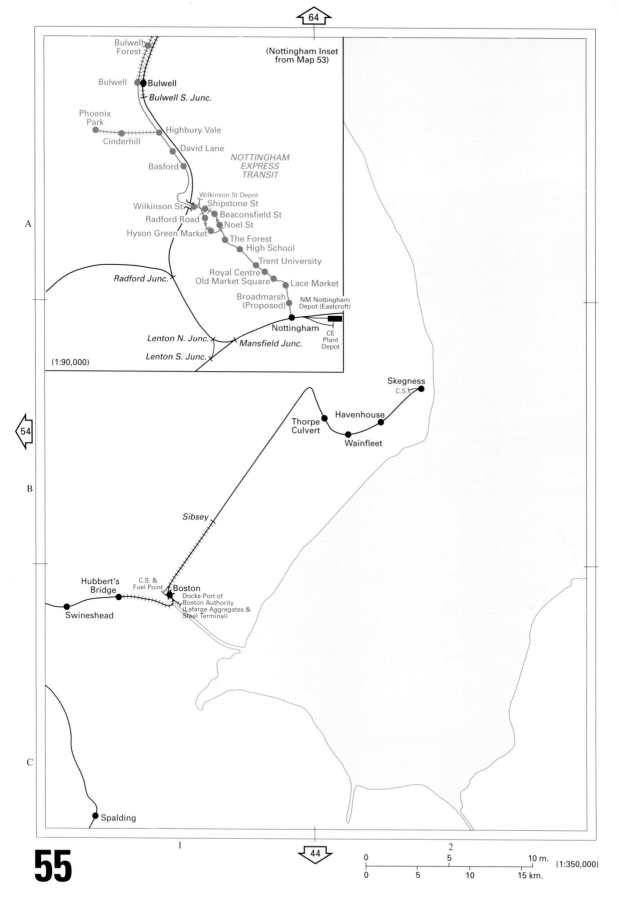

(Nottingham Inset
from Map 53)

Bulwell
Forest

Bulwell   ● Bulwell
          Bulwell S. Junc.

Phoenix
Park
          ● Highbury Vale
Cinderhill
          ● David Lane
Basford ●

*NOTTINGHAM
EXPRESS
TRANSIT*

Wilkinson St Depot
Shipstone St
Wilkinson St ●
          Beaconsfield St
Radford Road   Noel St
Hyson Green Market
          The Forest
          High School
          Trent University
          Royal Centre
Old Market Square   Lace Market

Radford Junc.

Broadmarsh
(Proposed)   NM Nottingham
                Depot (Eastcroft)

          ● Nottingham
Lenton N. Junc.   CE
          Mansfield Junc. Plant
                          Depot
Lenton S. Junc.

(1:90,000)

A

Skegness
          C.S.

Havenhouse
Thorpe   ●
Culvert   Wainfleet

54

B

Sibsey

Hubbert's   C.S. &
Bridge   Fuel Point ● Boston
                        Docks-Port of
                        Boston Authority
                        (Lafarge Aggregates &
Swineshead   Steel Terminal)

C

● Spalding

55

1   2

0   5   10 m.
|___|___|___|___|___|
0   5   10   15 km.

(1:350,000)

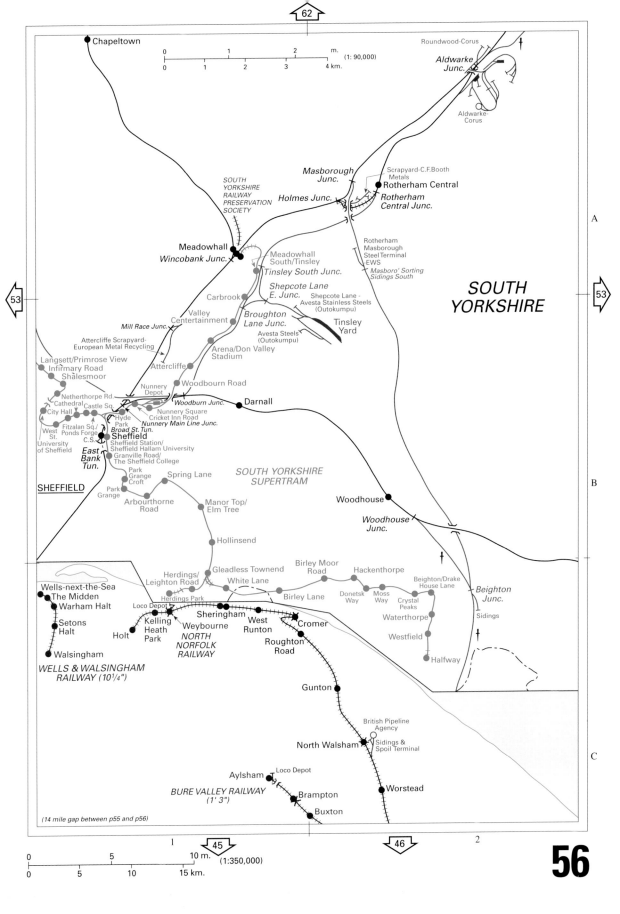

Chapeltown

0   1   2   m.   (1: 90,000)
0   1   2   3   4 km.

Roundwood-Corus

Aldwarke
Junc.

Aldwarke-
Corus

Masborough
Junc.

Scrapyard-C.F.Booth
Metals

Rotherham Central

Holmes Junc.

SOUTH
YORKSHIRE
RAILWAY
PRESERVATION
SOCIETY

Rotherham
Central Junc.

Meadowhall
Wincobank Junc.

Rotherham
Masborough
Steel Terminal
EWS

Meadowhall
South/Tinsley

Masboro' Sorting
Sidings South

Tinsley South Junc.

Carbrook

Shepcote Lane
E. Junc.

SOUTH
YORKSHIRE

Valley
Centertainment

Mill Race Junc.

Broughton
Lane Junc.

Shepcote Lane -
Avesta Stainless Steels
(Outokumpu)

Tinsley
Yard

Attercliffe Scrapyard-
European Metal Recycling

Avesta Steels
(Outokumpu)

Arena/Don Valley
Stadium

Langsett/Primrose View
Infirmary Road
Shalesmoor

Attercliffe

Woodbourn Road

Netherthorpe Rd.
Cathedral
City Hall Castle Sq.

Nunnery
Depot

Woodburn Junc.

Darnall

West
St.
University
of Sheffield

Hyde
Park
Fitzalan Sq./
Ponds Forge
C.S.

Broad St. Tun.

Sheffield

Nunnery Square
Cricket Inn Road
Nunnery Main Line Junc.

East
Bank
Tun.

Sheffield Station/
Sheffield Hallam University
Granville Road/
The Sheffield College

SOUTH YORKSHIRE
SUPERTRAM

SHEFFIELD

Park
Grange
Croft

Spring Lane

Woodhouse

Park
Grange

Arbourthorne
Road

Manor Top/
Elm Tree

Woodhouse
Junc.

Hollinsend

Wells-next-the-Sea
The Midden
Warham Halt

Herdings/
Leighton Road

Gleadless Townend

White Lane

Birley Moor
Road

Hackenthorpe

Beighton/Drake
House Lane

Beighton
Junc.

Setons
Halt

Herdings Park

Birley Lane

Donetsk
Way

Moss
Way

Crystal
Peaks

Sidings

Walsingham

Loco Depot

Holt

Kelling
Heath
Park

Sheringham

Weybourne

West
Runton

Cromer

Waterthorpe

Westfield

WELLS & WALSINGHAM
RAILWAY (10¼")

NORTH
NORFOLK
RAILWAY

Roughton
Road

Halfway

Gunton

British Pipeline
Agency

North Walsham

Sidings &
Spoil Terminal

Aylsham   Loco Depot

BURE VALLEY RAILWAY
(1' 3")

Brampton

Buxton

Worstead

(14 mile gap between p55 and p56)

0   5   10 m.
0   5   10   15 km.

(1:350,000)

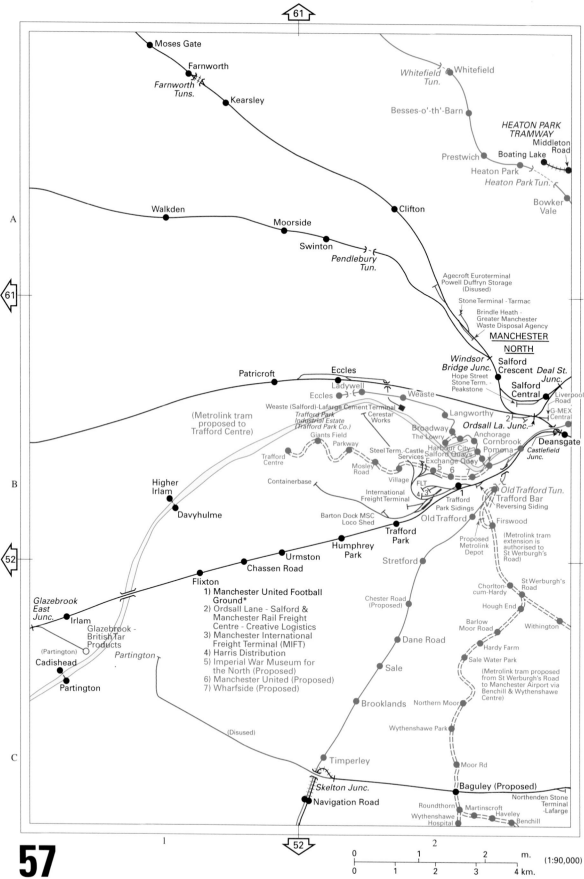

Moses Gate

Farnworth
Farnworth Tuns.

Kearsley

Whitefield Tun.
Whitefield

Besses-o'-th'-Barn

HEATON PARK
TRAMWAY
Middleton
Road

Prestwich
Boating Lake

Heaton Park

Heaton Park Tun.

Walkden

Clifton

Bowker
Vale

Moorside

Swinton

Pendlebury Tun.

Agecroft Euroterminal
Powell Duffryn Storage
(Disused)

Stone Terminal - Tarmac

Brindle Heath -
Greater Manchester
Waste Disposal Agency

MANCHESTER
NORTH

Patricroft

Eccles

Windsor
Bridge Junc.
Salford
Crescent
*Deal St.
Junc.*

Ladywell
Hope Street
Stone Term. -
Peakstone

Eccles
Weaste
Salford
Central

Liverpool
Road

Langworthy

G-MEX
Central

(Metrolink tram
proposed to
Trafford Centre)

Weaste (Salford)-Lafarge Cement Terminal
*Trafford Park
Industrial Estate
(Trafford Park Co.)*
Cerestar
Works

Ordsall La. Junc.

Broadway
The Lowry

Anchorage
Cornbrook

Deansgate

Giants Field
Parkway

Harbour City.-Castle
Services

Pomona
*Castlefield
Junc.*

Trafford
Centre

Steel Term.-Castle
Services

Salford Quays
Exchange Quay
5 6

Mosley
Road
Village

Containerbase

FLT

Higher
Irlam

International
Freight Terminal
4
Trafford
Park Sidings

Old Trafford Tun.
Trafford Bar
Reversing Siding

Davyhulme

Barton Dock MSC
Loco Shed
Old Trafford

Firswood

Trafford
Park

Proposed
Metrolink
Depot

(Metrolink tram
extension is
authorised to
St Werburgh's
Road)

Humphrey
Park

Stretford

Urmston

Chassen Road

Chorlton-
cum-Hardy
St Werburgh's
Road

Flixton

Chester Road
(Proposed)

Hough End

Barlow
Moor Road
Withington

Glazebrook
East
Junc.

Irlam

1) Manchester United Football
   Ground*
2) Ordsall Lane - Salford &
   Manchester Rail Freight
   Centre - Creative Logistics
3) Manchester International
   Freight Terminal (MIFT)
4) Harris Distribution
5) Imperial War Museum for
   the North (Proposed)
6) Manchester United (Proposed)
7) Wharfside (Proposed)

Dane Road

Hardy Farm

Sale Water Park

Glazebrook -
British Tar
Products

(Partington)

Partington

Sale

(Metrolink tram proposed
from St Werburgh's Road
to Manchester Airport via
Benchill & Wythenshawe
Centre)

Cadishead

Partington

Brooklands

Northern Moor

Wythenshawe Park

(Disused)

Moor Rd

Baguley (Proposed)

Timperley

Northenden Stone
Terminal -Lafarge

Skelton Junc.
Navigation Road

Roundthorn
Wythenshawe
Hospital

Martinscroft
Haveley

Benchill

1

2

0   1   2
m.
0   1   2   3   4 km.

(1:90,000)

A

B

52

C

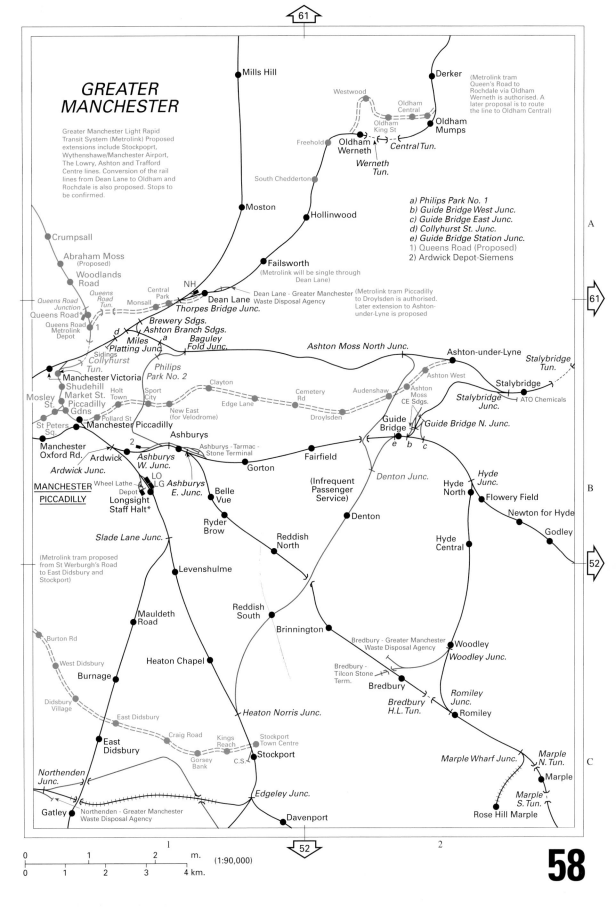

GREATER MANCHESTER

Greater Manchester Light Rapid Transit System (Metrolink) Proposed extensions include Stockpoprt, Wythenshawe/Manchester Airport, The Lowry, Ashton and Trafford Centre lines. Conversion of the rail lines from Dean Lane to Oldham and Rochdale is also proposed. Stops to be confirmed.

(Metrolink tram Queen's Road to Rochdale via Oldham Werneth is authorised. A later proposal is to route the line to Oldham Central)

Mills Hill

Derker

Westwood

Oldham Central

Oldham King St

Oldham Mumps

Central Tun.

Freehold

Oldham Werneth

Moston

South Chedderton

Werneth Tun.

Hollinwood

a) Philips Park No. 1
b) Guide Bridge West Junc.
c) Guide Bridge East Junc.
d) Collyhurst St. Junc.
e) Guide Bridge Station Junc.
1) Queens Road (Proposed)
2) Ardwick Depot-Siemens

Failsworth

(Metrolink will be single through Dean Lane)

Crumpsall

Abraham Moss (Proposed)

Woodlands Road

NH

Central Park

Queens Road Junction

Queens Road Tun.

Monsall

Dean Lane

Dean Lane - Greater Manchester Waste Disposal Agency

(Metrolink tram Piccadilly to Droylsden is authorised. Later extension to Ashton-under-Lyne is proposed)

Queens Road*

Thorpes Bridge Junc.

Queens Road Metrolink Depot

1

d

Brewery Sdgs.
Ashton Branch Sdgs.

Baguley Fold Junc.

Ashton Moss North Junc.

Ashton-under-Lyne

Stalybridge Tun.

a

Sidings

Miles Platting Junc.

Collyhurst Tun.

Philips Park No. 2

Ashton West

Stalybridge

Manchester Victoria

Clayton

Audenshaw

Stalybridge Junc.

ATO Chemicals

Shudehill

Mosley St.

Holt Town

Sport City

Cemetery Rd

Ashton Moss CE Sdgs.

Market St.

Piccadilly Gdns

Edge Lane

New East (for Velodrome)

Droylsden

Stalybridge Junc.

St Peters Sq.

Pollard St

Manchester Piccadilly

Ashburys

Guide Bridge

Guide Bridge N. Junc.

Manchester Oxford Rd.

Ardwick

Ardwick Junc.

2

Ashburys W. Junc.

Ashburys - Tarmac - Stone Terminal

Fairfield

e   b   c

Denton Junc.

Gorton

Hyde Junc.

MANCHESTER PICCADILLY

Wheel Lathe

LO

LG

Depot

Ashburys E. Junc.

Belle Vue

(Infrequent Passenger Service)

Hyde North

Flowery Field

*Longsight Staff Halt**

Ryder Brow

Newton for Hyde

Slade Lane Junc.

Reddish North

Denton

Hyde Central

Godley

(Metrolink tram proposed from St Werburgh's Road to East Didsbury and Stockport)

Levenshulme

Burton Rd

Mauldeth Road

Reddish South

Brinnington

Bredbury - Greater Manchester Waste Disposal Agency

Woodley

Woodley Junc.

West Didsbury

Heaton Chapel

Bredbury - Tilcon Stone Term.

Burnage

Bredbury

Romiley Junc.

Didsbury Village

East Didsbury

Bredbury H.L. Tun.

Romiley

Craig Road

Kings Reach

Stockport Town Centre

Marple Wharf Junc.

Marple N. Tun.

East Didsbury

Gorsey Bank

C.S.

Stockport

Marple

Northenden Junc.

Edgeley Junc.

Marple S. Tun.

Gatley

Northenden - Greater Manchester Waste Disposal Agency

Davenport

Rose Hill Marple

0   1   2   m.   (1:90,000)
0   1   2   3   4 km.

1   2

58

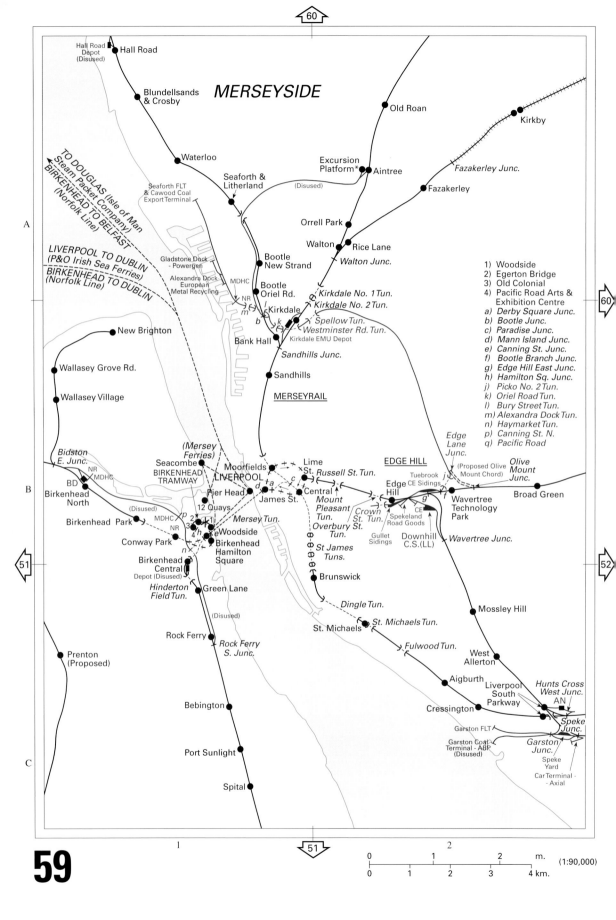

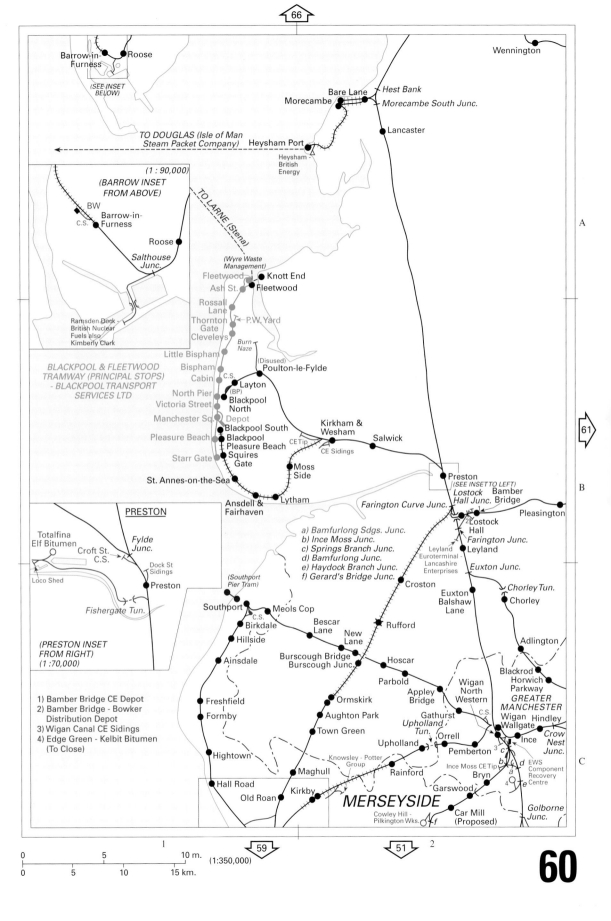

Wennington

Barrow-in-Furness   Roose   (SEE INSET BELOW)

Bare Lane   *Hest Bank*
Morecambe   *Morecambe South Junc.*

Lancaster

TO DOUGLAS (Isle of Man Steam Packet Company)   Heysham Port

Heysham - British Energy

(1 : 90,000)
(BARROW INSET FROM ABOVE)

BW
C.S.   Barrow-in-Furness
Roose

Salthouse Junc.

TO LARNE (Stena)

Ramsden Dock - British Nuclear Fuels also - Kimberly Clark

(Wyre Waste Management)

Fleetwood   Knott End
Ash St.   Fleetwood
Rossall Lane
Thornton   *P.W. Yard*
Gate
Cleveleys

Burn Naze

Little Bispham   (Disused)
Bispham   Poulton-le-Fylde
Cabin   C.S.
North Pier   Layton   (BP)
Victoria Street   Blackpool North
Manchester Sq.   Depot
Blackpool South   Kirkham & Wesham
Pleasure Beach   Blackpool Pleasure Beach   Salwick
Starr Gate   Squires Gate   *CE Tip*
St. Annes-on-the-Sea   Moss Side   CE Sidings

BLACKPOOL & FLEETWOOD TRAMWAY (PRINCIPAL STOPS) - BLACKPOOL TRANSPORT SERVICES LTD

Ansdell & Fairhaven   Lytham

Farington Curve Junc.   Preston   Bamber Bridge
    (SEE INSET TO LEFT)   Pleasington
    Lostock Hall Junc.

Totalfina Elf Bitumen
Croft St. C.S.   *Fylde Junc.*
Loco Shed   Dock St Sidings
Fishergate Tun.   Preston

(PRESTON INSET FROM RIGHT) (1 : 70,000)

a) Bamfurlong Sdgs. Junc.
b) Ince Moss Junc.
c) Springs Branch Junc.
d) Bamfurlong Junc.
e) Haydock Branch Junc.
f) Gerard's Bridge Junc.

Lostock Hall   *Farington Junc.*
Leyland
Leyland Euroterminal - Lancashire Enterprises   *Euxton Junc.*

Chorley Tun.   Chorley

1) Bamber Bridge CE Depot
2) Bamber Bridge - Bowker Distribution Depot
3) Wigan Canal CE Sidings
4) Edge Green - Kelbit Bitumen (To Close)

(Southport Pier Tram)   Croston   Euxton Balshaw Lane
Southport   Meols Cop
C.S.   Birkdale   Bescar Lane   Rufford
Hillside   New Lane   Adlington
Ainsdale   Hoscar
Burscough Bridge   Wigan North Western   Blackrod
Burscough Junc.   Parbold   Horwich Parkway
Freshfield   Ormskirk   Appley Bridge   Wigan   *GREATER MANCHESTER*
Formby   Aughton Park   Gathurst   North Western   C.S.
    Town Green   *Upholland Tun.*   Wigan Wallgate   Hindley
Hightown   Upholland   Orrell   Pemberton   Ince   *Crow Nest Junc.*
    Knowsley - Potter Group   Rainford   3 c   EWS Component Recovery Centre
Hall Road   Maghull   b d   Bryn
Old Roan   Kirkby   a   4 e
    MERSEYSIDE   Garswood
Cowley Hill - Pilkington Wks.   f   Car Mill (Proposed)   *Golborne Junc.*

Ince Moss CE Tip

0   5   10 m.
0   5   10   15 km.
(1:350,000)

A

61

B

C

1

2

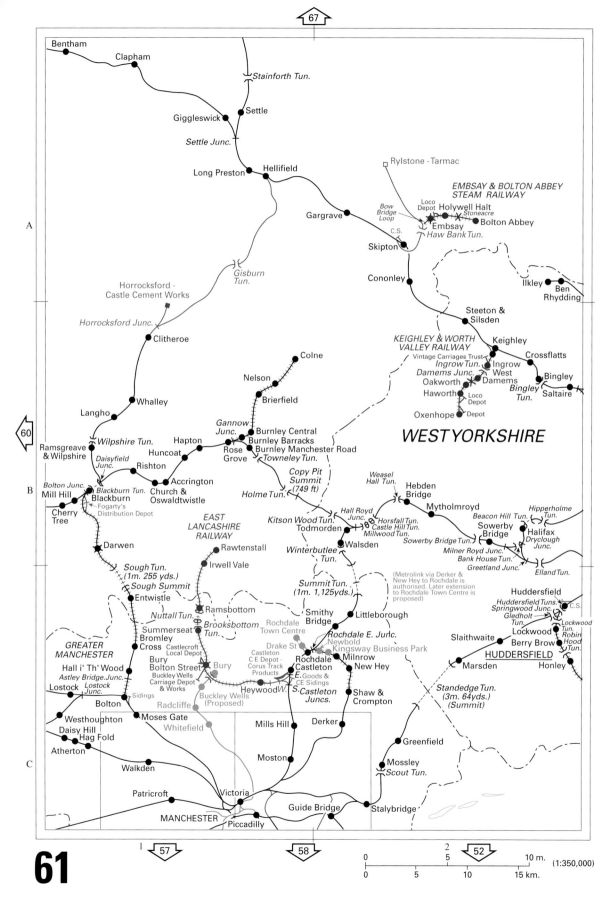

Bentham

Clapham

Stainforth Tun.

Settle

Giggleswick

Settle Junc.

Long Preston   Hellifield

Gargrave

RylStone - Tarmac

EMBSAY & BOLTON ABBEY STEAM RAILWAY

Bow Bridge Loop   Loco Depot   Holywell Halt
Stoneacre
Embsay   Bolton Abbey
C.S.   *Haw Bank Tun.*

A

Skipton

Cononley   Ilkley   Ben Rhydding

Steeton & Silsden

Gisburn Tun.

Horrocksford - Castle Cement Works

Keighley   Crossflatts

KEIGHLEY & WORTH VALLEY RAILWAY

Vintage Carriages Trust
Ingrow Tun.   Ingrow   Bingley
Horrocksford Junc.   Clitheroe   *Damems Junc.*   West
Oakworth   Damems   Saltaire
Colne   Haworth   *Bingley Tun.*

Nelson   Loco Depot
Oxenhope   Depot
Brierfield

Whalley   *WEST YORKSHIRE*

Langho

Gannow Junc.   Burnley Central

60   *Wilpshire Tun.*   Hapton   Burnley Barracks
Huncoat   Rose Grove   Burnley Manchester Road
Ramsgreave & Wilpshire   *Daisyfield Junc.*   Rishton   *Towneley Tun.*
Bolton Junc.   *Blackburn Tun.*   Accrington   *Copy Pit Summit (749 ft)*
Mill Hill   Blackburn   Church & Oswaldtwistle   *Holme Tun.*   *Weasel Hall Tun.*   Hebden Bridge

B   Cherry Tree   Fogarty's Distribution Depot   *Hall Royd Junc.*   Mytholmroyd
EAST LANCASHIRE RAILWAY   *Kitson Wood Tun.*   *Horsfall Tun.*   *Hipperholme Tun.*
Beacon Hill Tun.
Darwen   Todmorden   *Castle Hill Tun.*   Sowerby   Halifax
Rawtenstall   *Millwood Tun.*   Bridge   *Dryclough Junc.*
Sough Tun. (1m. 255 yds.)   Irwell Vale   *Winterbutlee Tun.*   Walsden   *Sowerby Bridge Tun.*   *Elland Tun.*
Sough Summit   *Milner Royd Junc.*
Entwistle   *Summit Tun. (1m. 1,125yds.)*   *Bank House Tun.*   Huddersfield
Nuttall Tun.   Ramsbottom   Greetland Junc.   *Huddersfield Tuns.*
Springwood Junc.   C.S.
Brooksbottom Tun.   (Metrolink via Derker & New Hey to Rochdale is authorised. Later extension to Rochdale Town Centre is proposed)   *Gledholt Tun.*   Lockwood
Summerseat   Littleborough   *Lockwood Tun.*
GREATER MANCHESTER   Bromley Cross   Smithy Bridge   Slaithwaite   Berry Brow   *Robin Hood Tun.*
Castlecroft Local Depot   *Rochdale Town Centre*   *Rochdale E. Junc.*
Hall i' Th' Wood   Bury   Drake St   Newbold   Honley
Astley Bridge Junc.   Bolton Street   Kingsway Business Park   *HUDDERSFIELD*
Lostock   Buckley Wells Carriage Depot & Works   Castleton C E Depot - Corus Track Products   Milnrow   Marsden
Lostock Junc.   Bury   Rochdale   New Hey
Sidings   Heywood   Castleton   *Standedge Tun. (3m. 64yds.) (Summit)*
Bolton   W.   E. Goods & CE Sidings   Shaw & Crompton
Buckley Wells (Proposed)   S. *Castleton Juncs.*
Radcliffe
Westhoughton   Moses Gate   Greenfield
Daisy Hill   Whitefield   Mills Hill   Derker
Hag Fold
Atherton   Moston   Mossley
Walkden   *Scout Tun.*

C   Patricroft   Victoria   Guide Bridge   Stalybridge

MANCHESTER   Piccadilly

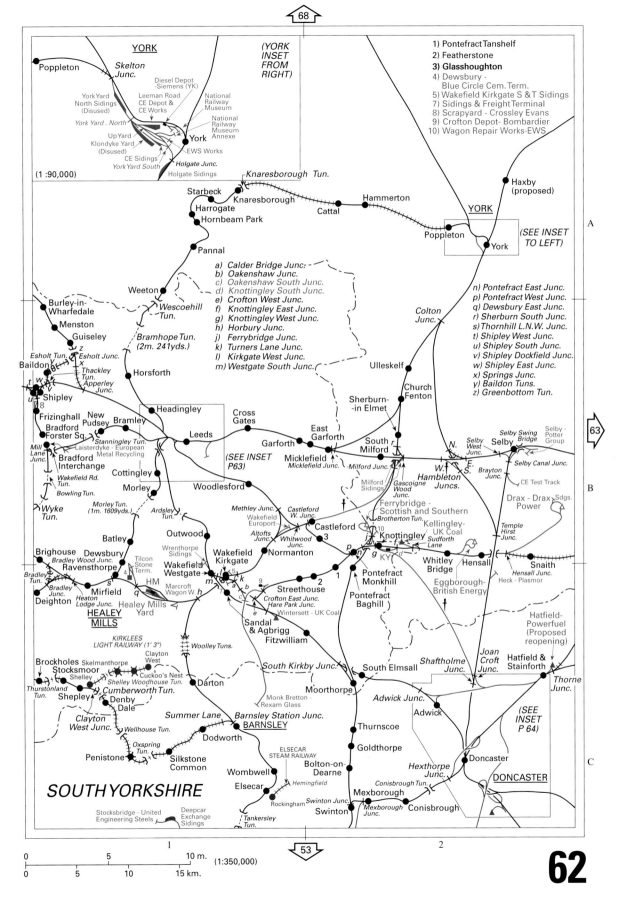

Bridlington Quay
Bridlington

Headingley

Burley Park

Nafferton

Driffield

(LEEDS INSET FROM MAP 62)

**WEST
YORKS.**

A

Hutton
Cranswick

Armley Junc.
*Whitehall
Junc.*

*Copley Hill
E. Junc.*
*Holbeck
Junc.*

*Copley Hill
W. Junc.*

*Marsh Lane
(Disused)*

*Richmond
Hill Tun.*
*Neville
Hill
West
Junc.*

*Neville
Hill
(NL)*

Leeds

Leeds W. Junc.
*Engine
Shed
Junc.*

*Whitehall
Road S & T
Sidings*

*Holbeck-CE
Plant Depot*

*Tarmac Stone
Terminal*

*Neville
Hill Up
Sidings*

Arram

1) Sinter Plant
2) Santon-Foreign Ore Term.
3) Scunthorpe Trent Yard
4) Loco Shed-Corus
a) Walton St. Junc.
b) West Parade N. Junc.
c) Hessle Road Junc.
d) Anlaby Road Junc.
e) Trent Junc.
f) Hessle East Junc.
g) North Lincoln Junc.

*Moor Row
(Hunslet)*

Shed

*Hunslet East
Cross Green-
Tarmac Stone Terminal*

Beverley

*Midland Road Loco Depot-
Freightliner (LD)*

*Hunslet Sidings
(Disused)*

Stone Term.-RMC

Stourton FLT

*MIDDLETON
RAILWAY*

D & F
Steels

Steel Terminal
-Corus

(1 : 90,000)

Cottingley

Park Halt

Cottingham

62

Wressle

Howden

Eastrington

Gilberdyke

Broomfleet

Brough

B

Hedon
Road Sidings

Kingston
Coal Term.

*Springbank
North Junc.*
a
b

BG

Hull

Sidings

Hull King
George Dock
-ABP

Saltend -
BP Chems.

Goole-Guardian
Glass

Saltmarshe

Melton- Omya U K

Ferriby

Sidings

Hessle

*Dairycoates-Tarmac
Freight
Terminal
(Disused)*

Dairycoates-Tarmac
Stone Term.

*Potters
Grange Junc.*

Goole

*Goole
Swing Bridge*

Barton-on-Humber

Barrow
Haven

New Holland

Oxmarsh Crossing

Goxhill

Killingholme

Rawcliffe

*Engine
Shed
Junc.*

Docks Goole Railfreight

Goole Yard

Thornton
Abbey

(SEE INSET P 64)

Roxby Landfill Site -
Waste Management

Immingham

Thorne
North

Flixborough Wharf-
RMS Europe Group

*Dragonby
Sidings*

Plant Depot-
Grant Rail

Scunthorpe Coal Term.-Corus

Anchor Yard

Foreign Ore Branch Junc.

Ulceby

Brocklesby Junc.

Habrough

*Normanby
Park*

e
3 g

Thorne
South

Hatfield
Peat
Works

Sidings

Crowle

Althorpe

Scunthorpe

4 2

*Scunthorpe
(Anchor Works)
-Corus*

Sidings
(Disused)

Barnetby

(3' Gauge)

Appleby-Frodingham RPS Excursion Platform
Heavy Section Mill-Corus

Blast
Furnaces

Basic
Oxygen
Steel Plant

Brigg

CE Sidings (Disused)

Wrawby Junc.

Hatfield
Peat Works-
The Scotts Co.

**SOUTH
YORKS.**

Corus Steelworks
Scunthorpe Complex

SCUNTHORPE
(Barnetby-Gainsborough
passenger service
operates Sats. only)

*Kirton
Lime
Sidings*

C

Kirton Tun.

Northorpe

Kirton
Lindsey

I

0   2
|---|---|---|---|
5   10 m. (1:350,000)

0   5   10
|---|---|---|
5   10   15 km.

63

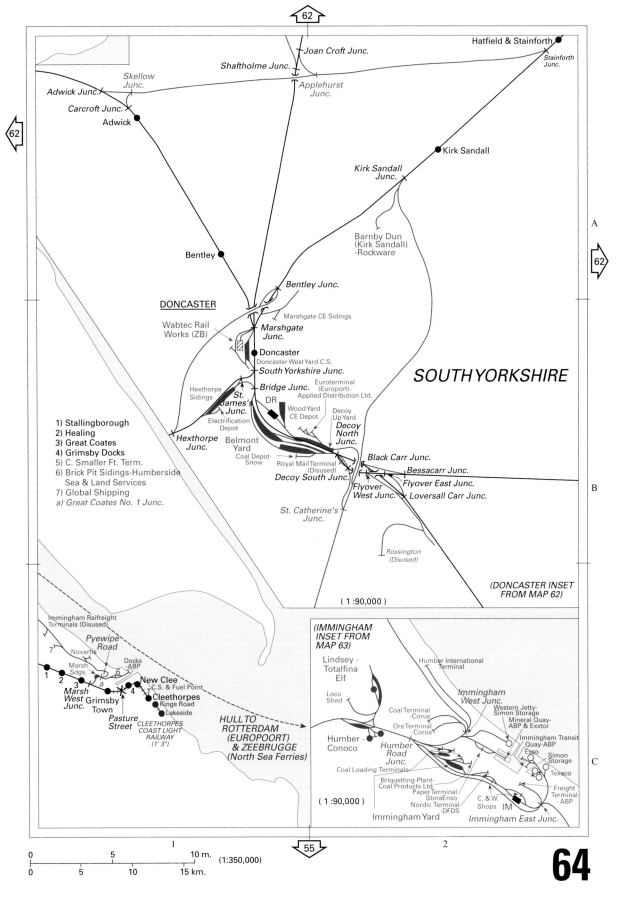

Hatfield & Stainforth

Stainforth Junc.

Joan Croft Junc.

Shaftholme Junc.

Skellow Junc.

Applehurst Junc.

Adwick Junc.

Carcroft Junc.

Adwick

Kirk Sandall

Kirk Sandall Junc.

A

Barnby Dun (Kirk Sandall) -Rockware

Bentley

Bentley Junc.

DONCASTER

Marshgate CE Sidings

Wabtec Rail Works (ZB)

Marshgate Junc.

SOUTH YORKSHIRE

Doncaster

Doncaster West Yard C.S.

South Yorkshire Junc.

Bridge Junc.

Euroterminal (Europort)- Applied Distribution Ltd.

Hexthorpe Sidings

St. James's Junc.

DR

Wood Yard CE Depot

Decoy Up Yard

Decoy North Junc.

Electrification Depot

Hexthorpe Junc.

Belmont Yard

1) Stallingborough
2) Healing
3) Great Coates
4) Grimsby Docks
5) C. Smaller Ft. Term.
6) Brick Pit Sidings-Humberside Sea & Land Services
7) Global Shipping
a) Great Coates No. 1 Junc.

Coal Depot- Snow

Royal Mail Terminal (Disused)

Decoy South Junc.

Black Carr Junc.

Bessacarr Junc.

Flyover East Junc.

Flyover West Junc.

Loversall Carr Junc.

B

St. Catherine's Junc.

Rossington (Disused)

(DONCASTER INSET FROM MAP 62)

(1 :90,000)

Immingham Railfreight Terminals (Disused)

Pyewipe Road

7

Novartis

Marsh Sdgs.

Docks -ABP

6

New Clee

C.S. & Fuel Point

1   2

3   *a*

4

Marsh West Junc.

Grimsby Town

Kings Road

Cleethorpes

Pasture Street

CLEETHORPES COAST LIGHT RAILWAY (1' 3")

Lakeside

HULL TO ROTTERDAM (EUROPOORT) & ZEEBRUGGE (North Sea Ferries)

(IMMINGHAM INSET FROM MAP 63)

Humber International Terminal

Lindsey - Totalfina Elf

Immingham West Junc.

Loco Shed

Coal Terminal -Corus

Western Jetty- Simon Storage

Mineral Quay- ABP & Exxtor

Ore Terminal -Corus

Immingham Transit Quay-ABP

Esso

Simon Storage

Humber - Conoco

Humber Road Junc.

Coal Loading Terminals

Texaco

Briquetting Plant- Coal Products Ltd.

Paper Terminal -StoraEnso

Nordic Terminal -DFDS

C. & W. Shops

IM

Freight Terminal - ABP

C

Immingham Yard

Immingham East Junc.

(1 :90,000)

0   5   10 m.   (1:350,000)

0   5   10   15 km.

64

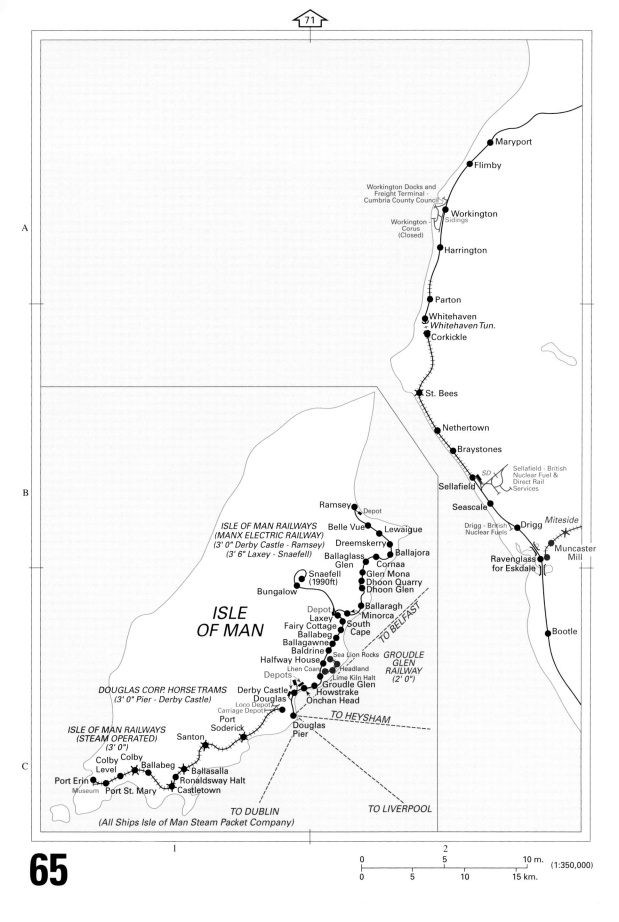

Maryport

Flimby

Workington Docks and
Freight Terminal -
Cumbria County Council

Workington - Corus
(Closed)

Sidings

Workington

A

Harrington

Parton

Whitehaven
Whitehaven Tun.

Corkickle

St. Bees

Nethertown

Braystones

Sellafield - British
Nuclear Fuel &
Direct Rail
Services

SD

Sellafield

Ramsey

Depot

Seascale

Belle Vue   Lewaigue

B

Drigg - British
Nuclear Fuels

Drigg

Miteside

ISLE OF MAN RAILWAYS
(MANX ELECTRIC RAILWAY)
(3' 0" Derby Castle - Ramsey)
(3' 6" Laxey - Snaefell)

Dreemskerry

Ballajora

Ballaglass
Glen   Cornaa

Glen Mona

Dhoon Quarry

Snaefell
(1990ft)

Dhoon Glen

Bungalow

Ballaragh

Muncaster
Mill

Ravenglass
for Eskdale

**ISLE
OF MAN**

Depot

Minorca

Laxey

Fairy Cottage   South
Cape

Ballabeg

TO BELFAST

Ballagawne

Baldrine

Sea Lion Rocks

*GROUDLE
GLEN
RAILWAY
(2' 0")*

Bootle

Halfway House

Lhen Coan   Headland

Depots

Lime Kiln Halt

DOUGLAS CORP. HORSE TRAMS
(3' 0" Pier - Derby Castle)

Derby Castle

Groudle Glen

Douglas

Howstrake

Loco Depot

Onchan Head

Carriage Depot

Port
Soderick

ISLE OF MAN RAILWAYS
(STEAM OPERATED)
(3' 0")

Santon

Douglas
Pier

TO HEYSHAM

Colby
Level   Colby

Ballabeg

Port Erin

Ballasalla

Museum

Port St. Mary

Ronaldsway Halt

Castletown

TO DUBLIN

TO LIVERPOOL

(All Ships Isle of Man Steam Packet Company)

65

0   5   10 m.   (1:350,000)

0   5   10   15 km.

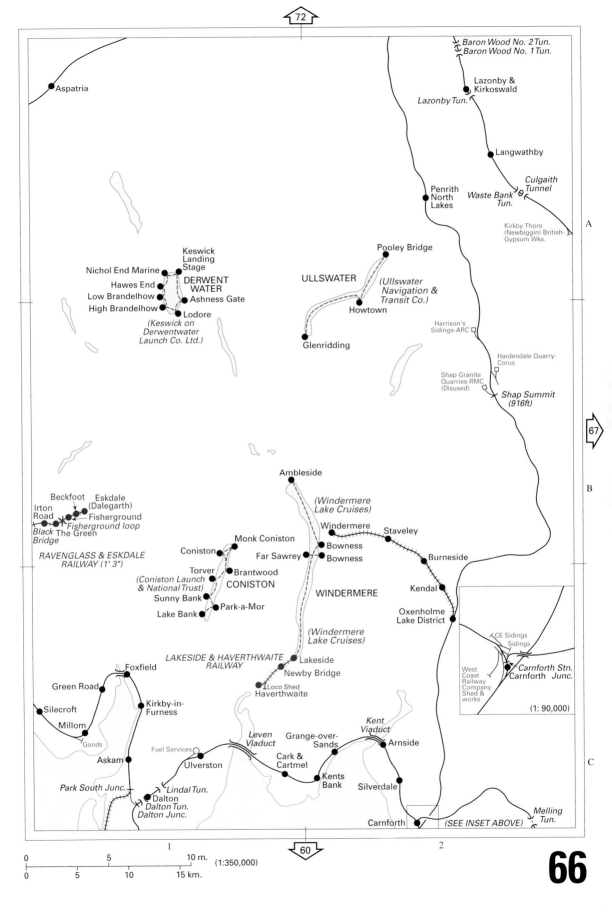

Baron Wood No. 2 Tun.
Baron Wood No. 1 Tun.

Lazonby &
Kirkoswald

Lazonby Tun.

Aspatria

Langwathby

Penrith
North
Lakes

*Culgaith
Tunnel*

*Waste Bank
Tun.*

A

Kirkby Thore
(Newbiggin) British-
Gypsum Wks.

Keswick
Landing
Stage

Nichol End Marine

Hawes End

Low Brandelhow

High Brandelhow

**DERWENT
WATER**

Ashness Gate

Lodore

*(Keswick
on Derwentwater
Launch Co. Ltd.)*

Pooley Bridge

ULLSWATER

*(Ullswater
Navigation &
Transit Co.)*

Howtown

Glenridding

Harrison's
Sidings-ARC

Hardendale Quarry-
Corus

Shap Granite
Quarries-RMC
(Disused)

*Shap Summit
(916ft)*

67

B

Ambleside

*(Windermere
Lake Cruises)*

Beckfoot

Eskdale
(Dalegarth)

Irton
Road

Fisherground

Fisherground loop

*Black
Bridge* The Green

*RAVENGLASS & ESKDALE
RAILWAY (1' 3")*

Monk Coniston

Coniston

Far Sawrey

Windermere

Bowness

Staveley

Bowness

Burneside

Torver

Brantwood

CONISTON

WINDERMERE

Kendal

*(Coniston Launch
& National Trust)*

Sunny Bank

Park-a-Mor

Lake Bank

Oxenholme
Lake District

*(Windermere
Lake Cruises)*

*LAKESIDE & HAVERTHWAITE
RAILWAY*

Lakeside

Newby Bridge

Foxfield

Green Road

Silecroft

Kirkby-in-
Furness

Millom

Loco Shed
Haverthwaite

CE Sidings
Sidings

West
Coast
Railway
Company
Shed &
works

Carnforth Stn.
Carnforth *Junc.*

(1: 90,000)

Goods

Fuel Services

*Leven
Viaduct*

Grange-over-
Sands

*Kent
Viaduct*

Askam

Ulverston

Cark &
Cartmel

Arnside

C

Park South Junc.

Lindal Tun.

Dalton

Kents
Bank

Silverdale

Dalton Tun.
Dalton Junc.

Carnforth

(SEE INSET ABOVE)

*Melling
Tun.*

0   5   10 m.   (1:350,000)

0   5   10   15 km.

1   2

66

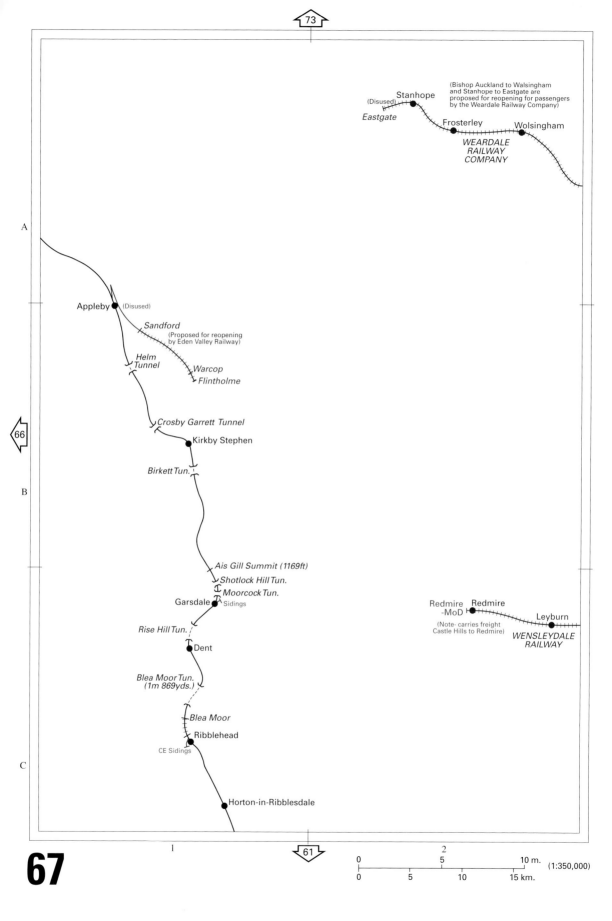

(Bishop Auckland to Walsingham
and Stanhope to Eastgate are
proposed for reopening for passengers
by the Weardale Railway Company)

Stanhope

(Disused)

Eastgate

Frosterley

Wolsingham

*WEARDALE
RAILWAY
COMPANY*

A

Appleby (Disused)

Sandford

(Proposed for reopening
by Eden Valley Railway)

*Helm
Tunnel*

Warcop

Flintholme

Crosby Garrett Tunnel

Kirkby Stephen

B

Birkett Tun.

Ais Gill Summit (1169ft)

Shotlock Hill Tun.

Moorcock Tun.

Garsdale *Sidings*

Redmire Redmire
-MoD

Leyburn

(Note- carries freight
Castle Hills to Redmire)

*WENSLEYDALE
RAILWAY*

Rise Hill Tun.

Dent

*Blea Moor Tun.
(1m 869yds.)*

Blea Moor

Ribblehead

CE Sidings

C

Horton-in-Ribblesdale

67

1

0   2   10 m.   (1:350,000)

0   5   10   15 km.

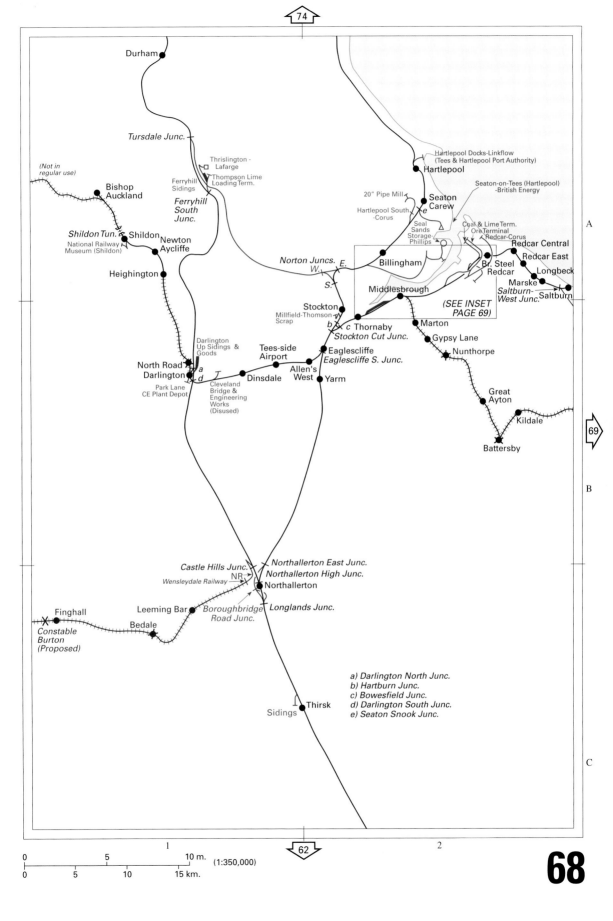

Durham

Tursdale Junc.

Thrislington - Lafarge
Thompson Lime Loading Term.
Ferryhill Sidings

Ferryhill South Junc.

(Not in regular use)

Bishop Auckland

Shildon Tun. Shildon
National Railway Museum (Shildon)
Newton Aycliffe

Heighington

Hartlepool Docks-Linkflow
(Tees & Hartlepool Port Authority)
Hartlepool

Seaton-on-Tees (Hartlepool)
-British Energy

20" Pipe Mill
Seaton Carew
e
Hartlepool South -Corus
Seal Sands Storage-Phillips
Coal & Lime Term.
Ore Terminal
Redcar-Corus
Redcar Central
Redcar East
Br. Steel Redcar
Longbeck
Marske
Saltburn-West Junc.
Saltburn

Norton Juncs. E.
W.
S.
Billingham
Middlesbrough

(SEE INSET PAGE 69)

Stockton
Millfield-Thomson Scrap
b c Thornaby
Stockton Cut Junc.
Marton
Gypsy Lane
Nunthorpe

Darlington Up Sidings & Goods

Tees-side Airport

Eaglescliffe
Eaglescliffe S. Junc.

North Road a
Darlington d
Park Lane CE Plant Depot
Cleveland Bridge & Engineering Works (Disused)
Dinsdale
Allen's West
Yarm

Great Ayton
Kildale

Battersby

A

B

Castle Hills Junc.
Wensleydale Railway
NR
Northallerton East Junc.
Northallerton High Junc.
Northallerton
Longlands Junc.

Finghall
Constable Burton (Proposed)
Bedale
Leeming Bar
Boroughbridge Road Junc.

a) Darlington North Junc.
b) Hartburn Junc.
c) Bowesfield Junc.
d) Darlington South Junc.
e) Seaton Snook Junc.

Sidings Thirsk

C

0   1   5   10 m.
0   5   10   15 km.
(1:350,000)

68

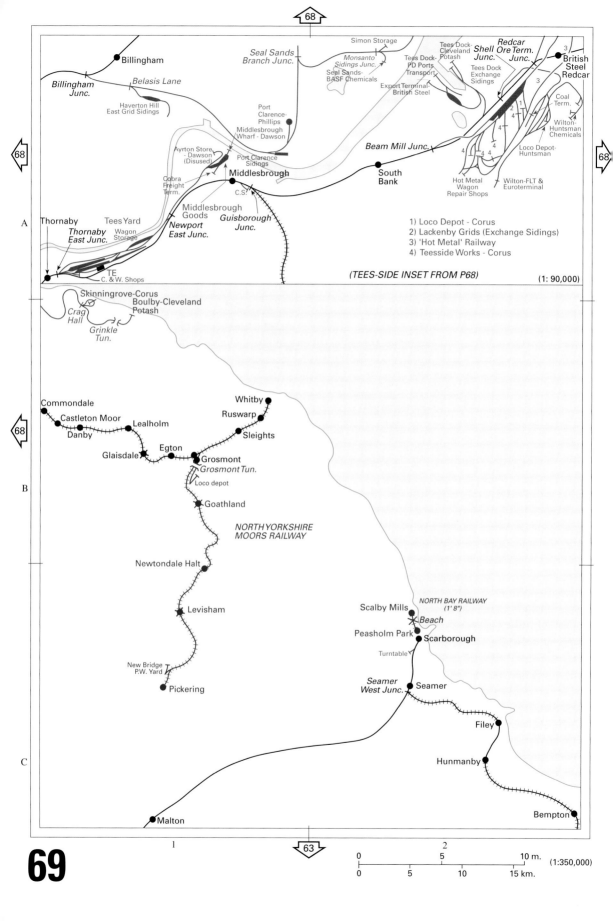

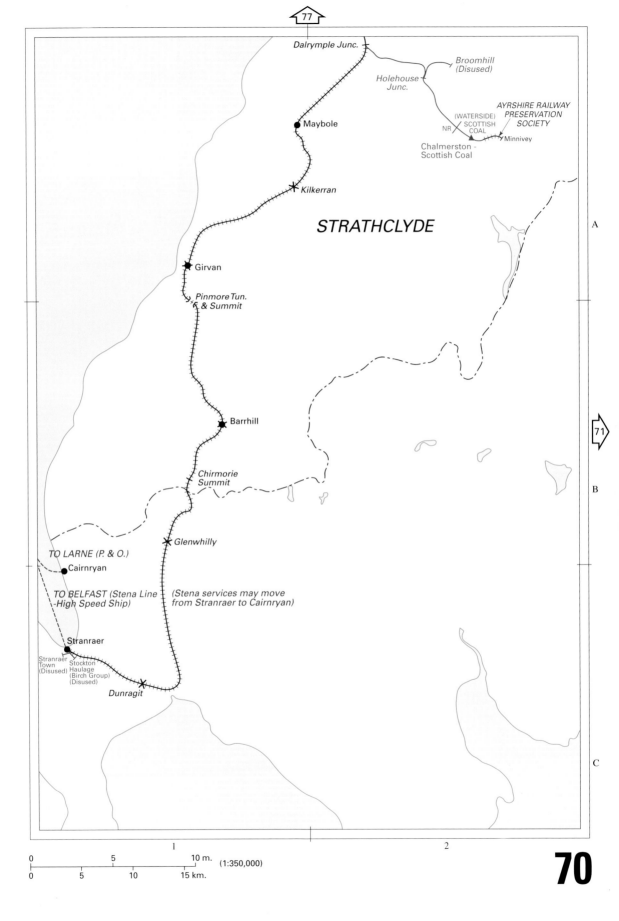

Dalrymple Junc.

Broomhill
(Disused)

Holehouse
Junc.

AYRSHIRE RAILWAY
PRESERVATION
SOCIETY

Maybole

(WATERSIDE)
SCOTTISH
COAL

NR

Minnivey

Chalmerston -
Scottish Coal

Kilkerran

STRATHCLYDE

Girvan

Pinmore Tun.
& Summit

Barrhill

Chirmorie
Summit

Glenwhilly

TO LARNE (P. & O.)

Cairnryan

TO BELFAST (Stena Line
-High Speed Ship)

(Stena services may move
from Stranraer to Cairnryan)

Stranraer

Stranraer
Town
(Disused)

Stockton
Haulage
(Birch Group)
(Disused)

Dunragit

0   5   10 m.   (1:350,000)

0   5   10   15 km.

1

2

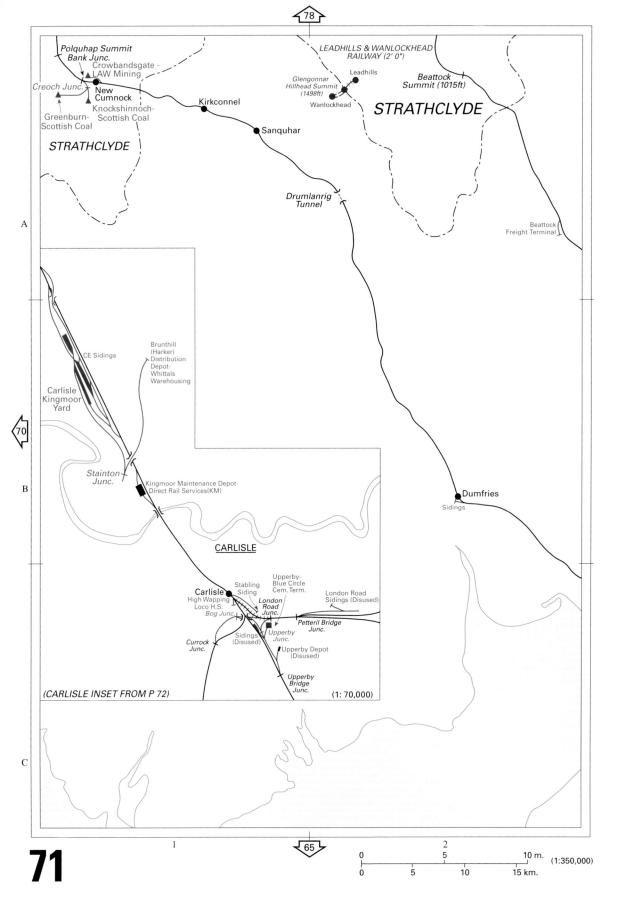

Polquhap Summit
Bank Junc.
Crowbandsgate -
▲ LAW Mining

Creoch Junc. ▲
New
Cumnock
▲ Knockshinnoch-
Scottish Coal
Greenburn-
Scottish Coal

LEADHILLS & WANLOCKHEAD
RAILWAY (2' 0")

*Glengonnar
Hillhead Summit
(1498ft)*
Leadhills
Wanlockhead

*Beattock
Summit (1015ft)*

STRATHCLYDE

STRATHCLYDE

Kirkconnel

Sanquhar

*Drumlanrig
Tunnel*

Beattock
Freight Terminal

A

CE Sidings

Brunthill
(Harker)
Distribution
Depot-
Whittals
Warehousing

Carlisle
Kingmoor
Yard

*Stainton
Junc.*

Kingmoor Maintenance Depot-
Direct Rail Services(KM)

B

Dumfries

Sidings

CARLISLE

Carlisle

Stabling
Siding
High Wapping
Loco H.S.
Bog Junc.

Upperby-
Blue Circle
Cem. Term.

*London
Road
Junc.*

London Road
Sidings (Disused)

*Petteril Bridge
Junc.*

*Currock
Junc.*

Sidings
(Disused)

*Upperby
Junc.*

Upperby Depot
(Disused)

*Upperby
Bridge
Junc.*

(CARLISLE INSET FROM P 72)

(1: 70,000)

C

71

0   5   10 m.   (1:350,000)

0   5   10   15 km.

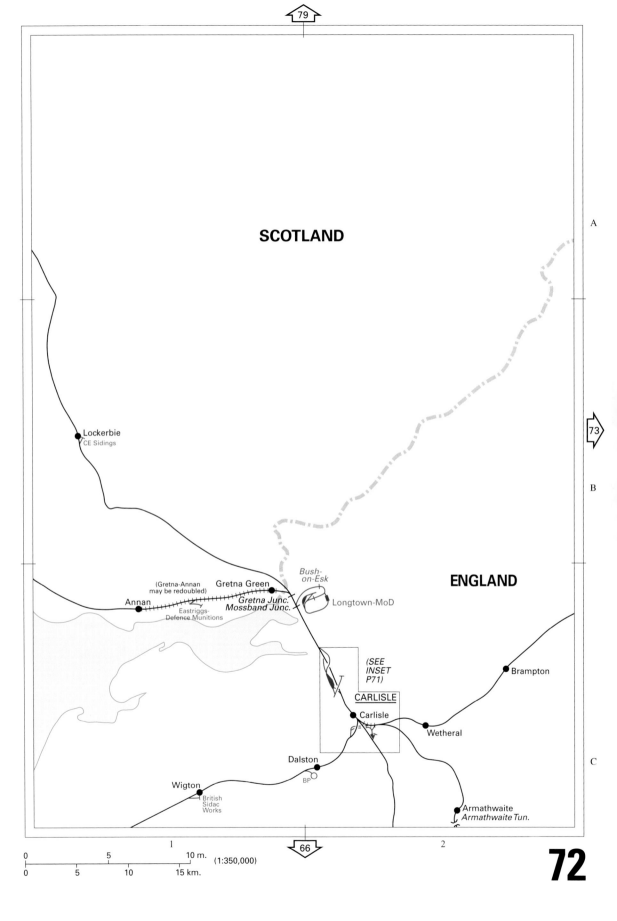

SCOTLAND

73

A

B

Lockerbie
CE Sidings

ENGLAND

Bush-
on-Esk

(Gretna-Annan
may be redoubled)   Gretna Green

Annan   Gretna Junc.   Longtown-MoD
Mossband Junc.
Eastriggs-
Defence Munitions

(SEE
INSET
P71)

Brampton

CARLISLE

Carlisle

Wetheral

C

Dalston

BP

Wigton   Armathwaite
British   Armathwaite Tun.
Sidac
Works

0   1   10 m.   (1:350,000)
5
0   5   10   15 km.

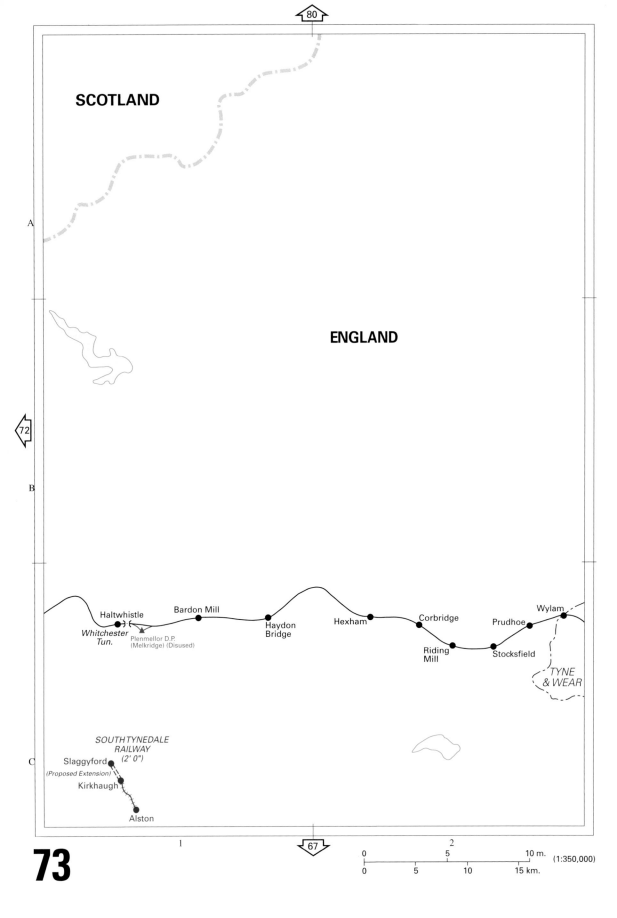

SCOTLAND

ENGLAND

A

72

B

Haltwhistle   Bardon Mill   Wylam

Whitchester   Hexham   Corbridge   Prudhoe
Tun.   Plenmellor D.P.   Haydon
                (Melkridge) (Disused)   Bridge   Riding   Stocksfield
                                                                       Mill
                                                                                  TYNE
                                                                                  & WEAR

C

SOUTH TYNEDALE
RAILWAY
Slaggyford   *(2' 0")*
(Proposed Extension)
Kirkhaugh

Alston

73

1

67

80

| 0 | | 5 | | 10 m. | (1:350,000) |
| 0 | 5 | 10 | 15 km. | | |

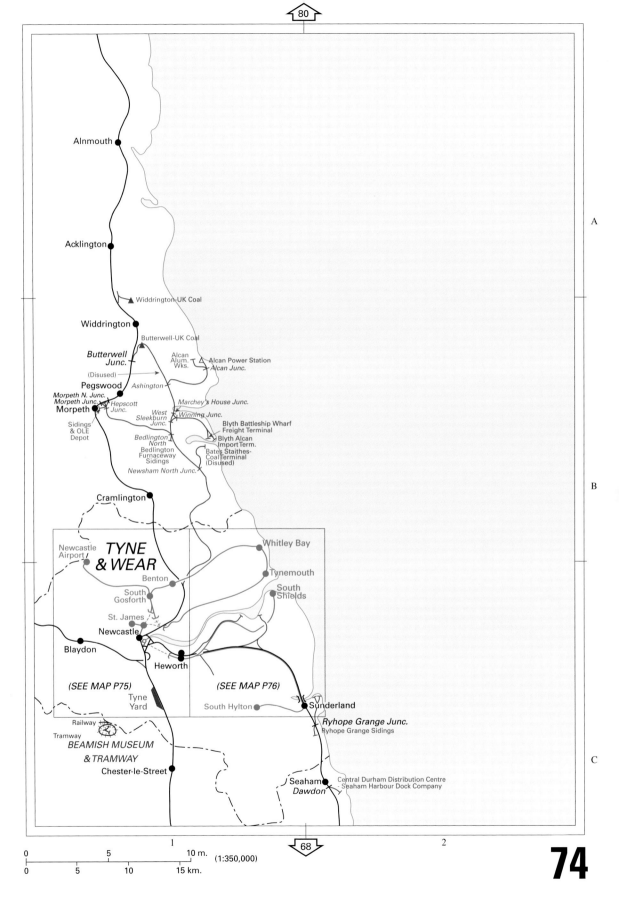

Alnmouth

Acklington

Widdrington-UK Coal

Widdrington

Butterwell-UK Coal

Butterwell Junc.

Alcan
Alum.
Wks.

Alcan Power Station
Alcan Junc.

(Disused)

Pegswood

Ashington

Morpeth N. Junc.
Morpeth Junc.

Hepscott Junc.

Marchey's House Junc.

Morpeth

West
Sleekburn
Junc.

Winning Junc.

Sidings
& OLE
Depot

Blyth Battleship Wharf
Freight Terminal

*Bedlington
North*
Bedlington
Furnaceway
Sidings

Blyth Alcan
Import Term.

Bates Staithes-
Coal Terminal
(Disused)

Newsham North Junc.

Cramlington

**TYNE
& WEAR**

Whitley Bay

Newcastle
Airport

Tynemouth

Benton

South
Gosforth

South
Shields

St. James

Newcastle

Blaydon

Heworth

(SEE MAP P75)

(SEE MAP P76)

Tyne
Yard

South Hylton

Sunderland

Railway

Ryhope Grange Junc.
Ryhope Grange Sidings

Tramway

**BEAMISH MUSEUM
& TRAMWAY**

Chester-le-Street

Seaham

Dawdon

Central Durham Distribution Centre
- Seaham Harbour Dock Company

A

B

C

| 0 | | 5 | | 10 m. | (1:350,000) |

0   5   10   15 km.

74

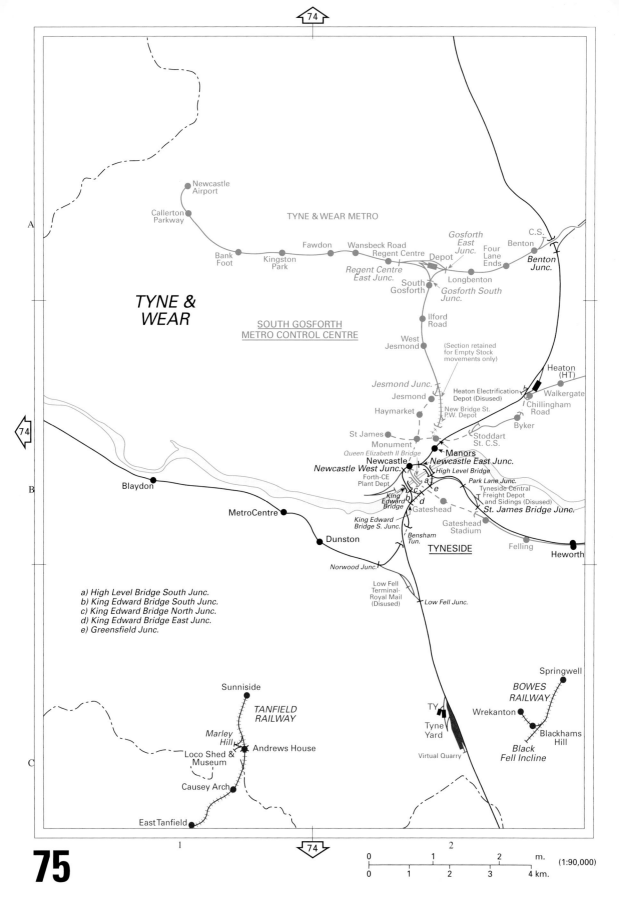

TYNE & WEAR METRO

Newcastle
Airport

Callerton
Parkway

A

TYNE &
WEAR

Bank
Foot

Kingston
Park

Fawdon

Wansbeck Road
Regent Centre

*Regent Centre
East Junc.*

South
Gosforth

SOUTH GOSFORTH
METRO CONTROL CENTRE

*Gosforth
East Junc.*

Depot

Four
Lane
Ends

C.S.

Benton

*Benton
Junc.*

Longbenton

*Gosforth South
Junc.*

Ilford
Road

West
Jesmond

(Section retained
for Empty Stock
movements only)

Heaton
(HT)

Walkergate

Jesmond Junc.

Jesmond

Haymarket

St James

Monument

Heaton Electrification
Depot (Disused)

New Bridge St.
P.W. Depot

Chillingham
Road

Byker

Stoddart
St. C.S.

Queen Elizabeth II Bridge

Newcastle

Newcastle West Junc.

Manors

Newcastle East Junc.

High Level Bridge

Forth-CE
Plant Dept

a

*King
Edward
Bridge*

b *c*

e

d

Park Lane Junc.

Tyneside Central
Freight Depot
and Sidings (Disused)

St. James Bridge Junc.

B

Blaydon

MetroCentre

Dunston

Gateshead

*King Edward
Bridge S. Junc.*

Gateshead
Stadium

TYNESIDE

Felling

Heworth

*Bensham
Tun.*

Norwood Junc.

Low Fell
Terminal-
Royal Mail
(Disused)

Low Fell Junc.

a) *High Level Bridge South Junc.*
b) *King Edward Bridge South Junc.*
c) *King Edward Bridge North Junc.*
d) *King Edward Bridge East Junc.*
e) *Greensfield Junc.*

Sunniside

*TANFIELD
RAILWAY*

Springwell

*BOWES
RAILWAY*

Wrekanton

*Marley
Hill*

Loco Shed &
Museum

Andrews House

TY

Tyne
Yard

Blackhams
Hill

*Black
Fell Incline*

Causey Arch

Virtual Quarry

C

East Tanfield

2

0   1   2   m.

0   1   2   3   4 km.

(1:90,000)

75

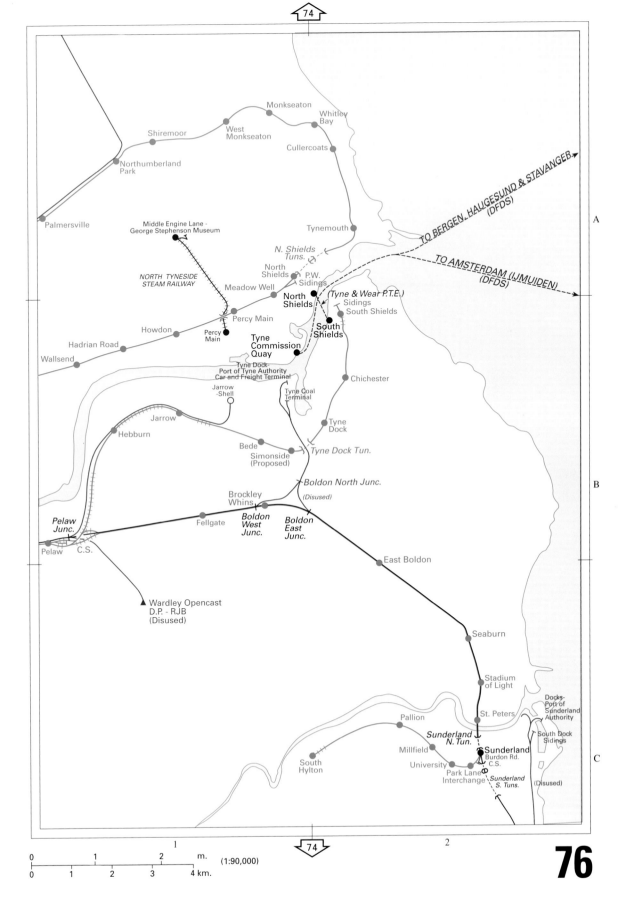

Monkseaton
Whitley Bay
Shiremoor
West Monkseaton
Cullercoats
Northumberland Park

Palmersville

Middle Engine Lane -
George Stephenson Museum

Tynemouth

TO BERGEN, HAUGESUND & STAVANGER
(DFDS)

A

N. Shields Tuns.

TO AMSTERDAM (IJMUIDEN)
(DFDS)

NORTH TYNESIDE
STEAM RAILWAY

North
Shields
P.W.
Sidings

Meadow Well

North Shields

(Tyne & Wear P.T.E.)

Sidings
South Shields

Percy Main

South Shields

Howdon

Percy Main

Tyne Commission Quay

Hadrian Road

Chichester

Wallsend

Tyne Dock
Port of Tyne Authority
Car and Freight Terminal

Jarrow
-Shell

Tyne Coal Terminal

Jarrow

Tyne Dock

Hebburn

Bede
Simonside
(Proposed)

Tyne Dock Tun.

Boldon North Junc.

Brockley Whins

(Disused)

Pelaw Junc.

Fellgate

Boldon West Junc.

Boldon East Junc.

Pelaw   C.S.

East Boldon

Wardley Opencast
D.P. - RJB
(Disused)

B

Seaburn

Stadium of Light

Docks-
Port of Sunderland Authority

Pallion

St. Peters

South Dock Sidings

Sunderland N. Tun.

Millfield

Sunderland
Burdon Rd.
C.S.

South Hylton

University

Park Lane Interchange

Sunderland S. Tuns.

(Disused)

C

1   m.   (1:90,000)   2

0   1   2
0   1   2   3   4 km.

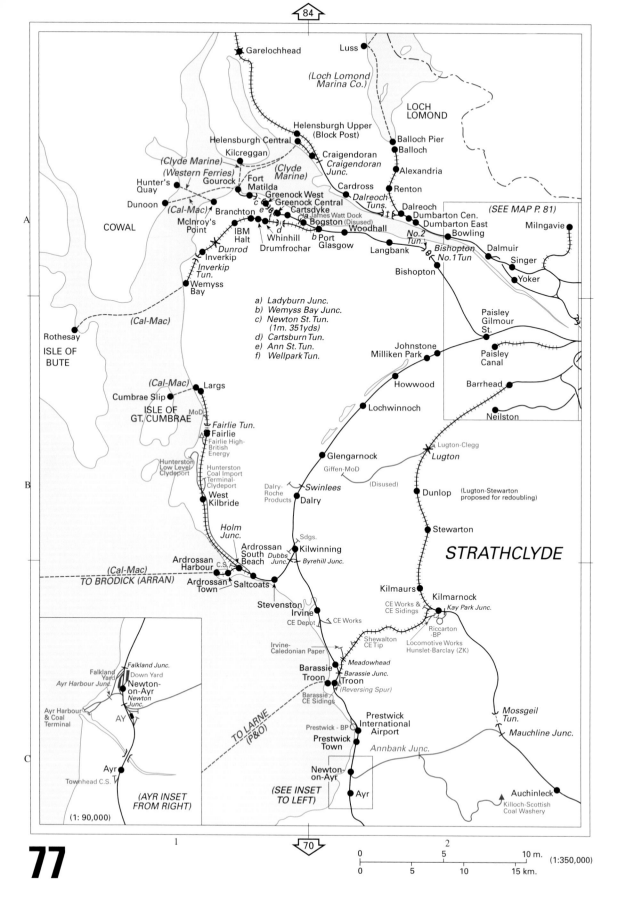

Garelochhead
Luss

(Loch Lomond Marina Co.)

LOCH LOMOND

Helensburgh Upper (Block Post)
Balloch Pier
Balloch
Helensburgh Central
Kilcreggan
Craigendoran
Craigendoran Junc.
Alexandria
(Clyde Marine)
(Western Ferries)
Gourock
Fort Matilda
Cardross
Renton
(Clyde Marine)
Hunter's Quay
Greenock West
Dalreoch Tuns.
Dalreoch
Dunoon
Greenock Central
Cartsdyke
Dumbarton Cen.
Milngavie
(Cal-Mac)
Branchton
c James Watt Dock
Dumbarton East
McInroy's Point
e Bogston (Disused)
Bowling
Dalmuir
COWAL
IBM Halt
Whinhill
a Woodhall
No.2 Tun.
Singer
Drumfrochar
d b Port Glasgow
Bishopton No.1 Tun
Yoker
Dunrod
Langbank
Inverkip
Bishopton
Inverkip Tun.
Wemyss Bay

a) Ladyburn Junc.
b) Wemyss Bay Junc.
c) Newton St. Tun.
   (1m. 351yds)
d) Cartsburn Tun.
e) Ann St. Tun.
f) Wellpark Tun.

Paisley Gilmour St.
(SEE MAP P. 81)

Rothesay
ISLE OF BUTE

(Cal-Mac)

Johnstone
Milliken Park
Paisley Canal

Largs
Cumbrae Slip
(Cal-Mac)
Howwood
Barrhead
ISLE OF GT. CUMBRAE
MoD
Neilston
Fairlie Tun.
Fairlie
Lochwinnoch
Fairlie High-British Energy
Hunterston Low Level Clydeport
Glengarnock
Lugton-Clegg
Hunterston Coal Import Terminal-Clydeport
Giffen-MoD
Lugton
West Kilbride
Dalry-Roche Products
Swinlees
(Disused)
Dunlop
(Lugton-Stewarton proposed for redoubling)
Dalry
Stewarton
Holm Junc.
Ardrossan South Beach
Dubbs Junc.
Sdgs.
Kilwinning
Byrehill Junc.
STRATHCLYDE
Ardrossan Harbour C.S.
Kilmaurs
(Cal-Mac) TO BRODICK (ARRAN)
Ardrossan Town
Saltcoats
Kilmarnock
CE Works & CE Sidings
Kay Park Junc.
Stevenston
Irvine
Riccarton -BP
CE Depot CE Works
Locomotive Works Hunslet-Barclay (ZK)
Irvine-Caledonian Paper
Shewalton CE Tip
Meadowhead
Mossgeil Tun.
Falkland Junc.
Falkland Yard
Ayr Harbour Junc.
Down Yard
Newton-on-Ayr
Barassie
Troon
Barassie Junc.
Troon
(Reversing Spur)
Mauchline Junc.
Ayr Harbour & Coal Terminal
AY
Newton Junc.
Barassie CE Sidings
TO LARNE (P&O)
Prestwick - BP
Prestwick International Airport
Annbank Junc.
Ayr
Townhead C.S.
Prestwick Town
Newton-on-Ayr
Auchinleck
(AYR INSET FROM RIGHT)
(SEE INSET TO LEFT)
Ayr
Killoch-Scottish Coal Washery
(1: 90,000)

1
2
0 5 10 m.
0 5 10 15 km.
(1:350,000)

70

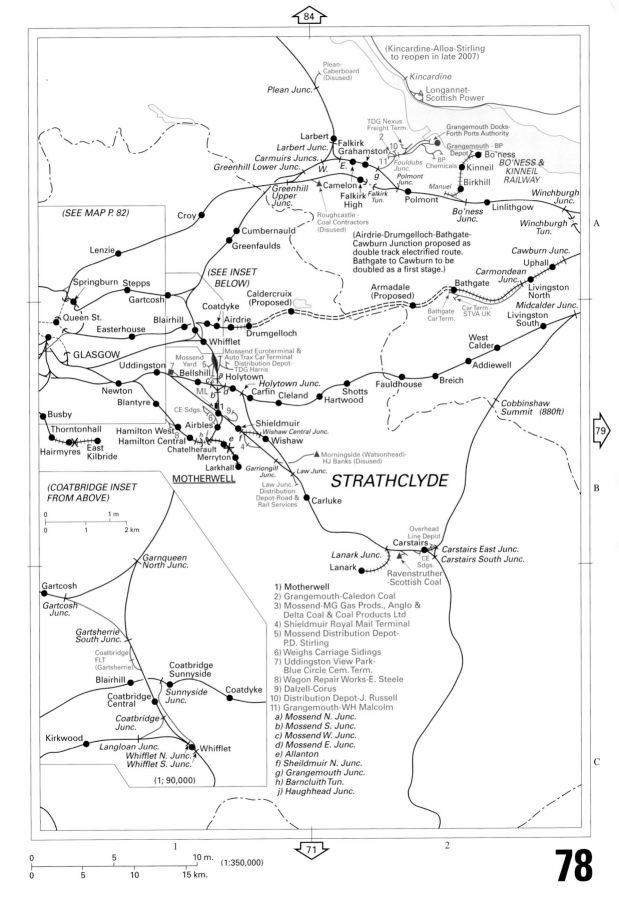

(Kincardine-Alloa-Stirling
to reopen in late 2007)

Kincardine

Plean-
Caberboard
(Disused)

Plean Junc.

Longannet-
Scottish Power

TDG Nexus
Freight Term.

Grangemouth Docks-
Forth Ports Authority

Larbert
Larbert Junc.
Carmuirs Juncs.
Greenhill Lower Junc.

Falkirk
Grahamston

2
10

Grangemouth - BP
Depot

Bo'ness

*BO'NESS &
KINNEIL
RAILWAY*

11

Fouldubs
Junc.

BP
Chemicals

Kinneil

W.   E.

Birkhill

*Greenhill Upper
Junc.*

Camelon

g

Polmont
Junc.

Falkirk
High

Falkirk
Tun.

Manuel

Polmont

*Bo'ness
Junc.*

Linlithgow

*Winchburgh
Junc.*

A

Croy

Roughcastle -
Coal Contractors
(Disused)

(Airdrie-Drumgelloch-Bathgate-
Cawburn Junction proposed as
double track electrified route.
Bathgate to Cawburn to be
doubled as a first stage.)

*Winchburgh
Tun.*

(SEE MAP P. 82)

Cumbernauld

Greenfaulds

Cawburn Junc.

Lenzie

*Carmondean
Junc.*

Uphall

Springburn Stepps

(SEE INSET
BELOW)

Caldercruix
(Proposed)

Armadale
(Proposed)

Bathgate

Livingston
North

Midcalder Junc.

Queen St.

Gartcosh

Coatdyke

Blairhill

Airdrie

Car Term.
STVA UK

Bathgate
Car Term.

Livingston
South

Easterhouse

Whifflet

Drumgelloch

West
Calder

GLASGOW

Mossend
Yard 5

Mossend Euroterminal &
Auto Trax Car Terminal
Distribution Depot-
TDG Harris

Addiewell

Uddingston 7

Bellshill *a*

Holytown

Holytown Junc.

Breich

Fauldhouse

Newton

ML

Carfin

Cleland

Shotts

Hartwood

Blantyre

b

c *3*

d

Busby

CE Sdgs.

(6) 11 *9*

Shieldmuir

Wishaw Central Junc.

*Cobbinshaw
Summit (880ft)*

Thorntonhall

Airbles

h *j*

Wishaw

e *f*

79

Hamilton West
Hamilton Central

8

Hairmyres

East
Kilbride

Chatelherault

Merryton

4

Larkhall

*Garriongill
Junc.*

Morningside (Watsonhead)-
HJ Banks (Disused)

STRATHCLYDE

MOTHERWELL

Law Junc.

Law Junc.
Distribution
Depot-Road &
Rail Services

Carluke

B

(COATBRIDGE INSET
FROM ABOVE)

0   1 m
0   1   2 km

Overhead
Line Depot

Carstairs

Carstairs East Junc.
Carstairs South Junc.

Lanark Junc.

CE
Sdgs.

*Garnqueen
North Junc.*

Lanark

Ravenstruther
-Scottish Coal

Gartcosh

1) Motherwell

*Gartcosh
Junc.*

2) Grangemouth-Caledon Coal
3) Mossend-MG Gas Prods., Anglo &
   Delta Coal & Coal Products Ltd
4) Shieldmuir Royal Mail Terminal

*Gartsherrie
South Junc.*

5) Mossend Distribution Depot-
   P.D. Stirling

Coatbridge
FLT
(Gartsherrie)

Coatbridge
Sunnyside

6) Weighs Carriage Sidings
7) Uddingston View Park-
   Blue Circle Cem. Term.

Blairhill

Coatdyke

8) Wagon Repair Works-E. Steele
9) Dalzell-Corus

Coatbridge
Central

*Sunnyside
Junc.*

10) Distribution Depot-J. Russell
11) Grangemouth-WH Malcolm

*Coatbridge
Junc.*

a) Mossend N. Junc.
b) Mossend S. Junc.

Kirkwood

c) Mossend W. Junc.
d) Mossend E. Junc.

Langloan Junc.
Whifflet N. Junc.
Whifflet S. Junc.

Whifflet

e) Allanton
f) Sheildmuir N. Junc.
g) Grangemouth Junc.

(1; 90,000)

h) Barncluith Tun.
j) Haughhead Junc.

C

1

0   5   10 m.
0   5   10   15 km.

(1:350,000)

2

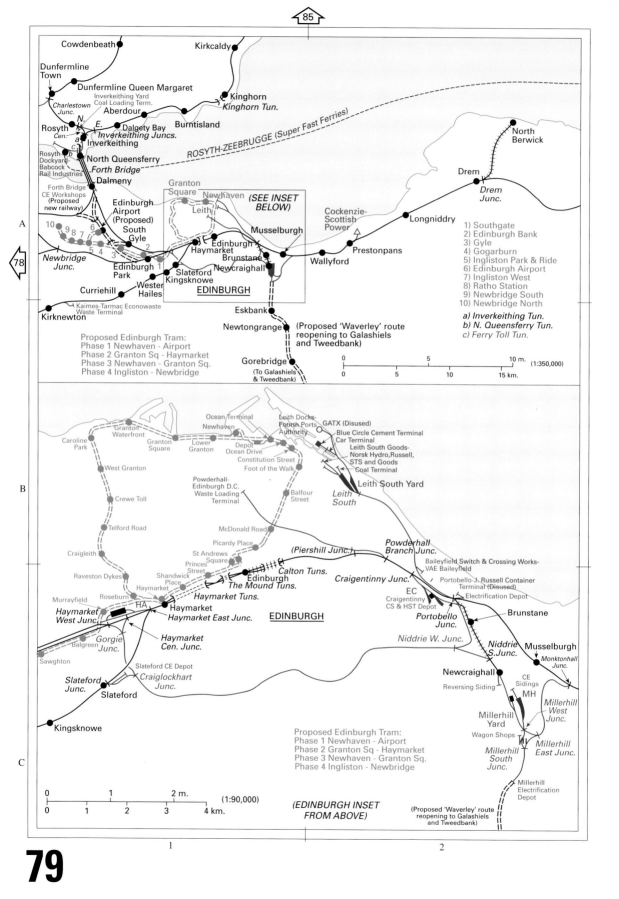

Cowdenbeath
Kirkcaldy
Dunfermline Town
Dunfermline Queen Margaret
Charlestown Junc.
Inverkeithing Yard
Coal Loading Term.
Aberdour
Kinghorn
Kinghorn Tun.
Burntisland
North Berwick
Rosyth Cen.
N.
E.
Dalgety Bay
Inverkeithing Juncs.
Inverkeithing
ROSYTH-ZEEBRUGGE (Super Fast Ferries)
Drem
Drem Junc.
Rosyth Dockyard-Babcock Rail Industries
C
North Queensferry
Forth Bridge
Dalmeny
Granton Square
Newhaven
Leith
(SEE INSET BELOW)
Cockenzie-Scottish Power
Longniddry
Forth Bridge CE Workshops (Proposed new railway)
Edinburgh Airport (Proposed)
South Gyle
Musselburgh
A
10
9
8
7
6
Edinburgh
Haymarket
Brunstane
Prestonpans
1) Southgate
2) Edinburgh Bank
3) Gyle
4) Gogarburn
5) Ingliston Park & Ride
6) Edinburgh Airport
7) Ingliston West
8) Ratho Station
9) Newbridge South
10) Newbridge North
78
Newbridge Junc.
5
4
3
2
1
Edinburgh Park
Slateford
Kingsknowe
Wester Hailes
Newcraighall
Wallyford
EDINBURGH
a) Inverkeithing Tun.
b) N. Queensferry Tun.
c) Ferry Toll Tun.
Curriehill
Kirknewton
Kaimes-Tarmac Econowaste Waste Terminal
Eskbank
Newtongrange
(Proposed 'Waverley' route reopening to Galashiels and Tweedbank)
Proposed Edinburgh Tram:
Phase 1 Newhaven - Airport
Phase 2 Granton Sq - Haymarket
Phase 3 Newhaven - Granton Sq.
Phase 4 Ingliston - Newbridge
Gorebridge
(To Galashiels & Tweedbank)
0   5   10 m.
0   5   10   15 km.   (1:350,000)

Caroline Park
Granton Waterfront
Ocean Terminal
Newhaven
Leith Docks-Fourth Ports Authority
GATX (Disused)
Blue Circle Cement Terminal
Car Terminal
Leith South Goods-
Norsk Hydro,Russell, STS and Goods
Coal Terminal
Granton Square
Lower Granton
Depot
Ocean Drive
Constitution Street
Foot of the Walk
Leith South Yard
West Granton
Leith South
B
Crewe Toll
Powderhall-Edinburgh D.C. Waste Loading Terminal
Balfour Street
Telford Road
McDonald Road
Picardy Place
Powderhall Branch Junc.
Baileyfield Switch & Crossing Works-VAE Baileyfield
Craigleith
St Andrews Square
(Piershill Junc.)
Raveston Dykes
Princes Street
Shandwick Place
Edinburgh
Calton Tuns.
The Mound Tuns.
Craigentinny Junc.
Portobello-J. Russell Container Terminal (Disused)
Electrification Depot
Murrayfield
Roseburn
Haymarket
Haymarket Tuns.
HA
Haymarket
Haymarket East Junc.
EC
Craigentinny CS & HST Depot
Portobello Junc.
Brunstane
Haymarket West Junc.
Gorgie Junc.
Balgreen
Haymarket Cen. Junc.
Niddrie W. Junc.
Niddrie S. Junc.
Musselburgh
Sawghton
EDINBURGH
Monktonhall Junc.
Slateford Junc.
Slateford CE Depot
Craiglockhart Junc.
Newcraighall
CE Sidings
MH
Millerhill West Junc.
Slateford
Reversing Siding
Kingsknowe
Millerhill Yard
Wagon Shops
Millerhill East Junc.
Millerhill South Junc.
Proposed Edinburgh Tram:
Phase 1 Newhaven - Airport
Phase 2 Granton Sq - Haymarket
Phase 3 Newhaven - Granton Sq.
Phase 4 Ingliston - Newbridge
Millerhill Electrification Depot
0   1   2 m.
0   1   2   3   4 km.   (1:90,000)
(EDINBURGH INSET FROM ABOVE)
(Proposed 'Waverley' route reopening to Galashiels and Tweedbank)

C

1
2

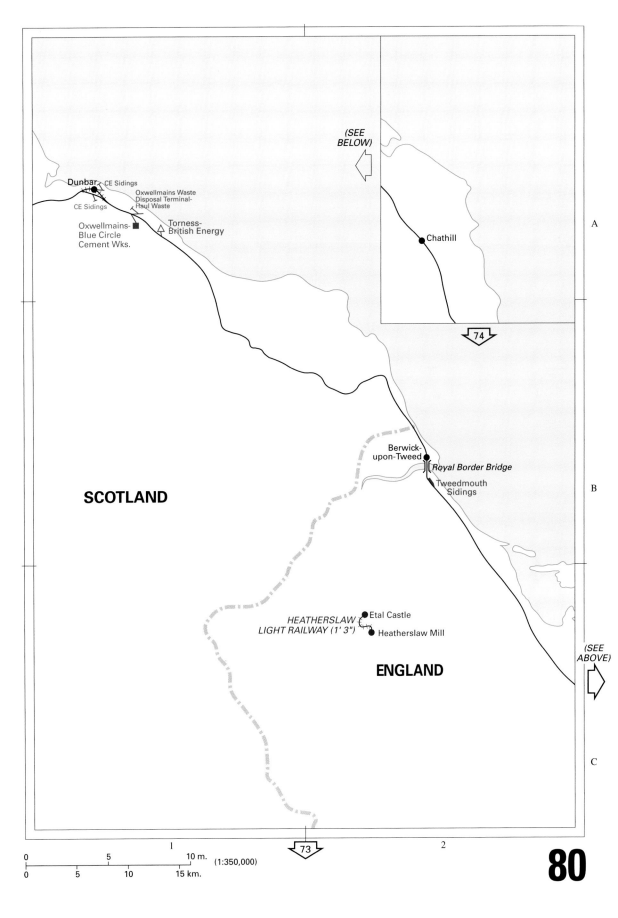

(SEE BELOW)

Dunbar CE Sidings

CE Sidings

Oxwellmains Waste
Disposal Terminal-
Haul Waste

Oxwellmains-
Blue Circle
Cement Wks.

Torness-
British Energy

Chathill

74

SCOTLAND

Berwick-
upon-Tweed

Royal Border Bridge

Tweedmouth
Sidings

B

HEATHERSLAW
LIGHT RAILWAY (1' 3")

Etal Castle

Heatherslaw Mill

ENGLAND

(SEE
ABOVE)

C

73

A

0   5   10 m.   (1:350,000)
0   5   10   15 km.

80

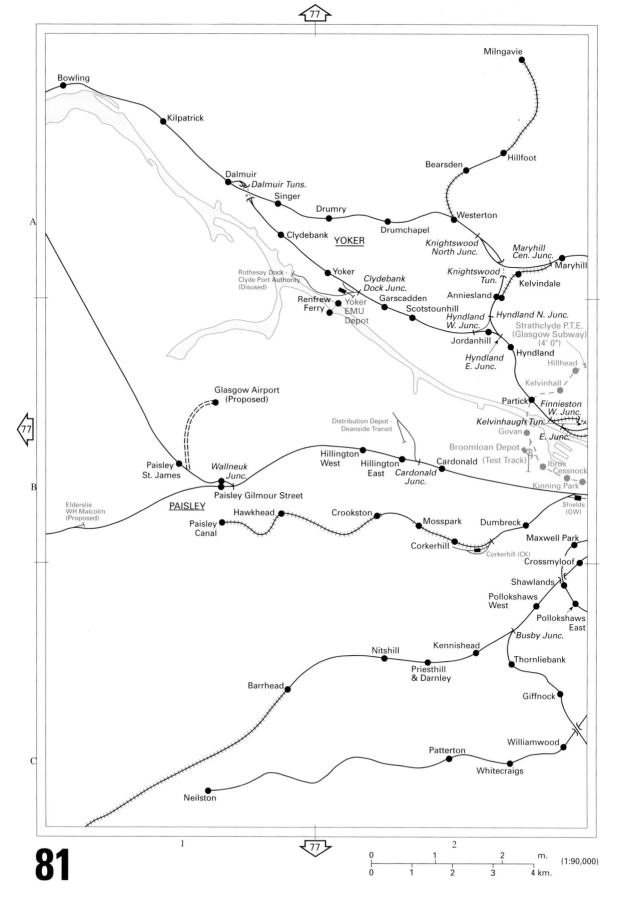

Milngavie

Bowling

Kilpatrick

Hillfoot

Bearsden

Dalmuir
Dalmuir Tuns.
Singer
Drumry
Drumchapel
Westerton

Clydebank
YOKER
Knightswood North Junc.
Maryhill Cen. Junc.
Maryhill

Yoker
Clydebank Dock Junc.
Knightswood Tun.
Kelvindale

Rothesay Dock -
Clyde Port Authority
(Disused)

Renfrew
Ferry
Yoker
EMU
Depot
Garscadden
Scotstounhill
Anniesland
Hyndland N. Junc.

Hyndland W. Junc.
Jordanhill
Strathclyde P.T.E.
(Glasgow Subway)
(4' 0")

Hyndland E. Junc.
Hyndland
Hillhead

Kelvinhall

Partick
Finnieston W. Junc.

Glasgow Airport
(Proposed)

Kelvinhaugh Tun.
Govan
E. Junc.

Broomloan Depot
(Test Track)
Ibrox
Cessnock

Paisley
St. James
Wallneuk Junc.
Hillington
West
Hillington
East
Cardonald
Cardonald Junc.
Kinning Park

Paisley Gilmour Street
PAISLEY
Shields
(GW)

Elderslie
WH Malcolm
(Proposed)
Hawkhead
Crookston
Mosspark
Dumbreck
Maxwell Park

Paisley
Canal
Corkerhill
Corkerhill (CK)
Crossmyloof

Shawlands

Pollokshaws
West
Pollokshaws
East

Nitshill
Kennishead
Busby Junc.
Thornliebank

Barrhead
Priesthill
& Darnley
Giffnock

Williamwood

Patterton
Whitecraigs

Neilston

A

B

C

1   2

81

0   1   2   m.   (1:90,000)
0   1   2   3   4 km.

Distribution Depot -
Deanside Transit

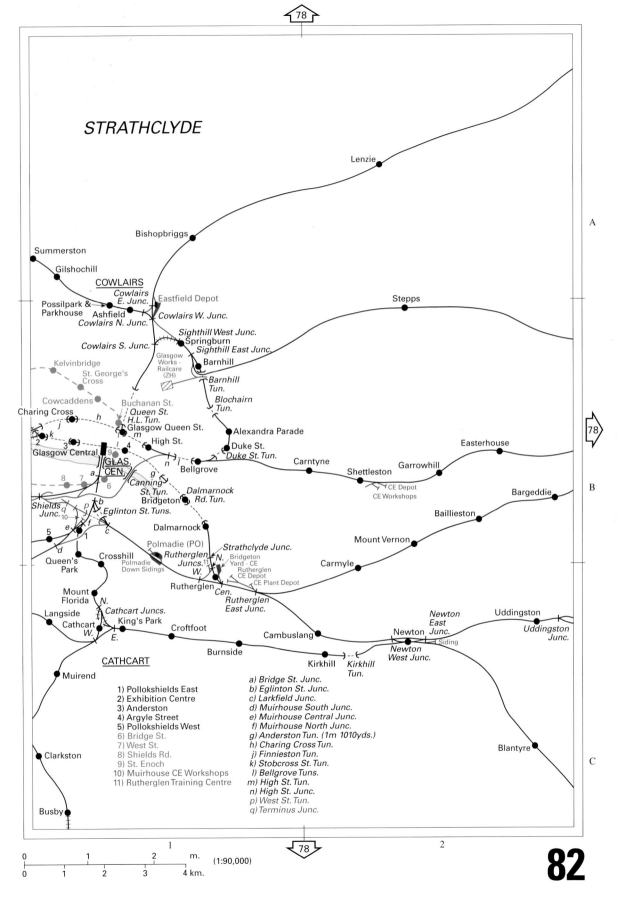

STRATHCLYDE

Lenzie

Bishopbriggs

Stepps

Summerston

Gilshochill

COWLAIRS

Cowlairs E. Junc.

Eastfield Depot

Possilpark & Parkhouse

Ashfield

Cowlairs W. Junc.

Cowlairs N. Junc.

Sighthill West Junc.

Springburn

Cowlairs S. Junc.

Sighthill East Junc.

Glasgow Works - Railcare (ZH)

Barnhill

Barnhill Tun.

Kelvinbridge

St. George's Cross

Blochairn Tun.

Cowcaddens

Buchanan St.

Charing Cross

Queen St. H.L. Tun.

Glasgow Queen St.

Alexandra Parade

h

j

k

High St.

Duke St.

2

3

Duke St. Tun.

Easterhouse

Glasgow Central

4

9

n

l

Carntyne

Garrowhill

GLAS. CEN.

Bellgrove

Shettleston

Bargeddie

8

7

a

g

CE Depot
CE Workshops

6

Canning St. Tun.

Dalmarnock Rd. Tun.

Bridgeton

Baillieston

Shields Junc.

p

b

Eglinton St. Tuns.

q

10

f

Dalmarnock

Mount Vernon

5

e

1

c

d

Polmadie (PO)

Strathclyde Junc.

Queen's Park

Crosshill

Rutherglen Juncs.

N.

Bridgeton Yard - CE
Rutherglen CE Depot

Carmyle

Polmadie Down Sidings

W.

11

CE Plant Depot

Mount Florida

N.

Rutherglen

Cen.

Newton East Junc.

Uddingston

Langside

Cathcart Juncs.

Rutherglen East Junc.

Uddingston Junc.

Cathcart

King's Park

W.

E.

Croftfoot

Cambuslang

Newton

Siding

Muirend

Burnside

Kirkhill

Newton West Junc.

CATHCART

Kirkhill Tun.

1) Pollokshields East
2) Exhibition Centre
3) Anderston
4) Argyle Street
5) Pollokshields West
6) Bridge St.
7) West St.
8) Shields Rd.
9) St. Enoch
10) Muirhouse CE Workshops
11) Rutherglen Training Centre

a) Bridge St. Junc.
b) Eglinton St. Junc.
c) Larkfield Junc.
d) Muirhouse South Junc.
e) Muirhouse Central Junc.
f) Muirhouse North Junc.
g) Anderston Tun. (1m 1010yds.)
h) Charing Cross Tun.
j) Finnieston Tun.
k) Stobcross St. Tun.
l) Bellgrove Tuns.
m) High St. Tun.
n) High St. Junc.
p) West St. Tun.
q) Terminus Junc.

Clarkston

Blantyre

Busby

A

78

B

C

0   1   2   m.   (1:90,000)

0   1   2   3   4 km.

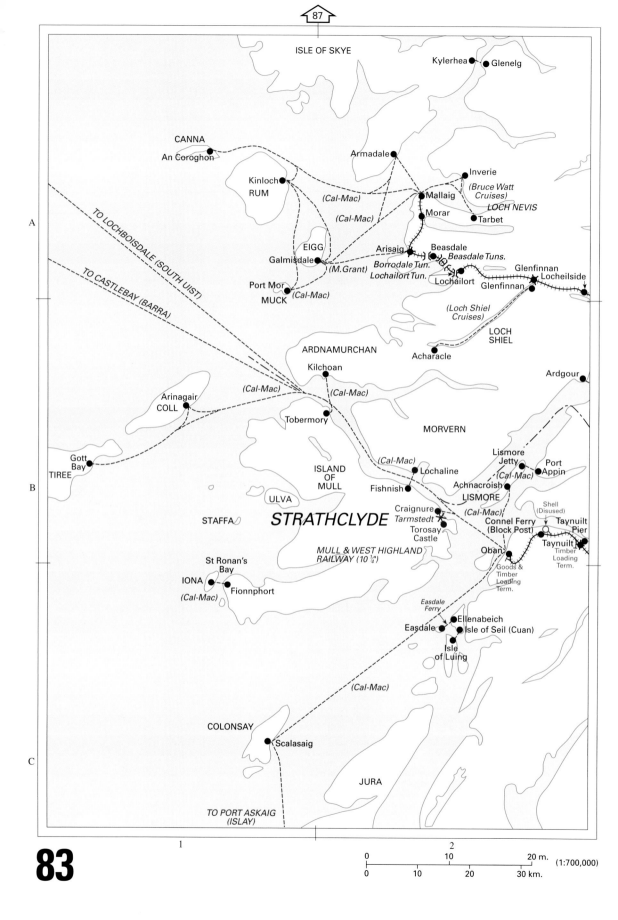

ISLE OF SKYE

Kylerhea • • Glenelg

CANNA
An Coroghon •

Armadale •

• Inverie
(Bruce Watt Cruises)

Kinloch •
RUM

(Cal-Mac)

• Mallaig
Morar •
LOCH NEVIS

(Cal-Mac)

• Tarbet

EIGG

Arisaig • Beasdale
Galmisdale • *Beasdale Tuns.*
Borrodale Tun.
Lochailort Tun.
Lochailort • Glenfinnan • Locheilside
Port Mor • Glenfinnan •
MUCK *(Cal-Mac)*

(M.Grant)

(Loch Shiel Cruises)

LOCH SHIEL

ARDNAMURCHAN

Kilchoan • Acharacle • Ardgour •

TO LOCHBOISDALE (SOUTH UIST)

TO CASTLEBAY (BARRA)

(Cal-Mac) *(Cal-Mac)*

Arinagair •
COLL
Tobermory •

MORVERN

Lismore
Jetty •
• Port
Appin
(Cal-Mac)

Gott Bay •
TIREE

(Cal-Mac)
Lochaline •
Fishnish •
Achnacroish •
LISMORE

ISLAND OF MULL

ULVA

STAFFA

STRATHCLYDE

Craignure
Tarmstedt
Torosay Castle

(Cal-Mac)

Connel Ferry
(Block Post)

Shell
(Disused)

Taynuilt
Pier

Taynuilt

MULL & WEST HIGHLAND RAILWAY (10¼")

Oban

Goods & Timber Loading Term.

Timber Loading Term.

St Ronan's Bay
IONA
(Cal-Mac) Fionnphort

Easdale Ferry
Easdale • • Ellenabeich
• Isle of Seil (Cuan)
Isle of Luing

(Cal-Mac)

COLONSAY
Scalasaig •

JURA

TO PORT ASKAIG (ISLAY)

83

1

2

0   10   20 m.
|———|———|———|
0   10   20   30 km.

(1:700,000)

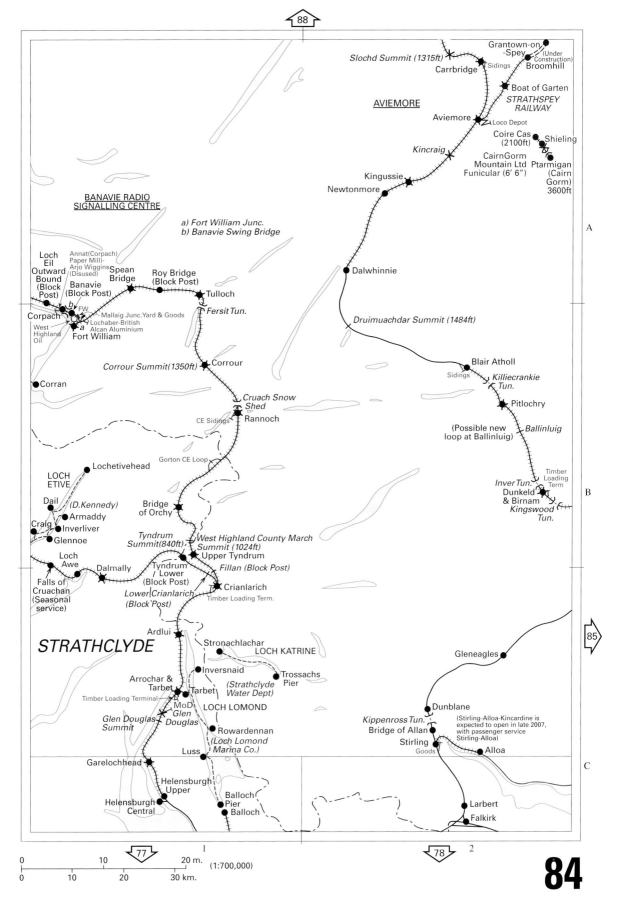

Grantown-on-Spey
(Under Construction)
Broomhill
Slochd Summit (1315ft)
Carrbridge
Sidings
Boat of Garten
STRATHSPEY RAILWAY
AVIEMORE
Aviemore
Loco Depot
Coire Cas (2100ft)
Shieling
Kincraig
CairnGorm Mountain Ltd Funicular (6' 6")
Ptarmigan (Cairn Gorm) 3600ft
Kingussie
Newtonmore

BANAVIE RADIO
SIGNALLING CENTRE

a) Fort William Junc.
b) Banavie Swing Bridge

A

Loch Eil Outward Bound (Block Post)
Annat(Corpach) Paper Mill)-Arjo Wiggins (Disused)
Spean Bridge
Roy Bridge (Block Post)
Banavie (Block Post)
b / FW
Tulloch
Corpach
Mallaig Junc.Yard & Goods
Fersit Tun.
West Highland Oil
a
Lochaber-British Alcan Aluminium
Fort William

Dalwhinnie

Druimuachdar Summit (1484ft)

Corran

Corrour Summit(1350ft)
Corrour

Blair Atholl
Sidings
Killiecrankie Tun.

Cruach Snow Shed
CE Sidings
Rannoch

Pitlochry

Ballinluig

Lochetivehead
Gorton CE Loop

(Possible new loop at Ballinluig)

B

LOCH ETIVE
Dail
(D.Kennedy)
Armaddy
Craig
Inverliver
Glennoe

Bridge of Orchy

Tyndrum Summit(840ft)
Upper Tyndrum
West Highland County March Summit (1024ft)
Fillan (Block Post)

Inver Tun.
Dunkeld & Birnam
Kingswood Tun.
Timber Loading Term.

Loch Awe
Dalmally
Tyndrum Lower (Block Post)
Crianlarich
Timber Loading Term.
Lower Crianlarich (Block Post)

Falls of Cruachan (Seasonal service)

Gleneagles

Ardlui

STRATHCLYDE

Stronachlachar
LOCH KATRINE
Inversnaid
(Strathclyde Water Dept)
Trossachs Pier

Arrochar & Tarbet
Timber Loading Terminal
Tarbet
MoD *Glen Douglas*
LOCH LOMOND
Glen Douglas Summit

Dunblane
Kippenross Tun.
Bridge of Allan
(Stirling-Alloa-Kincardine is expected to open in late 2007, with passenger service Stirling-Alloa)

Rowardennan
(Loch Lomond Marina Co.)

Stirling
Goods
Alloa

Luss

Garelochhead

C

Helensburgh Upper
Balloch Pier
Balloch
Helensburgh Central

Larbert
Falkirk

0   10   20 m.
0   10   20   30 km.
(1:700,000)

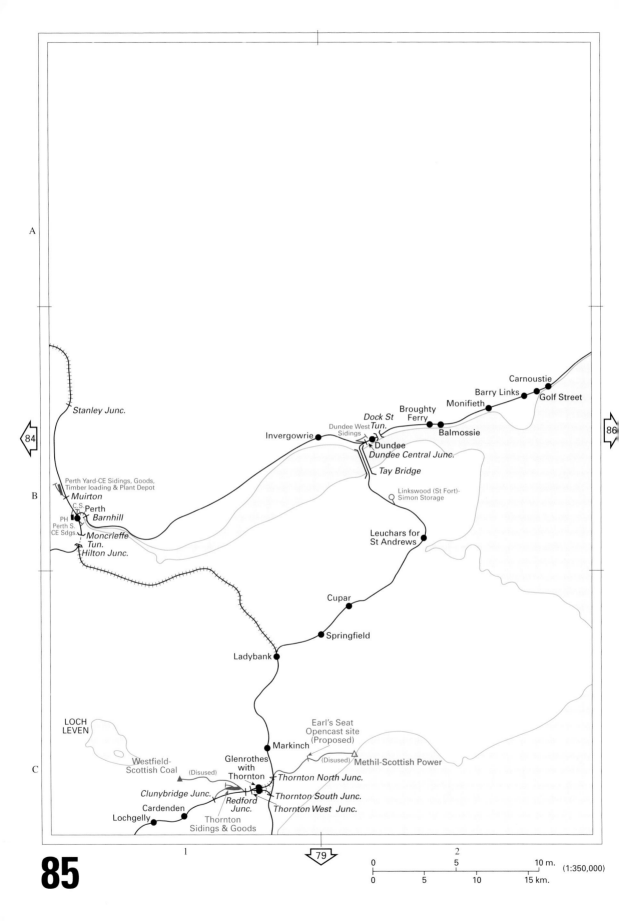

Carnoustie

Barry Links

Golf Street

Monifieth

Broughty
Ferry

*Dock St
Tun.*

Balmossie

Invergowrie

Dundee West
Sidings

Dundee

Dundee Central Junc.

Stanley Junc.

Perth Yard-CE Sidings, Goods,
Timber loading & Plant Depot

Muirton

C.S Perth

PH

Barnhill

Perth S.
CE Sdgs.

Tay Bridge

Linkswood (St Fort)-
Simon Storage

*Moncrieffe
Tun.*

Hilton Junc.

Leuchars for
St Andrews

Cupar

Springfield

Ladybank

LOCH
LEVEN

Earl's Seat
Opencast site
(Proposed)

Markinch

Westfield-
Scottish Coal

(Disused)

Glenrothes
with
Thornton

(Disused)

Methil-Scottish Power

Thornton North Junc.

Clunybridge Junc.

Cardenden

*Redford
Junc.*

Thornton South Junc.

Thornton West Junc.

Lochgelly

Thornton
Sidings & Goods

0   2

0   5   10 m.

(1:350,000)

0   5   10   15 km.

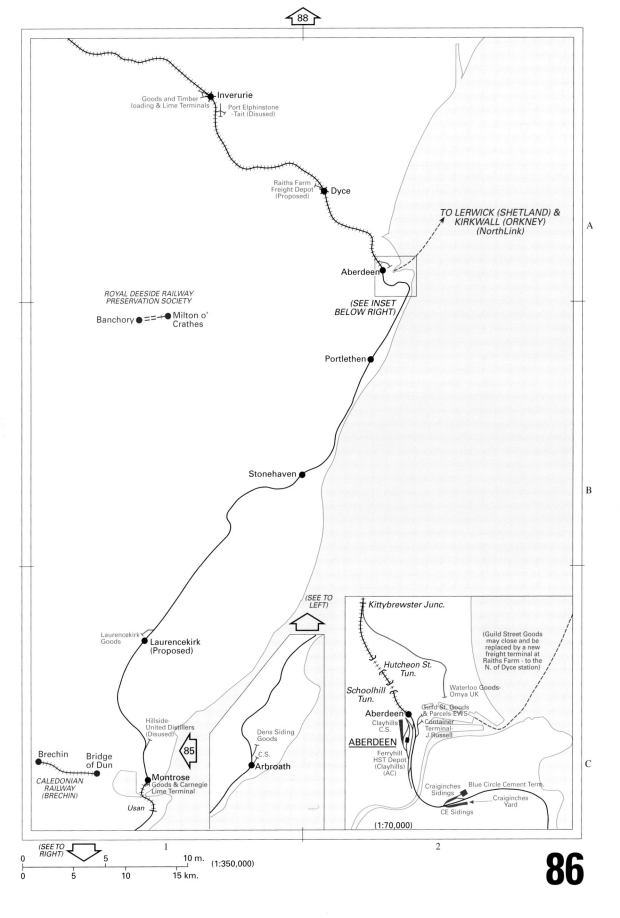

Inverurie

Goods and Timber
loading & Lime Terminals

Port Elphinstone
-Tait (Disused)

Raiths Farm
Freight Depot
(Proposed)

Dyce

TO LERWICK (SHETLAND) &
KIRKWALL (ORKNEY)
(NorthLink)

A

Aberdeen

*(SEE INSET
BELOW RIGHT)*

ROYAL DEESIDE RAILWAY
PRESERVATION SOCIETY

Banchory ● ═══ ● Milton o'
Crathes

Portlethen

Stonehaven

B

*(SEE TO
LEFT)*

Kittybrewster Junc.

(Guild Street Goods
may close and be
replaced by a new
freight terminal at
Raiths Farm - to the
N. of Dyce station)

Laurencekirk
Goods

Laurencekirk
(Proposed)

*Hutcheon St.
Tun.*

*Schoolhill
Tun.*

Waterloo Goods-
Omya UK

Aberdeen

Guild St. Goods
& Parcels-EWS

Hillside-
United Distillers
(Disused)

85

Dens Siding
Goods

Clayhills
C.S.

Container
Terminal-
J.Russell

ABERDEEN

C.S.

Ferryhill
HST Depot
(Clayhills)
(AC)

C

Brechin

Bridge
of Dun

Arbroath

*CALEDONIAN
RAILWAY
(BRECHIN)*

Montrose

Goods & Carnegie
Lime Terminal

Blue Circle Cement Term.

Craiginches
Sidings

Craiginches
Yard

Usan

CE Sidings

(1:70,000)

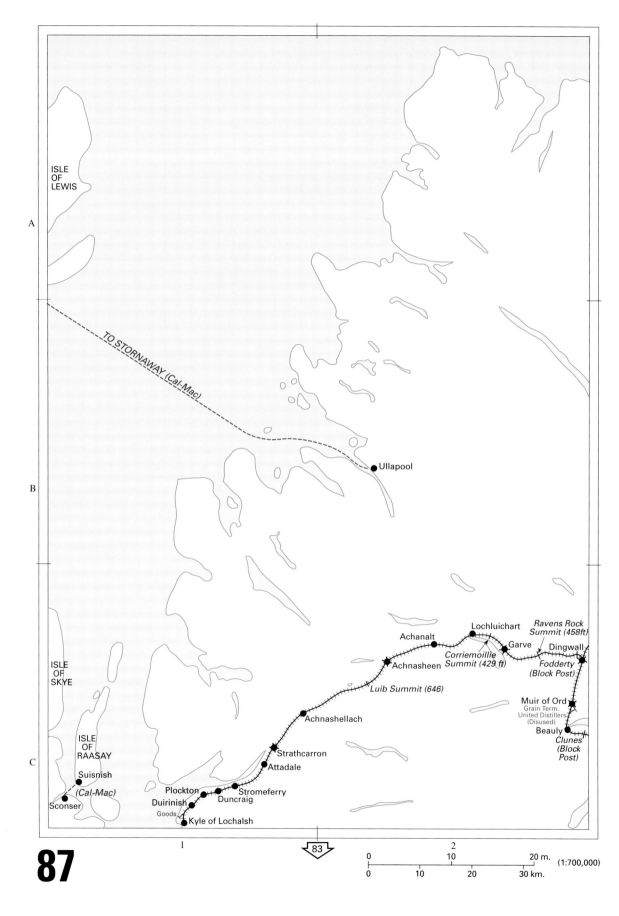

ISLE
OF
LEWIS

A

TO STORNAWAY (Cal-Mac)

Ullapool

B

ISLE
OF
SKYE

ISLE
OF
RAASAY

C

Suisnish

(Cal-Mac)

Sconser

Achanalt

Lochluichart

*Ravens Rock
Summit (458ft)*

*Corriemoillie
Summit (429 ft)*

Garve

Dingwall

Achnasheen

*Fodderty
(Block Post)*

Luib Summit (646)

Muir of Ord

Achnashellach

Grain Term.
United Distillers
(Disused)

Strathcarron

Beauly

*Clunes
(Block
Post)*

Attadale

Plockton

Stromeferry

Duirinish

Duncraig

Goods

Kyle of Lochalsh

87

1

83

2
10

20 m.

(1:700,000)

0

10

0

30 km.

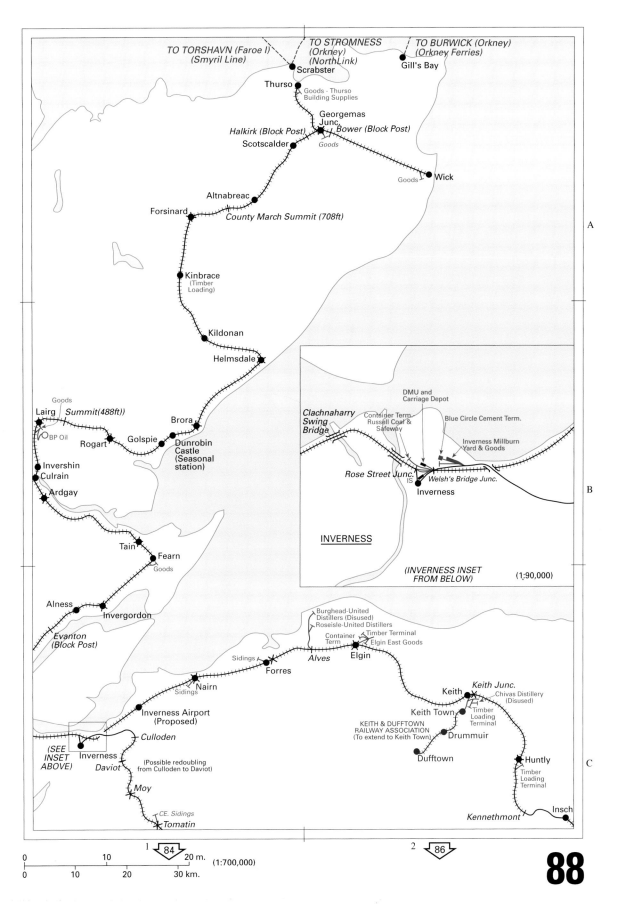

TO TORSHAVN (Faroe I) (Smyril Line)
TO STROMNESS (Orkney) (NorthLink)
TO BURWICK (Orkney) (Orkney Ferries)

Scrabster
Gill's Bay
Thurso
Goods - Thurso Building Supplies
Georgemas Junc.
Halkirk (Block Post)
Bower (Block Post)
Scotscalder
Goods
Goods
Wick
Altnabreac
Forsinard
County March Summit (708ft)
Kinbrace (Timber Loading)
Kildonan
Helmsdale

Goods
Lairg *Summit(488ft)*
Brora
BP Oil
Rogart
Golspie
Dunrobin Castle (Seasonal station)
Invershin
Culrain
Ardgay
Tain
Fearn
Goods

Alness
Invergordon
Evanton (Block Post)

INVERNESS

Clachnaharry Swing Bridge
DMU and Carriage Depot
Container Term. Russell Coal & Safeway
Blue Circle Cement Term.
Inverness Millburn Yard & Goods
Rose Street Junc.
IS
Welsh's Bridge Junc.
Inverness

(INVERNESS INSET FROM BELOW)
(1:90,000)

Burghead-United Distillers (Disused)
Roseisle-United Distillers
Container Term.
Timber Terminal
Elgin East Goods
Sidings
Alves
Elgin
Forres
Sidings
Nairn
Keith
Keith Junc.
Chivas Distillery (Disused)
Keith Town
Timber Loading Terminal
Inverness Airport (Proposed)
Culloden
KEITH & DUFFTOWN RAILWAY ASSOCIATION (To extend to Keith Town)
Drummuir
(SEE INSET ABOVE)
Inverness
Daviot
Dufftown
(Possible redoubling from Culloden to Daviot)
Huntly
Timber Loading Terminal
Moy
CE. Sidings
Tomatin
Kennethmont
Insch

0   10   20 m.
1 ⟨84⟩   2 ⟨86⟩
(1:700,000)
0   10   20   30 km.

A

B

C

88

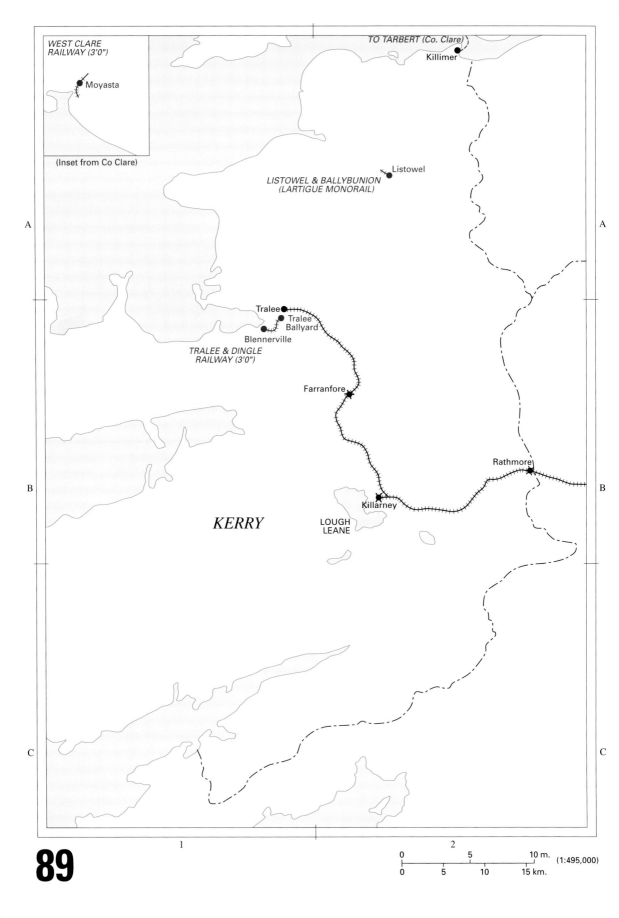

WEST CLARE
RAILWAY (3'0")

● Moyasta

(Inset from Co Clare)

TO TARBERT (Co. Clare)
● Killimer

● Listowel
LISTOWEL & BALLYBUNION
(LARTIGUE MONORAIL)

A

Tralee ●
● Tralee
Ballyard
● Blennerville
TRALEE & DINGLE
RAILWAY (3'0")

Farranfore

Rathmore

B

KERRY

Killarney
LOUGH
LEANE

C

1   2

0   5   10 m.
├────┬────┬────┤   (1:495,000)
0   5   10   15 km.

89

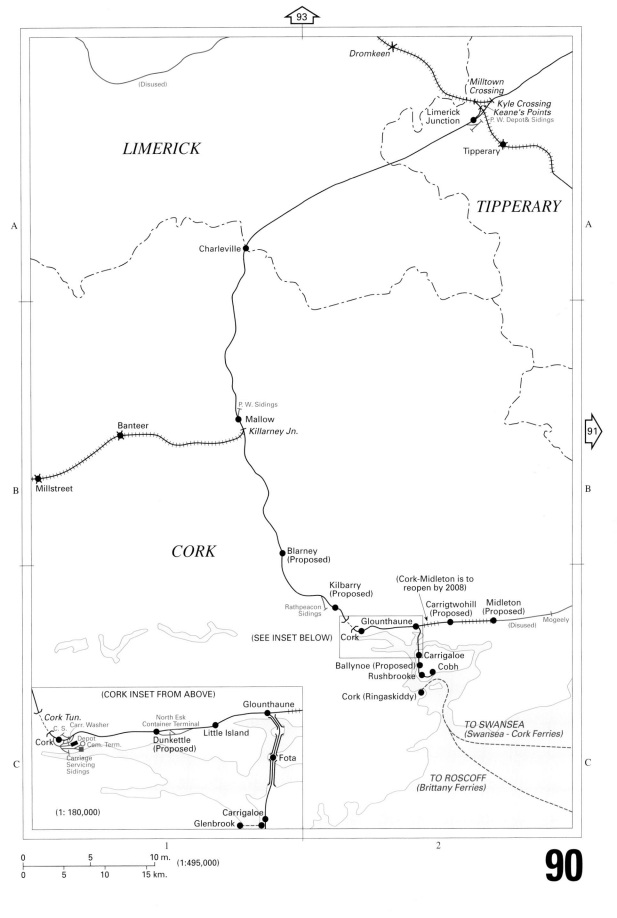

Dromkeen

Milltown Crossing

Kyle Crossing
Keane's Points
P. W. Depot & Sidings

Limerick Junction

LIMERICK

Tipperary

TIPPERARY

Charleville

91

P. W. Sidings

Banteer

Mallow
Killarney Jn.

CORK

B Millstreet

Blarney
(Proposed)

Kilbarry
(Proposed)

(Cork-Midleton is to
reopen by 2008)

Carrigtwohill
(Proposed)

Midleton
(Proposed)

Rathpeacon
Sidings

Glounthaune

Cork

(SEE INSET BELOW)

Carrigaloe

Ballynoe (Proposed)

Rushbrooke

Cobh

Cork (Ringaskiddy)

(Disused) Mogeely

TO SWANSEA
(Swansea - Cork Ferries)

TO ROSCOFF
(Brittany Ferries)

(CORK INSET FROM ABOVE)

Cork Tun.
C. S.   Carr. Washer

North Esk
Container Terminal

Glounthaune

Cork
Depot
Cem. Term.

Dunkettle
(Proposed)

Little Island

Fota

Carriage
Servicing
Sidings

(1: 180,000)

Carrigaloe

Glenbrook

0   5   10 m.
0   5   10   15 km.
1   (1:495,000)

2

90

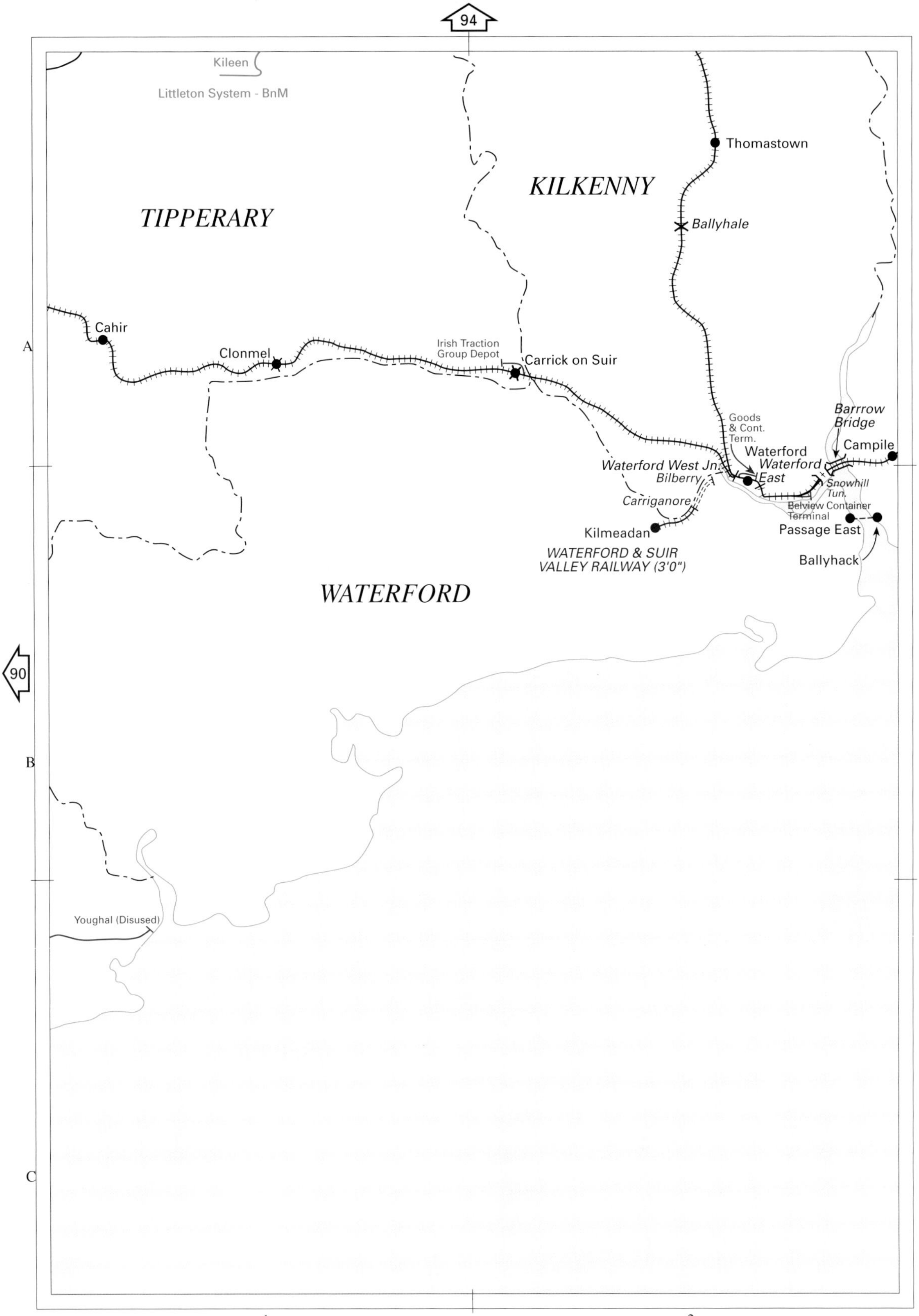

Kileen

Littleton System - BnM

KILKENNY

TIPPERARY

● Thomastown

✕ *Ballyhale*

A ● Cahir

Clonmel ●

Irish Traction
Group Depot

Carrick on Suir

Barrrow
Bridge

● Campile

Goods
& Cont.
Term.

Waterford
Waterford
East

A

Waterford West Jn.
Bilberry

Carriganore

Snowhill
Tun.

Belview Container
Terminal

● Kilmeadan

WATERFORD & SUIR
VALLEY RAILWAY (3'0")

Passage East

Ballyhack

WATERFORD

90

B

B

Youghal (Disused)

C

C

1

2

0   5   10 m.   (1:495,000)

0   5   10   15 km.

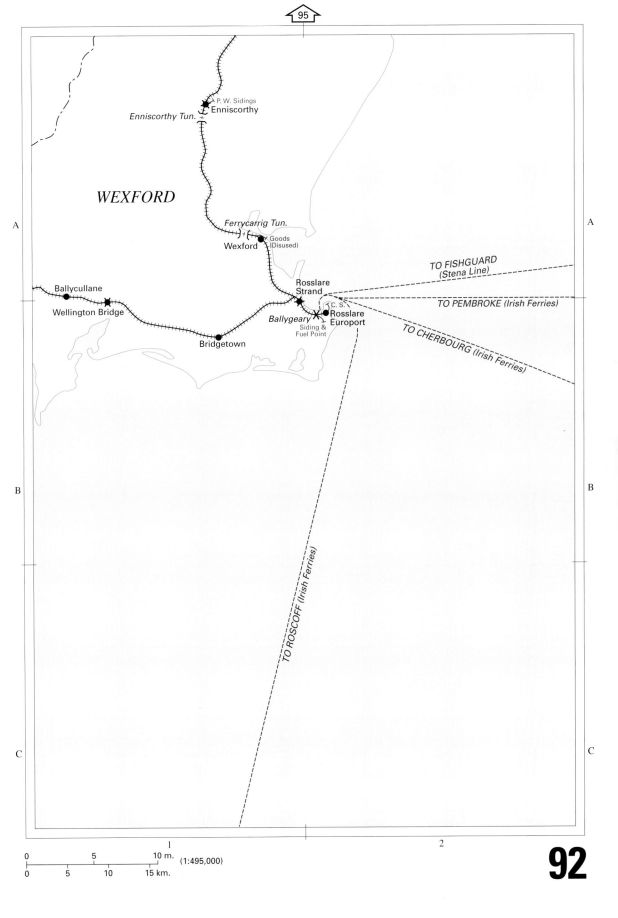

A

WEXFORD

P. W. Sidings
Enniscorthy

Enniscorthy Tun.

Ferrycarrig Tun.

Wexford

Goods
(Disused)

Rosslare
Strand

Ballycullane

Wellington Bridge

Bridgetown

Ballygeary

C. S.

Rosslare
Europort

Siding &
Fuel Point

TO FISHGUARD
(Stena Line)

TO PEMBROKE (Irish Ferries)

TO CHERBOURG (Irish Ferries)

TO ROSCOFF (Irish Ferries)

A

B

B

C

C

0   5   10 m.   (1:495,000)
0   5   10   15 km.

ROSCOMMON

Tuam ✕

Derryfadda
- BnM

(Athenry to Clonmarris may
reopen to passengers)

(Disused)

Clonkeen - Attymon
Peat Co-op Soc.

Woodlawn

Clooniff

Ballinasloe

Cullaghmore

Athenry

Attymon

Sidings

Attymon -
Attymon Peat Co-op Soc.

Lismanny
West Offaly-BSL

Garryduff

Oranmor
(Proposed)

Galway

Sidings ✕

A

A

Craughwell

GALWAY

Ardrahan

(Athenry to Ennis to reopen as
a single line to passengers by
2008/9, with new stations
between Galway, Athenry and
Limerick)

Gort

B

B

LOUGH
DERG

Cloughjordan

(Not in regular use)

CLARE

Nenagh

Ennis

Kilmastulla
Shale Siding

TIPPERARY

Sixmilebridge
(Proposed)

Birdhill

Castleconnell

C

C

Limerick

Burmah

Killonan Jn.

LIMERICK

Castlemungret-Limerick
Cement Factory

Sdgs.

Wagon Works &
Plant Depot

*Limerick
Check*

Foynes
(Disused)

93

1		2	

0   5   10 m.   (1:495,000)

0   5   10   15 km.

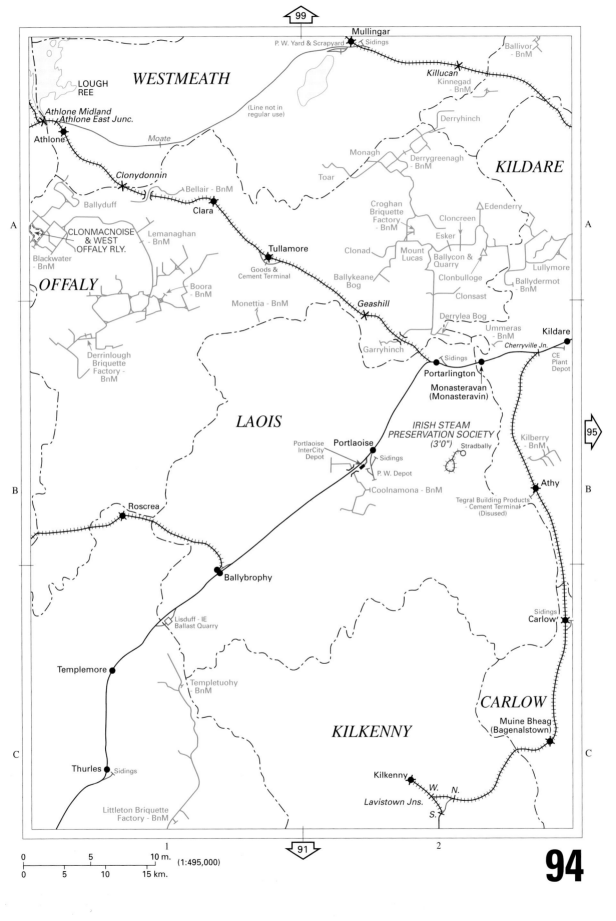

WESTMEATH

LOUGH
REE

P. W. Yard & Scrapyard   Mullingar
                          Sidings
                                              Ballivor -
                                              BnM
                                    Killucan
                                          Kinnegad -
                                          BnM
                         Derryhinch

(Line not in
regular use)

Athlone Midland
Athlone East Junc.
Athlone
                                                      KILDARE
          Moate
                              Monagh
                                        Derrygreenagh
                                        - BnM
              Clonydonnin   Toar
                          Bellair - BnM
Ballyduff   Clara
                                        Croghan
                                        Briquette   Edenderry
                                        Factory   Cloncreen
A   - BnM   Esker   A
CLONMACNOISE
& WEST   Lemanaghan -   Clonad   Ballycon &
OFFALY RLY.   BnM   Mount   Quarry   Lullymore
          Tullamore   Lucas
Blackwater   Clonbulloge   Ballydermot
- BnM   Goods &   Ballykeane   - BnM
OFFALY   Cement Terminal   Bog   Clonsast
                    Boora -
                    BnM
          Monettia - BnM   Geashill   Derrylea Bog
                                                              Ummeras   Kildare
                                        Garryhinch   - BnM
Derrinlough   Cherryville Jn.
Briquette   Sidings   CE
Factory -   Portarlington   Plant
BnM   Depot
                                        Monasteravan
                                        (Monasteravin)

                    LAOIS   IRISH STEAM
                                        PRESERVATION
                                        SOCIETY
                    Portlaoise   (3'0")   Kilberry
          Portlaoise   InterCity   Stradbally   - BnM
          Depot   Sidings
B   P. W. Depot   Athy   B
                    Coolnamona - BnM
          Roscrea   Tegral Building Products
                                        - Cement Terminal
                                        (Disused)

                    Ballybrophy   Sidings
          Lisduff - IE   Carlow
          Ballast Quarry

Templemore   Templetuohy   CARLOW
                    - BnM
                    KILKENNY   Muine Bheag
                                        (Bagenalstown)
C   C
Thurles   Sidings
                                        Kilkenny
          Littleton Briquette   W.   N.
          Factory - BnM   Lavistown Jns.
                                        S.

0   1   10 m.
0   5   15 km.   (1:495,000)

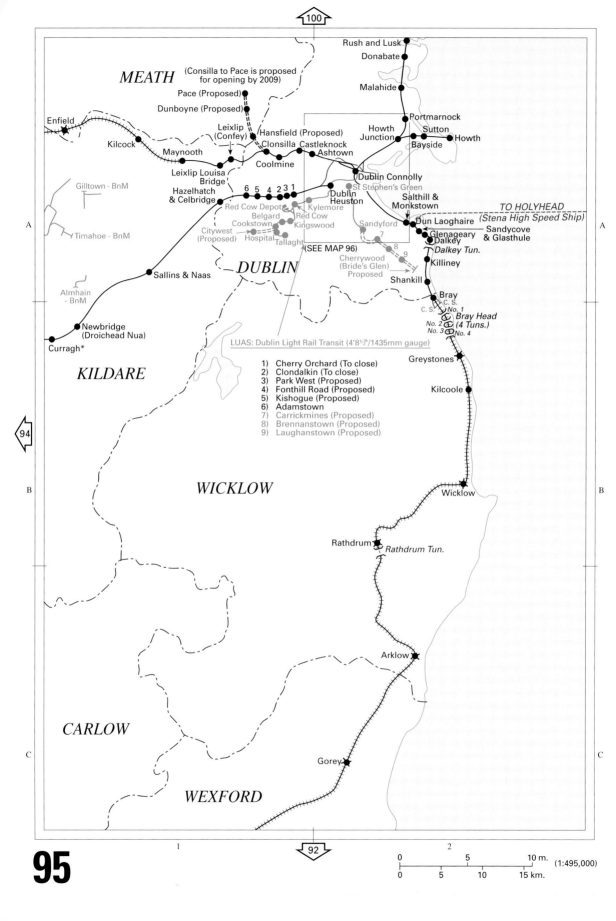

MEATH

Rush and Lusk
Donabate
Malahide

(Consilla to Pace is proposed
for opening by 2009)

Pace (Proposed)
Dunboyne (Proposed)

Enfield

Portmarnock
Howth
Junction
Sutton
Bayside
Howth

Leixlip
(Confey)
Hansfield (Proposed)
Clonsilla
Castleknock
Ashtown

Kilcock

Maynooth
Coolmine

Leixlip Louisa
Bridge

Dublin Connolly

Hazelhatch
& Celbridge

6 5 4 3 2 1

Dublin
Heuston

St Stephen's Green

Salthill &
Monkstown

TO HOLYHEAD
(Stena High Speed Ship)

Gilltown - BnM

Red Cow Depot
Belgard
Cookstown
Kylemore
Red Cow
Kingswood
Sandyford

Dun Laoghaire
Sandycove
& Glasthule

Timahoe - BnM

Citywest
(Proposed)
Hospital
Tallaght

(SEE MAP 96)

7

Glenageary
Dalkey
Dalkey Tun.

Cherrywood
(Bride's Glen)
Proposed

8

9

Killiney

Shankill

Sallins & Naas

DUBLIN

Bray
C. S.
C. S. No. 1
No. 2 *Bray Head*
No. 3 *(4 Tuns.)*
No. 4

Almhain
- BnM

LUAS: Dublin Light Rail Transit (4'8¹/₂"/1435mm gauge)

Newbridge
(Droichead Nua)

Curragh*

KILDARE

1) Cherry Orchard (To close)
2) Clondalkin (To close)
3) Park West (Proposed)
4) Fonthill Road (Proposed)
5) Kishogue (Proposed)
6) Adamstown
7) Carrickmines (Proposed)
8) Brennanstown (Proposed)
9) Laughanstown (Proposed)

Greystones

Kilcoole

WICKLOW

Wicklow

Rathdrum
Rathdrum Tun.

CARLOW

Arklow

WEXFORD

Gorey

A

B

C

94

92

1

2

0   5   10 m.
0   5   10   15 km.

(1:495,000)

95

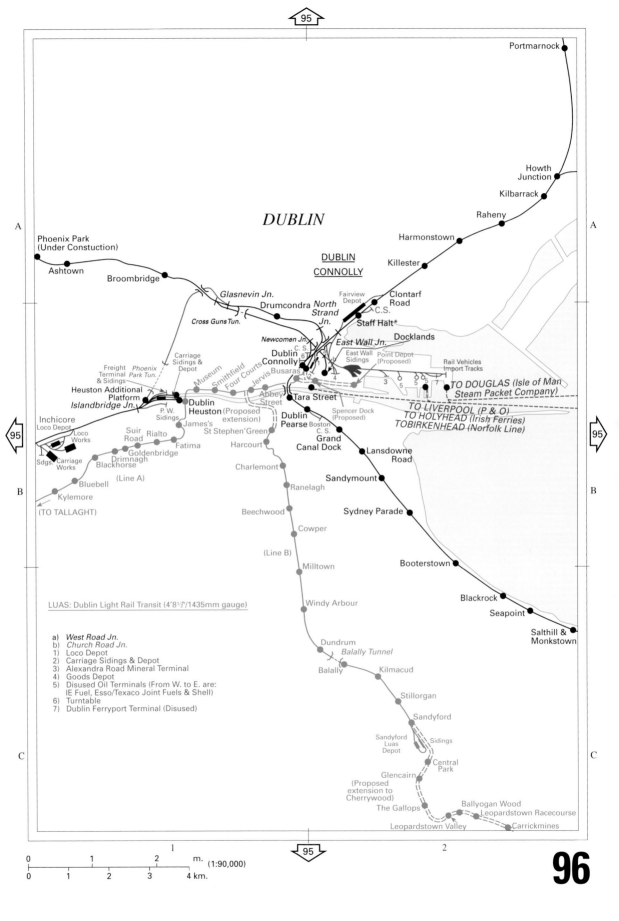

Portmarnock

DUBLIN

Howth
Junction

Kilbarrack

Raheny

Harmonstown

Killester

**DUBLIN
CONNOLLY**

A

Phoenix Park
(Under Constuction)

Ashtown

Broombridge

Glasnevin Jn.

Drumcondra

*North
Strand
Jn.*

Fairview
Depot

Clontarf
Road

C.S.

Staff Halt*

Cross Guns Tun.

Newcomen Jn.

East Wall Jn.

Docklands

**Dublin
Connolly**

Carriage Sidings &
Depot

Freight
Terminal
& Sidings

*Phoenix
Park Tun.*

Heuston Additional
Platform

Islandbridge Jn.

P.W.
Sidings

Museum

Smithfield

Four Courts

Jervis

Busaras

Abbey
Street

Tara Street

**Dublin
Heuston**

(Proposed
extension)

James's

St Stephen'Green

**Dublin
Pearse**

Boston
C.S.

Spencer Dock
(Proposed)

C. S.
6

East Wall
Sidings

Point Depot
(Proposed)

Rail Vehicles
Import Tracks

*TO DOUGLAS (Isle of Man
Steam Packet Company)*

TO LIVERPOOL (P & O)
TO HOLYHEAD (Irish Ferries)
TOBIRKENHEAD (Norfolk Line)

Inchicore
Loco Depot

Loco
Works

Suir
Road

Rialto

Goldenbridge

Fatima

Harcourt

**Grand
Canal Dock**

Lansdowne
Road

Sgds.
Carriage
Works

Drimnagh

Blackhorse

(Line A)

Charlemont

Sandymount

Bluebell

Ranelagh

Sydney Parade

Kylemore

(TO TALLAGHT)

Beechwood

Booterstown

Cowper

(Line B)

Milltown

Blackrock

Seapoint

Windy Arbour

LUAS: Dublin Light Rail Transit (4'8½'/1435mm gauge)

Salthill &
Monkstown

a) *West Road Jn.*
b) *Church Road Jn.*
1) Loco Depot
2) Carriage Sidings & Depot
3) Alexandra Road Mineral Terminal
4) Goods Depot
5) Disused Oil Terminals (From W. to E. are:
   IE Fuel, Esso/Texaco Joint Fuels & Shell)
6) Turntable
7) Dublin Ferryport Terminal (Disused)

Dundrum

Balally Tunnel

Balally

Kilmacud

Stillorgan

Sandyford

Sandyford
Luas Depot

Sidings

Central
Park

Glencairn

(Proposed
extension to
Cherrywood)

The Gallops

Ballyogan Wood

Leopardstown Racecourse

Leopardstown Valley

Carrickmines

C

0   1   2   m. (1:90,000)

0   1   2   3   4 km.

96

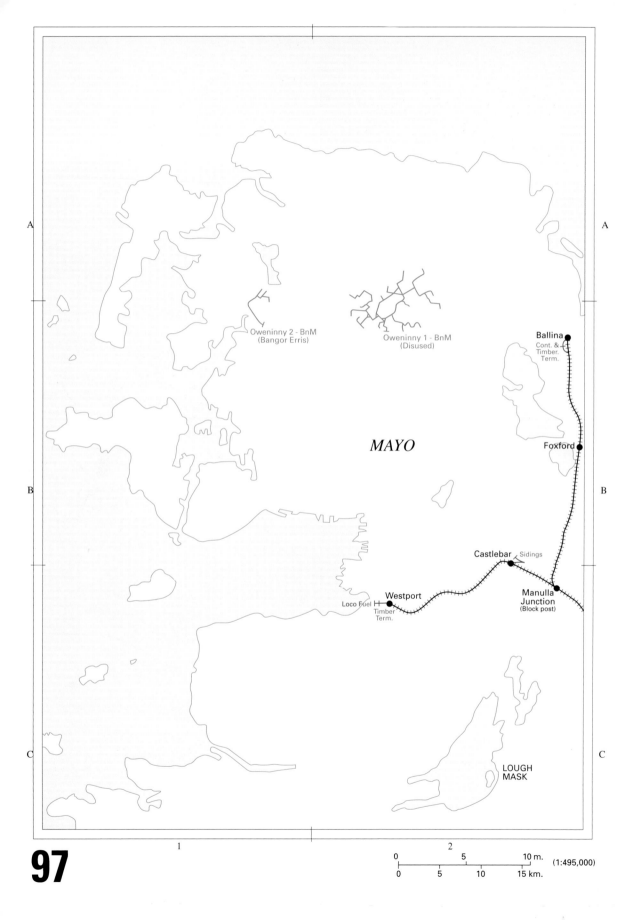

Oweninny 2 - BnM
(Bangor Erris)

Oweninny 1 - BnM
(Disused)

Ballina
Cont. &
Timber.
Term.

MAYO

Foxford

Castlebar — Sidings

Manulla
Junction
(Block post)

Westport

Loco Fuel
Timber.
Term.

LOUGH
MASK

97

0   5   10 m.
0   5   10   15 km.

(1:495,000)

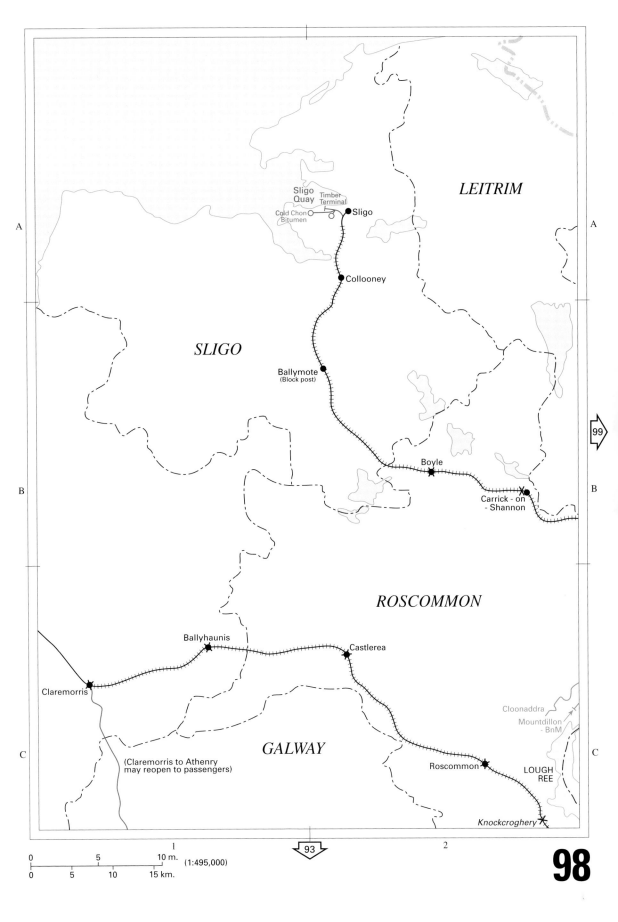

LEITRIM

Sligo
Quay
Timber
Terminal
Cold Chon
Bitumen
● Sligo

SLIGO

● Collooney

Ballymote
(Block post)

Boyle

Carrick - on
- Shannon

ROSCOMMON

Ballyhaunis
Castlerea

Claremorris

(Claremorris to Athenry
may reopen to passengers)

GALWAY

Cloonaddra

Mountdillon
- BnM

Roscommon

LOUGH
REE

Knockcroghery

99

93

0   5   10 m.   (1:495,000)

0   5   10   15 km.

1   2

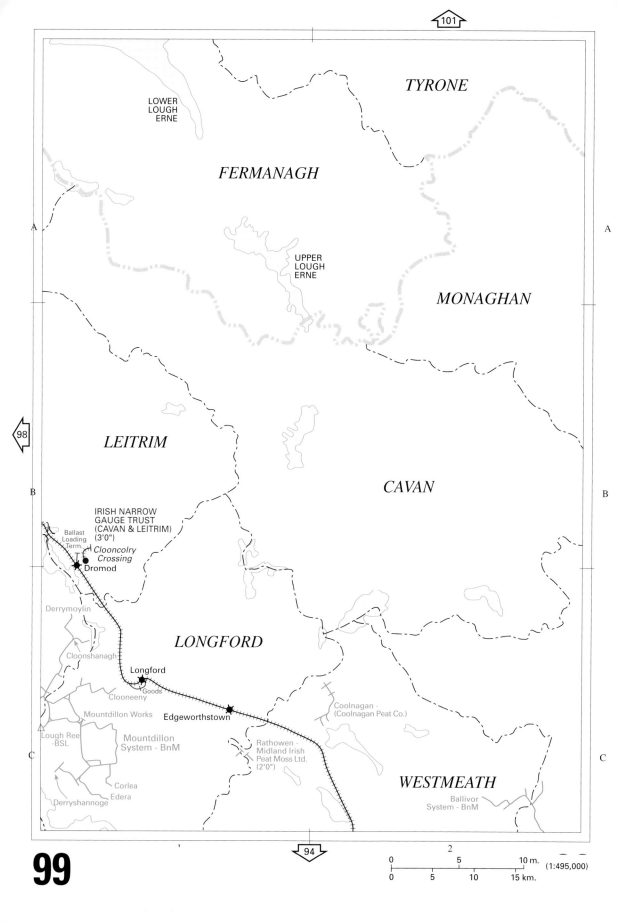

TYRONE

LOWER
LOUGH
ERNE

FERMANAGH

UPPER
LOUGH
ERNE

MONAGHAN

A

LEITRIM

CAVAN

B

B

IRISH NARROW
GAUGE TRUST
(CAVAN & LEITRIM)
(3'0")

Ballast
Loading
Term.

*Clooncolry
Crossing*
Dromod

Derrymoylin

LONGFORD

Cloonshanagh

Longford

Goods

Clooneeny

Coolnagan -
(Coolnagan Peat Co.)

Mountdillon Works

Edgeworthstown

Lough Ree
-BSL

Mountdillon
System - BnM

Rathowen -
Midland Irish
Peat Moss Ltd.
(2'0")

C

C

Corlea
Edera

WESTMEATH

Derryshannoge

Ballivor
System - BnM

99

2

0   5   10 m.
(1:495,000)
0   5   10   15 km.

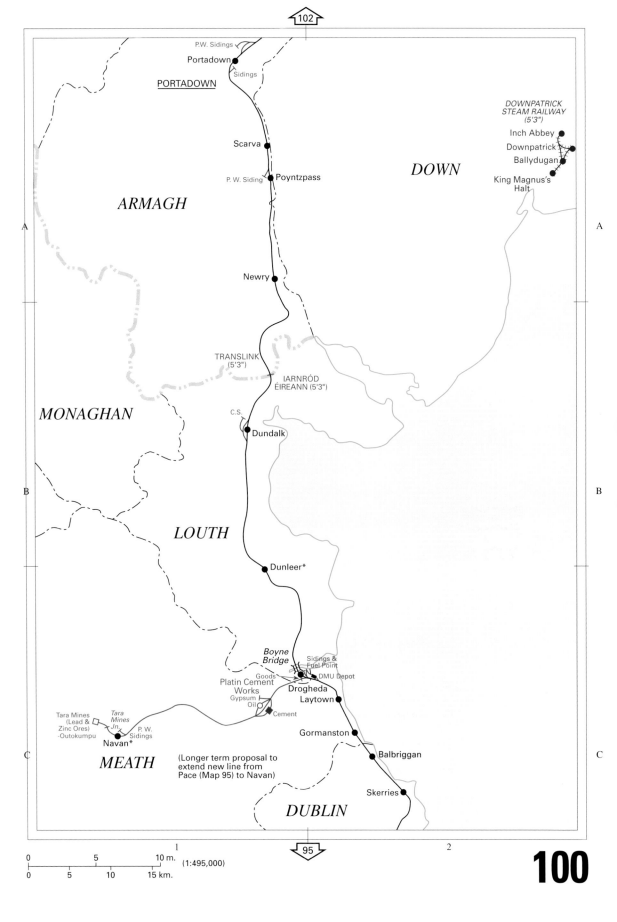

P.W. Sidings

Portadown

PORTADOWN

Sidings

DOWNPATRICK
STEAM RAILWAY
(5'3")

Inch Abbey

Scarva

Downpatrick

Ballydugan

DOWN

King Magnus's
Halt

Poyntzpass

P. W. Siding

ARMAGH

A

A

Newry

TRANSLINK
(5'3")

IARNRÓD
ÉIREANN (5'3")

MONAGHAN

C.S.

Dundalk

B

B

LOUTH

Dunleer*

Boyne
Bridge

Sidings &
Fuel Point

Goods

DMU Depot

Platin Cement
Works

Drogheda

Gypsum

Laytown

Oil

Cement

Tara Mines
(Lead &
Zinc Ores)
-Outokumpu

Tara
Mines
Jn.

P. W.
Sidings

Gormanston

Navan*

Balbriggan

C

C

MEATH

(Longer term proposal to
extend new line from
Pace (Map 95) to Navan)

Skerries

DUBLIN

1

2

0   5   10 m.   (1:495,000)

0   5   10   15 km.

100

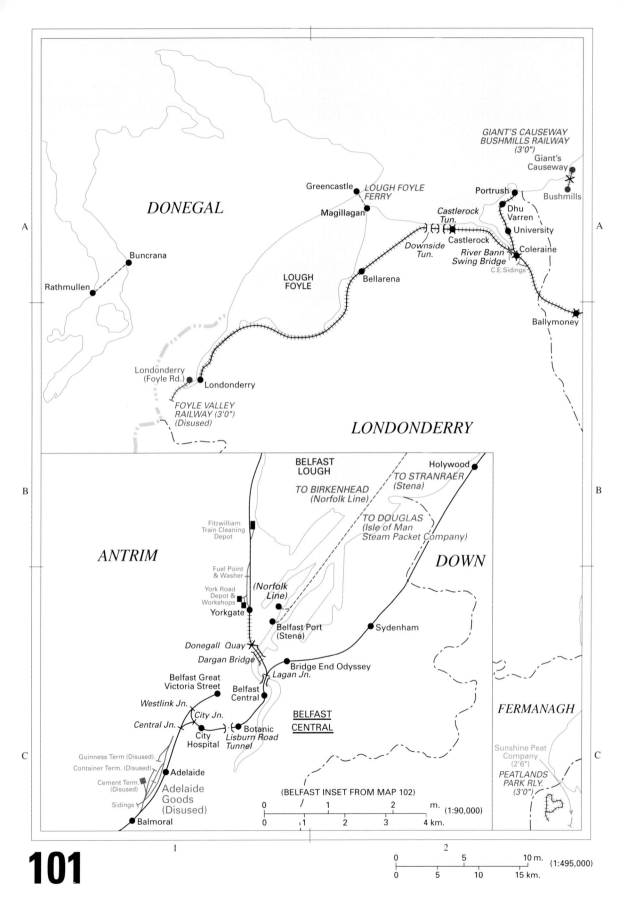

DONEGAL

Buncrana

Rathmullen

LOUGH
FOYLE

Greencastle

*LOUGH FOYLE
FERRY*

Magillagan

Bellarena

*Downside
Tun.*

*Castlerock
Tun.*

Castlerock

*River Bann
Swing Bridge*

C.E.Sidings

GIANT'S CAUSEWAY
BUSHMILLS RAILWAY
(3'0")

Giant's
Causeway

Bushmills

Portrush

Dhu
Varren

University

Coleraine

Ballymoney

Londonderry
(Foyle Rd.)

Londonderry

*FOYLE VALLEY
RAILWAY (3'0")
(Disused)*

LONDONDERRY

A

B

BELFAST
LOUGH

*TO BIRKENHEAD
(Norfolk Line)*

*TO STRANRAER
(Stena)*

*TO DOUGLAS
(Isle of Man
Steam Packet Company)*

Holywood

Fitzwilliam
Train Cleaning
Depot

Fuel Point
& Washer

York Road
Depot &
Workshops

Yorkgate

*(Norfolk
Line)*

Belfast Port
(Stena)

Sydenham

ANTRIM

DOWN

Donegall Quay

Dargan Bridge

Bridge End Odyssey

Lagan Jn.

Belfast Great
Victoria Street

Belfast
Central

Westlink Jn.

City Jn.

Central Jn.

City
Hospital

Botanic

*Lisburn
Road
Tunnel*

BELFAST
CENTRAL

FERMANAGH

Guinness Term (Disused)

Container Term. (Disused)

Adelaide

Cement Term.
(Disused)

Adelaide
Goods
(Disused)

Sidings

Balmoral

Sunshine Peat
Company
(2'6")

PEATLANDS
PARK RLY.
(3'0")

(BELFAST INSET FROM MAP 102)

0   1   2   m. (1:90,000)

0   1   2   3   4 km.

C

101

0   2

0   5   10 m. (1:495,000)

0   5   10   15 km.

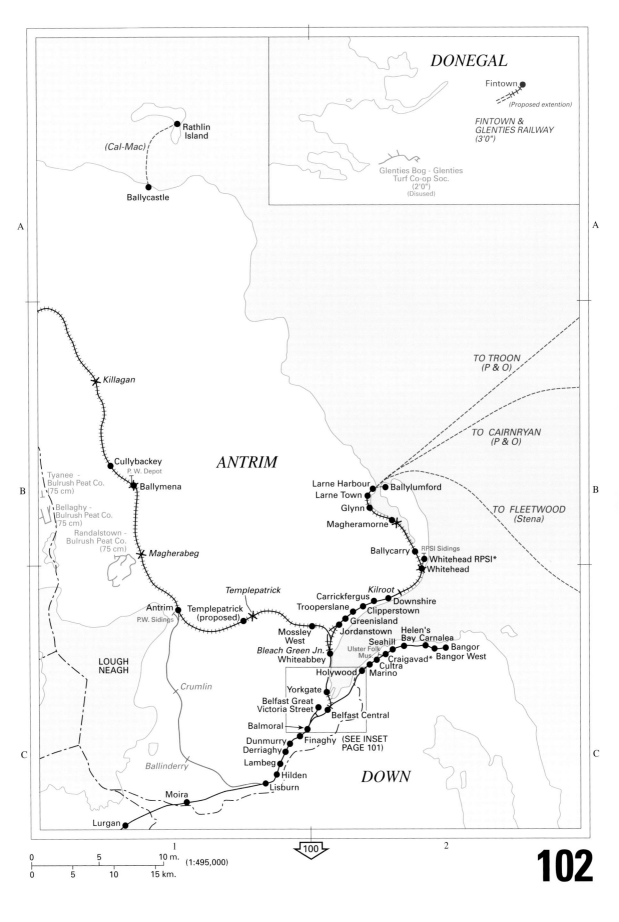

DONEGAL

Fintown

(Proposed extention)

FINTOWN &
GLENTIES RAILWAY
(3'0")

Glenties Bog - Glenties
Turf Co-op Soc.
(2'0")
(Disused)

Rathlin
Island

(Cal-Mac)

Ballycastle

TO TROON
(P & O)

TO CAIRNRYAN
(P & O)

Killagan

ANTRIM

Cullybackey
P. W. Depot
Ballymena

Tyanee -
Bulrush Peat Co.
(75 cm)

Bellaghy -
Bulrush Peat Co.
(75 cm)

Randalstown -
Bulrush Peat Co.
(75 cm)

Magherabeg

Templepatrick

Antrim
P.W. Sidings

Templepatrick
(proposed)

Larne Harbour
Larne Town
Ballylumford

Glynn

Magheramorne

TO FLEETWOOD
(Stena)

Ballycarry
RPSI Sidings
Whitehead RPSI*
Whitehead

Kilroot
Carrickfergus   Downshire
Trooperslane   Clipperstown
                   Greenisland
Mossley   Jordanstown
West
Bleach Green Jn.   Seahill   Helen's
Whiteabbey   Ulster Folk   Bay Carnalea
                    Mus.   Bangor
                    Cultra   Bangor West
            Holywood Marino Craigavad*

LOUGH
NEAGH

Crumlin

Yorkgate

Belfast Great
Victoria Street

Balmoral

Dunmurry
Derriaghy
Lambeg
Hilden
Lisburn

Finaghy

Belfast Central

(SEE INSET
PAGE 101)

DOWN

Moira

Ballinderry

Lurgan

1   2

0   5   10 m.
─────────────────   (1:495,000)
0   5   10
          15 km.

100

102

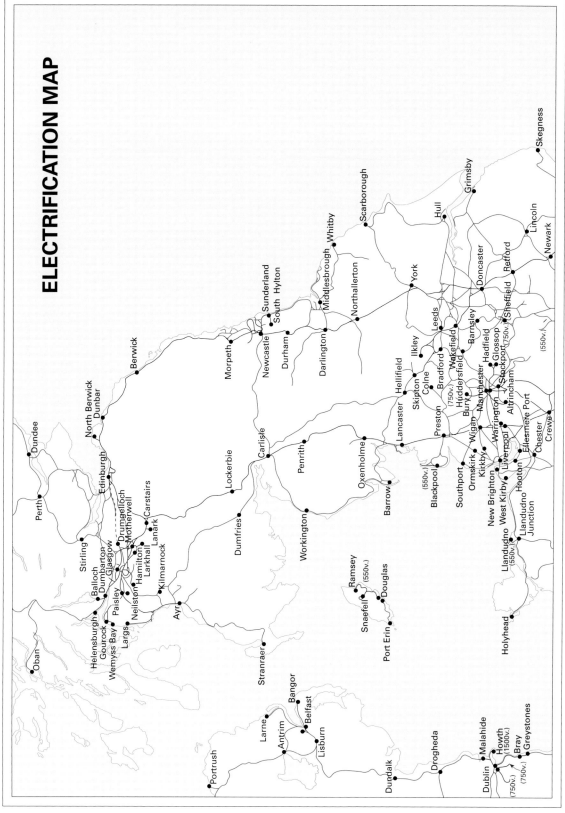

ELECTRIFICATION MAP

103

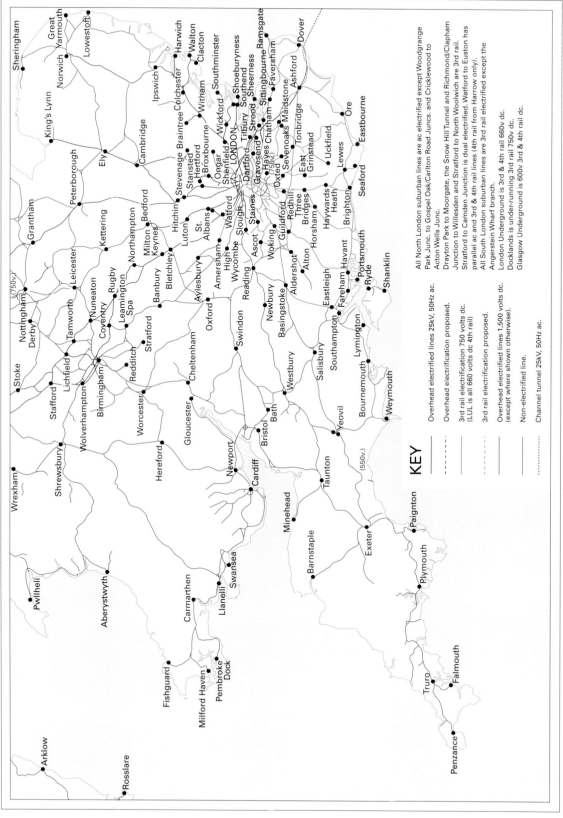

KEY

— — —	Overhead electrified lines 25kV, 50Hz ac.
- - - - -	Overhead electrification proposed.
————	3rd rail electrification 750 volts dc. (LUL is all 660 volts dc 4th rail)
- - - - -	3rd rail electrification proposed.
————	Overhead electrified lines 1,500 volts dc. (except where shown otherwise).
————	Non-electrified line.
· · · · ·	Channel tunnel 25kV, 50Hz ac.

All North London suburban lines are ac electrified except Woodgrange Park Junc. to Gospel Oak/Carlton Road Juncs. and Cricklewood to Acton Junc.

Drayton Park to Moorgate, the Snow Hill Tunnel and Richmond/Clapham Junction to Willesden and Stratford to North Woolwich are 3rd rail. Stratford to Camden Junction is dual electrified. Watford to Euston has parallel ac and 3rd & 4th rail lines (4th rail from Harrow only).

All South London suburban lines are 3rd rail electrified except the Angerstein Wharf branch.

London Underground is 3rd & 4th rail 660v dc.
Docklands is under-running 3rd rail 750v dc.
Glasgow Underground is 600v 3rd & 4th rail dc.

104

INDEX

All passenger stations are included in this index. Freight terminals, junction names, tunnels and other significant locations are indexed where their names or map references differ from a passenger station.

denotes an unadvertised or excursion station. (eg Curragh)

106

Location	Page No.	Page Ref.
Blair Atholl	84	B2
Blairhill	78	C1
Blake Street	48	A2
Blakedown	41	B1
Blantyre	82	C2
Blarney (Proposed)	90	C1
Blatchbridge Junction	9	B1
Blaydon	75	B1
Blea Moor	67	C1
Bleach Green Junction	102	C2
Bleasby	54	B1
Bledlow Bridge Halt	35	B1
Blennerville	89	B1
Bletchingley Tunnel	12	A1
Bletchley	35	A1
Blochairn Tunnel	82	B1
Blodwell	51	C1
Bloxwich	47	A2
Bloxwich North	41	A2
Blue Anchor	7	B2
Bluebell	96	B1
Blundellsands & Crosby	59	A1
Blunsdon	33	C2
Blyth	74	B1
Blythe Bridge	52	C2
Blythe Bridge (Caverswall Road)	52	C2
Boating Lake	57	A2
Boat of Garten	84	A2
Bodiam	13	B1
Bodmin General	2	B1
Bodmin Parkway	2	B1
Bodorgan	49	B2
Bog Junction	71	C1
Bognor Regis	11	C1
Bogston	77	A1
Boldon Junctions	76	B1
Bolton	61	C1
Bolton Abbey	61	A2
Bolton Junction	61	B1
Bolton-on-Dearne	62	C2
Bond Street	21	B1
Bo'ness Junction	78	A2
Bontnewydd	49	B2
Bonwm	50	C2
Bookham	11	A2
Boora	94	A1
Booterstown	96	C2
Bootle (Cumbria)	65	C2
Bootle Branch Junction	59	B2
Bootle New Strand	59	A1
Bootle Oriel Road	59	A1
Bopeep Junction & Tunnel	13	C1
Bordesley	48	C1
Borough	21	B2
Borough Green & Wrotham	12	A2
Borough Market Junction	21	B2
Boroughbridge Road Junction	68	C1
Borrodale Tunnel	83	A2
Borth	38	B2
Boscarne Junction	1	B2
Bosham	11	C1
Boston	55	C1
Boston Lodge	49	C2
Boston Manor	20	C1
Botanic	101	C1
Botley	10	C2
Bottesford	54	C1
Boughton Crossing	43	C1
Boulby	69	B1
Boultham Junction	54	B2
Bounds Green	25	C2
Bourne End	35	C1
Bournemouth	5	A2
Bournville	41	B2
Bow	22	B1
Bow Brickhill	35	A1
Bow Bridge	61	A2
Bow Church	22	B1
Bow Road	22	B1
Bower	88	A2
Bowes Park	25	C2
Bowesfield Junction	68	B2
Bowker Vale	57	A2
Bowling	81	A1
Bowling Tunnel	62	B1
Box Tunnel	9	A1
Boxhill & Westhumble	11	A2
Boyle	98	B2
Boyne Bridge	100	C1
Bracknell	11	A1
Bradford Forster Square	62	B1
Bradford Interchange	62	B1
Bradford-on-Avon	9	A1
Brading	6	A2
Bradley Junction & Tunnel	62	C1
Bradley Lane	47	B1
Bradway Tunnel	53	A1
Bradwell	37	B1
Braintree	37	A1
Braintree Freeport	37	A1
Bramdean	18	A2
Bramhall	52	A1
Bramhope Tunnel	62	B1
Bramley (Hampshire)	10	A2
Bramley (West Yorkshire)	62	B1
Brampton (Cumbria)	72	C2
Brampton (Norfolk)	56	C1
Brampton (Suffolk)	46	B1
Branchton	77	A1
Brancliffe East Junction	53	A2
Brandon	45	B1
Branksome	5	A2
Branston Junction	53	C1
Braunstone Gate	42	A2
Bray	95	B2
Braye Road	5	C1
Braystones	65	B2
Brayton	62	B2
Brechin	86	C1
Bredbury	58	C2
Breich	78	B2
Brent	20	A2
Brent Cross	20	A2
Brentford	20	C1
Brentwood	36	C2
Brereton Sidings	41	A2
Brewery Sidings	58	B1
Breydon Junction	46	A1
Brick Pit	64	C1
Bricket Wood	23	A2
Bridge End Odyssey	101	C1
Bridge Junction	64	B1
Bridge of Allan	84	C2
Bridge of Dun	86	C1
Bridge of Orchy	84	B1
Bridge Street (Glasgow)	82	B1
Bridgend	31	C2
Bridgeton	82	B1
Bridgetown	92	B1
Bridgnorth	41	B1
Bridgwater	8	B1
Bridlington	63	A2
Brierfield	61	B1
Brierley Hill	47	C1
Brigg	63	C2
Briggs Sidlings	52	B2
Brighouse	62	B1
Brighton	12	C1
Brill Tunnel	34	B2
Brimsdown	26	B1
Brindle Heath	57	B2
Brinnington	58	C2
Bristol Parkway	28	B2
Bristol Temple Meads	28	C2
Britannia Bridge	49	B2
Brithdir	32	B1
British Steel (Redcar)	69	A2
Briton Ferry	32	A1
Brixton	21	C2
Broad Green	59	B2
Broad Street Tunnel	56	B1
Broadbottom	52	A2
Broadmarsh (Proposed)	55	B1
Broadstairs	14	A1
Broadway	57	B2
Brockenhurst	10	C1
Brockholes	62	C1
Brocklesby Junction	63	C2
Brockley	22	C1
Brockley Whins	76	B1
Bromborough	51	A1
Bromborough Rake	51	A1
Bromford Bridge	48	B2
Bromley Cross	61	C1
Bromley Junction	17	B2
Bromley North	18	B2
Bromley South	18	B2
Bromley-by-Bow	22	B1
Bromsgrove	41	C2
Brondesbury	21	B1
Brondesbury Park	21	B1
Bronwydd Arms	30	A2
Brook C. S.	52	C1
Brookgate	12	A2
Brooklands	57	C2
Brookman's Park	24	A2
Brooksbottom Tunnel	61	C1
Brookwood	11	A1
Broombridge	96	A1
Broome	40	B2
Broomfleet	63	B1
Broomhill (Ayrshire)	70	A2
Broomhill (Highland)	84	A2
Broomloan Depot	81	B2
Brora	88	B1
Brotherton Tunnel	62	B2
Brough	63	B2
Broughton Lane Junction	56	B1
Broughty Ferry	85	B2
Brownhills West	41	A2
Brownqueen Tunnel	2	B1
Broxbourne	36	B1
Bruce Grove	25	C2
Brundall	46	A1
Brundall Gardens	46	A1
Brunswick	59	C2
Brunthill	71	B1
Brunstane	79	C2
Bruton	9	B1
Bryn	60	C2
Bryn Hynod	50	C2
Brynglas	38	A2
Brynteg	31	B1
Buchanan Street	82	B1
Buckenham	46	A1
Buckfastleigh	3	B1
Buckhorn Weston Tunnel	9	B1
Buckhurst Hill	26	C2
Buckland Junction	14	B1
Buckley	51	B1
Buckley Wells	61	C1
Bucknell	40	B1
Buckshead Tunnel	1	C2
Bugle	1	B2
Builth Road	39	C2
Bulwell	53	C2
Bulwell Forest	55	A1
Bungalow	65	C1
Burdon Road	76	C2
Bures	37	A1
Burgess Hill	12	C1
Burghead	88	C2
Buriton Tunnel	11	C1
Burley Park	63	A1
Burley-in-Wharfedale	62	A1
Burmarsh Road Halt*	13	B2
Burn Naze	60	B1
Burnage	58	C1
Burneside	66	C2
Burngullow	1	B2
Burnham	35	C1
Burnham-on-Crouch	37	C1
Burnley Barracks	61	B1
Burnley Central	61	B1
Burnley Manchester Road	61	B1
Burnside	82	C1
Burnt Oak	24	C2
Burntisland	79	A1
Burroughs Tunnel	20	A2
Burrows Sidings	31	A2
Burscough Bridge	60	C2
Burscough Junction	60	C2
Bursledon	10	C2
Burton Joyce	53	C2
Burton-on-Trent	53	C1
Bury	61	C1
Bury Bolton Street	61	C1
Bury St. Edmunds	45	C1
Bury Street Junction	25	B2
Bury Street Tunnel	59	B1
Busaras	96	B1
Busby	82	C1
Busby Junction	81	C2
Bush Hill Park	25	B2
Bush-on-Esk	72	C2
Bushbury Junction	47	A1
Bushey	23	B2
Bushmills	101	A2
Butlers Hill	53	B2
Butlers Lane	48	A2
Butterwell	74	B1
Buxted	12	B2
Buxton (Derbyshire)	52	A2
Buxton (Norfolk)	56	C2
Byfleet & New Haw	15	C1
Byker	75	B2
Bynea	30	B2
Byrehill Junction	77	C1
Cabin	60	B1
Cabot Park	28	B1
Cadoxton	27	C1
Caergwrie	51	B1
Caernarfon	49	B2
Caerphilly	32	C1
Caersws	39	B2
Caerwent	32	C2

111

112

118

119

INDEX TO LOCOMOTIVE and MULTIPLE UNIT STABLING POINTS, CARRIAGE DEPOTS and RAILWAY WORKS